THE FINANCING
OF TERROR

THE FINANCING OF TERROR

James Adams

NEW ENGLISH LIBRARY

Copyright © 1986 by The Adams Partnership

First published in Great Britain in 1986 by
New English Library, Mill Road, Dunton Green, Sevenoaks, Kent.
Editorial office: 47 Bedford Square, London WC1B 3DP.

Typeset by Rowland Phototypesetting Ltd,
Bury St Edmunds, Suffolk

Printed in Great Britain by
St Edmundsbury Press, Bury St Edmunds, Suffolk

British Library C.I.P.

Adams, James
    The financing of terror.
    1. Terrorism – Finance
    I. Title
    322.4'2   HV6431

ISBN 0 450 06086 1

To Frances

Contents

Acknowledgements

I would like to thank my researchers in Washington, Zaira Steele and Elizabeth Bode, for doing such good work. In addition, Hirsh Goodman, Dalbert Hallenstein and Chris Ryder went to a great deal of trouble to make sure I got access to the right people. By the nature of the subject, there are many others who made a significant contribution but who wish to remain anonymous. I am most grateful to them all, particularly to those who, at some personal risk, checked facts and verified descriptions on my behalf.

Alice Mayhew and Henry Ferris in America and Colin Honnor, Alice Atkin and Nancy Duin in England did a wonderful job of editing the manuscript. Because of their astonishing eye for detail, my mistakes were corrected and errors of logic made more sensible.

Denzil Murray-Lee introduced me to the joys and frustrations of the word processor, and patiently talked me through my endless blunders, whatever the time of day or night.

My wife Patricia, who found the research and writing of this book an especially worrying experience, deserves my grateful thanks. Not only did she nurse me through hepatitis contracted while researching the book, but her comments were always helpful and her advice sound. Without her support, this book would not have been possible.

Preface

The Financing of Terror began in 1979 when I was working as a reporter for *8 Days*, a weekly news magazine specialising in the Middle East. Inevitably, given the Arab ownership, the magazine devoted a large amount of effort to covering the Palestinians and, in particular, the Palestine Liberation Organisation. However, in all the material that was written about the PLO, I found nothing about their finances: they were obviously a large and well-funded operation, but where did the money come from?

With the encouragement of my editors, I spent some two months looking at the subject. It was extraordinarily difficult to obtain hard information, but with the help of friends and contacts within the PLO and in the intelligence community, a picture emerged of a powerful and rich multinational 'corporation' which owed its survival more to the business acumen of its leadership than to the donations of the faithful in the Lebanon's refugee camps.

A cover story for the magazine was prepared and laid out. The copy then reached the Arab paymasters and the article was suppressed. To many journalists, this is a familiar story of special interests interfering with a free press and, to some extent, it is part of the give-and-take of the news business. However, in this case, special circumstances pertained. The Arabs were unwilling to have the PLO portrayed other than as a self-sacrificing, highly motivated group working for the good of the Palestinians. This conventional, accepted image of the PLO did not conform to the portrait of PLO fat cats in their villas in Amman and the South of France or to the gilt-edged investment portfolio of the PLO.

Over the next few years, I saw various aspects of terrorism first hand. I was the first European journalist into Tehran after the American Embassy was seized, and I covered the bombing of the Iraqi nuclear reactor by Israel, guerrilla warfare in Africa, the killing of a British policewoman in London by Libyan terrorists, and the attempted assassination of Prime Minister Margaret Thatcher in Brighton by IRA terrorists in 1984.

In all the blood and horror that resulted, one aspect emerged quite clearly: no government seemed to be capable of responding to the threat of international terrorism until after the event had occurred – and by then it was always too late. This book is the result of that initial observation.

To build up an accurate picture of the financial resources of terrorism, original research had to be done in Washington, London, Paris, Bonn, Brussels, Beirut, Damascus, Rome, Tel Aviv, Jerusalem and Geneva. The subject of this book is of particular sensitivity to some terrorist groups, and I received a number of quite specific warnings not to go to certain cities. In two particular cases, I relied on the good offices of a friend and colleague who, at considerable personal risk, obtained some specific answers for me.

All the material that appears in this book, from whatever source, has been checked. Information supplied by an intelligence agency has been checked (if possible) with the terrorist organisation concerned or, at the very least, with an agency in another country which is a more impartial observer. In addition, the manuscript has been read by a number of experts with field experience in countering terrorism, and any errors which they pointed out have been removed.

However, this is an inexact science and it would be naïve of me to pretend that what you will read is a full and perfect account of the financing of international terrorism. I have approached the subject with no bias other than believing that terrorism of the left or right is wrong, and I hope that dispassionate analysis has helped to sift fact from propaganda.

Of the terrorists and their opposite numbers in intelligence or specialist counter-terrorist agencies whom I have interviewed, few would agree to have their names used and I am forced to respect their wishes. This will undoubtedly raise questions about the authenticity of my sources, which, under the circumstances, I will be unable adequately to answer. However, there are extensive notes for each chapter: these cite all published sources when they have been used; and where it has not been possible to name specific people, I have given an indication of the strength of the source.

For the sake of consistency and because terrorists mostly deal in them, I have used United States dollars throughout this book, except for domestic UK cases where the sterling sum is given followed by the dollar equivalent in brackets. To simplify matters, conversions were done on the basis that £1 is roughly equivalent to US$1.50.

Introduction

Controlling Terrorism: An Alternative Approach

TERRORISM MUST, of course, always in part dictate the counter-terrorist response, as governments must react to the nature of the threat. But since terrorism first appeared on the scene at the end of the 1960s, that response has always been inadequate.

In 1970 when, according to the US State Department, 302 terrorist acts occurred around the world, the Western governments found they had no common response and nor did they have the men and equipment to counter terrorism. The result was a painful examination that concentrated on two areas: combating terrorists on the ground and looking for the causes of terrorism.

To combat terrorism, various élite units, either working within existing armed forces or as an adjunct to the police, were established or strengthened. Their job was to act as a specialised quick-reaction force to deal with terrorism wherever it might appear, and they placed special emphasis on countering hijackings, kidnappings and assassinations. By the mid-1970s, no self-respecting democracy was without its own élite counter-terrorist unit.

The second response – to find the cause of the phenomenon – was more difficult. No matter how revolting the methods used by terrorists, some part of the announced reasons for a group's existence – the wrongs they proclaim they will right – will evoke sympathy. However, any admission that even the smallest part of the terrorists' cause may be justified can be seen as weakness. Therefore, counter-terrorist propaganda tends to portray the terrorist as all evil, and politicians and journalists talk of an international terrorist conspiracy. The theory suggests that, behind the bombings, the kidnappings and the killings,

1

there is a single force directing attempts to destabilise and eventually cause the collapse of the Western democratic system.

Such conspiracy theories link a series of otherwise unconnected facts to prove the argument. They also tend, at the least, to ignore any evidence to the contrary, if not to distort the evidence. In a document entitled *Patterns of International Terrorism: 1982*, the US Department of State supports the conspiracy line:

> The Soviet Union and its allies have provided training, arms and other direct and indirect support to a variety of national insurgent and separatist groups. Many of these groups commit international terrorist attacks as part of their program of revolutionary violence. Moreover, some of the individuals trained and equipped by the Soviets make their way into strictly terrorist groups with little revolutionary history or potential.

The Reagan administration firmly believes that the USSR is the mastermind of world terrorism, and the Soviets believe the United States is aggressive and determined to expand its sphere of influence – through terrorism if necessary. Such convictions imply an ability and a sophistication in both East and West which is far from the reality. In the case of both the CIA and the KGB, their operations are marked by a high degree of opportunism, little evidence of concentrated long-term strategies and a singular inability to manage complex political operations successfully.

However, both the superpowers and their allies do get involved in international terrorism. They may not directly finance individual groups but both seek to turn political instability to their own advantage. In the case of the Eastern Bloc, support for different terrorist groups often occurs because the Soviets see a healthy financial profit in the relationship. In Chapter 1, I shall look at the involvement of both the Soviet Union and the United States with terrorism, and will show that this is less than is generally believed and that there is little evidence to support the theory of an international terrorist conspiracy of left or right.

If that is the case, has society understood the nature of the terrorist threat and has our response been the right one? I intend to argue that counter-terrorism has been largely stagnant since the early 1970s while terrorists in different countries have all learned from their mistakes to evolve into richer and more sophisticated forces.

Although there is an enormous body of literature on the subject of terrorism, much of it is biased and/or shows varying degrees of ignorance. The same criticisms can be applied to most serious studies, which are dependent on prejudice for their starting point rather than on dispassionate analysis. For example, the story goes that, just after the publication of Claire Sterling's book, *The Terror Network*, which laid the responsibility for international terrorism firmly at the door of the KGB, a meeting of senior directors of the CIA took place at their headquarters in Langley, Virginia. William Casey, then head of the CIA, was in the chair. He had with him a copy of the book to which he drew the attention of his staff, saying that the CIA must make sure the book received maximum exposure as it proved everything they had been saying about the Soviets masterminding terrorism. Then one of the deputy directors pointed out that the book was largely a product of the CIA's disinformation department. The story may well be apocryphal but it does illustrate how terrorism is a potential tool of the superpowers.

This book attempts, through an objective examination of the evidence, to sort out the myth from the reality in the context of the financial resources of different terrorist groups. In all that has been written on terrorism, I have not discovered any serious study which deals with where the terrorists get their money and how they spend it. This is surprising, given the size of the multi-billion-dollar business that terrorism has become. Even where the subject is discussed in passing, the same assumptions of widespread Communist funding and the hand-to-mouth existence of terrorist groups are repeated in identical fashion by different authors, citing either the same sources or each other.

This book is not intended to be an exhaustive study of each and every terrorist group. I have structured it so that some of the accepted beliefs about the funding of international terrorism can be re-examined. I have then taken a number of specific examples which illustrate how terrorism has evolved from idealistic and poverty-stricken beginnings in the early 1970s, to the sophisticated multinational corporations that some terrorist groups resemble today. Each group is examined in the context of its finances, but rather than attempt to produce a balance-sheet for each organisation, I have attempted to use a particular group to illustrate one or more aspects of financing. So, for example, the Red Brigade, which has evolved similarly to the IRA, is looked at only in the context of kidnap and ransom, which they have turned into a lucrative trade. Some groups, such as ETA or FP25, have largely been ignored, not because they are insignificant but simply because they illustrate points that can be better illustrated by other groups.

As the Soviet Union is commonly seen as the main sponsor of international terrorism, it seemed appropriate to deal with their financial involvement with terrorism early on. I have done this in Chapter 2, in the context of the Palestine Liberation Organisation, which is not only the most financially successful terrorist group but is also the one terrorist organisation that is supposed to have benefited consistently from Kremlin help.

However, the facts suggest that the USSR's financing of terrorism is minimal. That is not to suggest that the Soviets do not benefit from international terrorism: they do and their propaganda effort in support of 'revolutionary movements' is considerable. Yet, if the experience of the PLO is anything to go by, they are mean allies who give very little and expect a great deal in return. By contrast, China, which has succeeded in maintaining a very low profile, is a far more generous friend.

The general pattern that emerges from looking at superpower support for terrorist groups is that it is only when a terrorist organisation develops into a guerrilla force with popular support that funding is forthcoming. The United States, for example, has generally supported groups such as UNITA in Angola and the Contras in Nicaragua but has ignored smaller organisations. I have not dealt with support for such groups as they fall outside my definition of terrorism, although it is quite clear that state support for guerrilla forces is growing.

As far as the PLO is concerned, the Arab countries have been the main source of outside income, but this has declined in recent years as the organisation has become increasingly self-sufficient, developing its own infrastructure which makes it independent. In two chapters I have examined this structure in the context of the Lebanon and its investments around the world which now provide it with an annual income of $1.25 billion from assets of $5 billion. The PLO is important because it shows what a terrorist group can achieve if the government opposing it – in this case, the Israelis – concentrates its counter-terrorist effort in the wrong direction. So, while the Israelis try to prevent the next bombing or killing, the PLO quietly get on with business, to such an extent that they are now impossible to eliminate through conventional counter-terrorist means.

The IRA have developed in a less sophisticated fashion, although they too have benefited from a British government that has failed to understand the changing face of terrorism. The IRA does not have as many Swiss bank accounts as the PLO, but it does have protection rackets and money-laundering operations that are more reminiscent of the Mafia than a Marxist organisation. The United States is generally thought to be the main supplier of cash to the IRA, but I have looked at this and, again, have found the truth to be very different from the impression that both the British government and the IRA wish to foster. America actually makes a very small contribution to the IRA coffers, and I have devoted a chapter to showing exactly how this is the case.

Kidnapping for ransom has become big business all over the world. Italy has turned this particular method of terrorist financing into something resembling an art form, with professional teams being hired to carry out the kidnap, guard the safe-house and handle the negotiations for the victim's release. To match this, Lloyd's of London have organised insurance for potential victims and have helped to set up a company which will negotiate a ransom for the insurers. This civilised process has made a great deal of money for terrorists, Lloyd's and the negotiators. The kidnap-and-ransom business is an interesting example of commerce adapting to a terrorist threat, accommodating it and then turning it to a profit. Chapter 8 explains how this business has developed and looks at what can be done to break the chain.

While business can turn terrorism to profit, the lesson can work in the other direction. Terrorism in Colombia was insignificant until the beginning of the 1980s, when the two main terrorist groups in the country – FARC and M19 – decided to capitalise on the growing drugs traffic. The two groups now provide 'protection' to the drug growers, and in four years, the followers of each group have increased in number from 150 to over 10,000. They are well armed and financed and are a potent political force in the country, and all this has occurred in the face of a massive US effort to stem the flow of drugs from Colombia. However, this effort has totally ignored the threat posed by the growth of terrorism in the country and has misunderstood how significant a healthy income can be to the success of a terrorist group.

Since the purpose of this book is to encourage a re-examination of the way society views terrorism, I hope that the examples I have given lead to the conclusion that a refocusing of the counter-terrorist effort is now necessary. It surely makes sense for democratic governments to take the initiative against international terrorism. However, this has traditionally brought with it the repression of the civil liberties which democratic societies tend to revere. In addition, draconian laws can in turn give ammunition to a terrorist who portrays the State as an oppressive machine which is the enemy of the people. However, instead of attacking the people, law enforcement agencies could go for the money that pays the terrorists.

In this book I have attempted to show how governments and law enforcement agencies have failed to adapt to the changing nature of terrorism and I hope I have set the agenda for a new debate on the terrorist phenomenon which is undermining the fabric of modern society. It is imperative that governments learn the lessons from the past and address themselves to this threat, before it is too late.

Defining Terrorism

In 1980, the Central Intelligence Agency adopted a definition of terrorism which has since been accepted by the US State Department. It reads:

> TERRORISM: The threat or use of violence for political purposes by individuals or groups, whether acting for or in opposition to established governmental authority, when such actions are intended to shock, stun, or intimidate a target group wider than the immediate victims. Terrorism has involved groups seeking to overthrow specific regimes, to rectify perceived national or group grievances, or to undermine international order as an end in itself.

This kind of all-embracing definition has led to a misunderstanding of the nature of terrorism. For example, this formula would include the French Resistance in Nazi-occupied France during World War II, the Contras in Nicaragua and the IRA in Northern Ireland. This tendency to group all forms of unconventional warfare under the umbrella of terrorism enables us to attach a 'terrorist' label to every act of violence, a label that is often of considerable propaganda value to the opposing governments. So, the mujahedeen in Afghanistan are classed as terrorists along with the Red Brigade in Italy even though they are different forces with different aims and methods of operation.

Every terrorist group has at its heart a core of legitimacy. The IRA claim to represent the Catholics in Northern Ireland who have suffered centuries of discrimination by the Protestants; the Red Brigade would claim to operate on behalf of the oppressed working classes of Milan, Naples and other industrial centres of Italy where corruption is rife and

the workers have little say in their own affairs; the Shi'ite fundamentalists who have launched so many attacks against Arab and Western targets
over the past few years believe they are the spearhead of an Islamic
revival which will restore their sect to the prominence it deserves and
make up for the exploitation they have suffered at the hands of their
enemies – the Sunnis and the Christians. Of course, legitimate com-
plaints against the society in which they operate does not excuse the
terrorism of such groups but can, in part, explain it.

Some terrorist groups may also operate within what society con-
siders to be proper legal boundaries. The IRA gun down soldiers and
policemen, but run clubs and taxis; the PLO blow up school buses in
Jerusalem, but have investment accounts in Wall Street. Similarly,
those who oppose terrorism and do so in the name of an existing society
may themselves commit acts of terrorism. The British commandos in
World War II were specifically established to terrorise the German
army, and some of the actions of the US army in Vietnam, such as My
Lai, could be classed as 'terrorist'.

Too wide a definition of terrorism tends to dissipate the counter-
terrorist effort, which inevitably becomes too broadly based. Not only do
the terms 'war' and 'terrorism' become confused but so also does the
identity of the terrorist as compared to the guerrilla fighter, the soldier or
the social worker.

The British government, in the Prevention of Terrorism Act of
1974, which was promulgated to combat the IRA, defines terrorism in
the same broad terms as have confused the fight against terrorism.
' "Terrorism" means the use of violence for political ends, and includes
any use of violence for the purpose of putting the public or any section of
the community in fear.'

The definition of terrorism should not be restricted by political or
national barriers. However, for the American and British governments,
and others, the word 'terrorist' has come to mean any form of violent
activity with which a particular government happens to disagree.
Terrorism has thus become a propaganda tool. For example, the British
refer to the IRA as *terrorists* but to the PLO as *guerrillas*, a distinction
that has always infuriated the Israelis who see no difference.

In the counter-terrorist war, this kind of broad definition of the enemy
is of help on two levels: First, the government, by labelling an opposition
group 'terrorist', hopes to draw away support from moderates who will
not wish to be associated with the violence implied by underwriting
terrorism. Second, in opposing what has officially been described as

7

'terrorism', the public will tolerate a far stronger reaction by police forces than would be allowed if a threat were posed to the government by a non-violent underground group, or by people who enjoyed widespread public support. The label 'terrorist' isolates the opposition forces and allows the aggressive use of force to combat the threat.

Such subjective judgements give rise to the cliché that 'one man's terrorist is another man's freedom fighter'. But terrorism exists on the left or right, and a bomb is just as dangerous whether it is planted on Capitol Hill, Washington DC or in Red Square, Moscow.

In 1976, the US State Department sponsored a conference of terrorist specialists who attempted to define the phenomenon, but even this group failed to arrive at a common definition. One of the participants, Chalmers Johnson, recalled another delegate's definition of terrorism:

> Let us strip away the masks of terrorist illusions and expose the deathhead of murder beneath [said the delegate]. Terrorists are fond of using romantic euphemisms for their murderous crimes. They claim to be revolutionary heroes yet they commit cowardly acts and lack the heroic qualities of humanity and magnanimity. They profess to be revolutionary soldiers yet they attack only by stealth, murder and maim the innocent, and disdain all rules and conventions of war. They claim to bring 'liberation' when in reality they seek power for themselves. Some claim that their violence ennobles them: history shows that it is totally corrupting and ultimately is turned against the revolutionary society itself. They frequently profess that they administer 'revolutionary justice': in truth, they make war on all ethics and legality and substitute the whim of their own tyranny.

Such an emotional response expresses our revulsion, but it does not help to define terrorism.

The Palestine Liberation Organisation, and others unfriendly to Israel, compare the activities of the Zionist Irgun Zva'i Leumi and the Stern Gang in Palestine in the 1940s, to those of the PLO in Israel today. The Zionist gangs murdered a number of senior British officials, hung two British army sergeants, blew up the King David Hotel and carried out a widespread campaign of intimidation, bombing and assassination. The campaign was ruthless and undoubtedly contributed to the British decision to leave Palestine. The British believed the Jews of the Stern Gang and the Irgun were terrorists; the Zionists believed they were freedom fighters in a war of national liberation. The Zionist terrorists achieved their aims and, in the Western world at least, the methods used to establish the State of Israel have for the most part been forgotten. The PLO, who have not achieved anything of significance in their political campaign, are still labelled terrorists by many Western countries although their sympathisers, such as Britain, see them as guerrillas – that is, they operate with some evidence of popular support.

While some aspects of the definition of a terrorist must be subjective, there are certain common elements to the problem. In climbing the ladder from peaceful civil demonstration to full-scale civil war, stopping at terrorism and guerrilla warfare along the way, the revolutionary will acquire a number of distinct characteristics that divide each stage.

For example, those who oppose abortion in the United States and Europe would generally characterise themselves as Christian and law-abiding citizens. They oppose abortion on quite clear grounds, believing that each abortion is an act of murder against an unborn child. They make their views known in a number of ways: they write to their government representatives and they demonstrate peacefully. However, in their ranks are some more extreme people who believe that the only way to persuade doctors of the justice of their cause is through violence. So, they throw petrol bombs at doctors' offices and issue death threats. This is terrorism at its most basic level.

A similar evolutionary pattern can be traced through more politically orientated groups such as the PLO and the Red Brigade. The roots of such groups lie in a social dissatisfaction among a minority of the population that fails to find expression through the normal democratic channels. Some or all of the group then turn to what they see as the only method to achieve their aims. In its infancy, terrorism operates with little evidence of public support. Safe-houses may be provided for the terrorist on the run, but this is a long way from the mass demonstrations that would be classed as 'popular' support. In the last days of the Shah's Iran, for example, it was common to see over one million people crowding on to the streets as a popular revolution evolved from what, for some years previously, had simply been a small and rather ineffective terrorist campaign.

The PLO, by contrast, have never managed to generate the kind of public support among the Palestinians in Israel and on the West Bank (where the great majority of Palestinians live) that would turn them from a terrorist organisation into an effective guerrilla force. There has never been any real evidence of popular support for the organisation, and this has resulted in them having to operate outside Israel – primarily from the Lebanon – from where they launch their terrorist attacks.

The Financing of Terror

Part of the aim of a terrorist group is to commit acts of such barbarity that they will provoke the government they oppose into acts of repression. These acts – house-to-house searches, imprisonment without trial, or laws that restrict freedom – generally win recruits to the terrorist cause and may allow a terrorist group to graduate to guerrilla warfare. In trying to provoke that repressive reaction, terrorists, typically, will treat civilians as legitimate targets. Guerrillas, relying as they do on a broader political base, tend to concentrate more on military targets as they push a country towards civil war.

For the purposes of this book, I prefer a narrower definition of terrorism:

> A terrorist is an individual or member of a group that wishes to achieve political ends using violent means, often at the cost of casualties to innocent civilians and with the support of only a minority of the people they claim to represent.

Some people may disagree with the groups I label as terrorist, but part of my intention has been to encourage a re-examination of the way modern society sees terrorism and terrorists. I shall use my definition only as a starting point.

Part One

STATE TERROR

1

Terrorism: the multinational corporation

THE GROWTH of revolutionary movements has given both the Soviet Union and the United States a unique opportunity to encourage destabilisation. Today, conventional warfare and gunboat diplomacy brings with it the danger of escalation into nuclear war and the annihilation of humanity. In both Washington and Moscow, there is agreement that the future of modern warfare lies in a low-intensity conflict – the surgical use of highly trained specialist forces to wage clandestine warfare in foreign countries. To fight such wars in places such as Nicaragua, Angola or Afghanistan, both the USSR and the United States, helped by their allies, have in the past few years devoted hundreds of millions of dollars to the training and supplying of secret armies.

The result of this new tactical emphasis has been a number of small and generally very savage conflicts – forty in 1984 – in which the superpowers battle for supremacy. These conflicts take place at two distinct levels. On the one hand, the major powers can use their own special forces to intervene secretly in another country's affairs, and on the other, they can fund and train foreign troops to fight a guerrilla war on their behalf.

Terrorists, as aspiring guerrillas, provide the major powers with an opportunity to get in early with the cash which buys the influence that can lead to real power sometime in the future. However, terrorist groups are both unstable and lacking in the pragmatism that is essential for political success. Few have achieved their political goals, and while terrorism can cause considerable economic and political damage, there is little evidence that it is a viable political force for change.

There are also certain inherent dangers in supporting terrorist movements. The Soviets worry that if they support groups that directly

13

threaten the United States or their allies, the favour might be returned. Both the United States and the USSR would be very vulnerable to terrorist attack, although neither has yet suffered anything resembling co-ordinated action.

However, within certain limitations, both superpowers have an interest in encouraging a degree of instability in areas under the control of their enemy or in areas where they wish to increase their influence: destabilisation can ultimately topple governments and produce a new ally. And, of course, every terrorist act or guerrilla war directs valuable resources away from countering a more conventional or nuclear threat. All countries of both east and west, appreciate that support begins with hard cash. Wherever instability is fostered, outside forces fund the anti-government movements, whether it be the mujahedeen in Afghanistan, the contras in Nicaragua or the African National Congress in South Africa. Without such aid, guerrilla or terrorist groups stagnate or die and present no real threat. For example, it was only after the CIA began substantial covert support of the guerrillas in Afghanistan that the mujahedeen gained real momentum and military credibility. It is a curious anomaly of covert warfare that governments understand the importance of financing groups they support, but fail to appreciate how vital cash is to the terrorist forces they oppose.

Financial support is not the only method of supporting terrorist groups. Favourable propaganda provides useful international credibility, and arms and training the fighting tools. For the Soviet Union and her allies, one of the main motives for involvement with terrorism seems to be simple profit.

One of the countries that has been a target of Communist subversion is Turkey, which occupies a crucial position on the eastern flank of NATO. In September 1980, a dictatorship led by General Kenan Evren took control of Turkey, a military coup that ended more than two years of steadily escalating political violence which had already killed 2000 people (an average of twenty-eight dying every day). Over the next six months, the military government arrested more than 40,000 people – both Fascist and Communist – who were allegedly involved in the wave of bombings and assassinations.

In the course of the purge, the government confiscated 633,724 illegal arms, valued at $250 million. The Turks concerned had purchased (with cash and drugs) the vast majority of these from the Bulgarians, but out of this huge quantity of small arms, only 1371 were Soviet-made Kalashnikov AK47 rifles, the favoured guerrilla weapon.

According to the Turkish security authorities, sixty per cent of the captured arms and ammunition had Western brand names and serial numbers, but when they tried to trace the serial numbers on the weapons, they found that most had not been manufactured in the countries designated on the guns. For example, French 'Unique' brand pistols were imitations and Beretta pistols had been manufactured in Bulgaria under licence from the Italian company. Of the remaining forty per cent of the captured arms, thirty per cent had been manufactured in Eastern Europe and the remainder had been made in Turkey.

Although much of the terrorism in Turkey was organised by groups who wished to bring about a Communist-led government, most of the arms were used by local gangsters involved in drug production, smuggling and other crime. The local mafia had built up extremely close relations with the authorities in Bulgaria, which of all Eastern Bloc countries is the most willing to co-operate with criminals and has the most corrupt leadership in Europe.

The Hotel Vitosha–New Otani in Sofia, the capital of Bulgaria, symbolises the mixture of greed, capitalism and political opportunism so apparent in the Communist world's attitude towards international terrorism, and the hotel's marble halls are a meeting-place for a cross-section of the criminal élite and politically motivated. Arabs from George Habbash's PFLP meet with Turkish drug smugglers and Bulgarian currency dealers and arms manufacturers. Deals made here invariably bring much-needed foreign currency to the Eastern Bloc while spreading the illegal flow of arms and drugs to the West.

Turkish officials believe that as many as six drug-smuggling rings dealing in heroin (brought in from Turkey and then passed on to West Germany and the United States) operate from the Hotel Vitosha. In addition, Bulgaria's association with the major criminal movements in Europe and the Middle East is of considerable importance to its intelligence network and to that of the KGB.

With this association come certain obligations. Little doubt remains that the Bulgarians were heavily involved in the plot to assassinate Pope John Paul II in May 1981. Mehmet Ali Agca, the assassin, has confessed that some members of the Bulgarian secret service helped him and that he stayed for a time in the comforts of the Hotel Vitosha. The Bulgars had also supplied Agca with a gun and money as well as putting him in touch with their agents in Rome.

In this particular case, there is strong evidence that the Bulgarians knew the purpose of Agca's visit and therefore condoned and encouraged it. If the Bulgarians knew of it, the KGB most likely did, too. While there may have been a reason why the Bulgarians and the Soviets wanted the Pope killed, this incident is not a convincing argument to suggest that either country is orchestrating the terrorism perpetrated by the large numbers of independent groups operating all over the world.

Bulgaria has a long record of giving sanctuary to terrorists on the run and of supplying documents and guns to different groups – the Israelis believe that more than eighty per cent of the PLO's arms come from the Bulgarian port of Varna – but this is hardly surprising given that an estimated $1 billion is involved annually in the illegal trade in guns and drugs in Bulgaria.

Fortunately, such a forthright approach to the business of terrorism is rare. Most so-called support for terrorist groups by various countries is actually characterised by disloyalty and whim. This makes life a misery for terrorists, who nearly always appear to be short of cash and totally unable to plan policy or strategy from one year to the next.

However, not all international terrorism is based simply on cash. Political idealism is obviously a prime motivator and nowhere is this more apparent than in Fidel Castro's Cuba. Since he came to power with Soviet backing in 1959, he has consistently supported revolutions around the world.

When Castro overthrew the Batista regime, he announced that capitalism and big business would be tolerated in Cuba provided their operations complied with local laws. This was a modest offering of moderation from a man whom the United States feared as the first example of the 'red menace' to threaten the American mainland. The United States countered by offering economic aid to Cuba but only under the most rigid conditions, hoping that the economic disaster that would inevitably accompany the revolution would bring Cuba back into the US fold. Understandably, Castro turned to a more sympathetic ally, the Soviet Union, who sent aid and engineered a heavily subsidised oil-for-sugar deal which underpinned the revolution by ensuring some measure of economic stability.

Once Cuba started to deal overtly with the USSR, American oil companies, which had stayed in the country after the revolution, began to withdraw. The ones that remained refused to refine Soviet oil delivered to Cuba and so they were nationalised, and the radicalisation of the revolution continued. The Soviets, arch proponents of the long-term view, were content to subsidise the Cuban economy and support the Castro revolution. They knew that the closer the ties became

16

between the two countries, the more rigid would be the response from the United States, thus forcing Castro ever deeper into the Soviet embrace.

In 1975, the US Senate committee investigating assassination plots against foreign leaders found a memorandum written by CIA director Richard Helms, dated 14 April 1967, which shows how radical US policy had become. The committee was told:

> Through the years the Cuban problem was discussed in terms such as 'dispose of Castro', 'remove Castro', 'knock off Castro', etc. and this meant the overthrow of the Communist government in Cuba and the replacing of it with a democratic régime. Terms such as the above appear in many working papers, memoranda for the record, etc., and, as stated, all refer to a change in the Cuban government.

This robust policy against Cuba resulted in a series of disastrous plots and assassination attempts that convinced Castro – if he ever had any doubts – that not only had the United States opposed the revolution but it was unwilling to allow any form of revolution to survive, whatever the wishes of the Cuban people. Castro's position became quite clear: he would do what he could for those countries that wished to fight what he saw as the yoke of colonialism, and would give support to what he would describe as 'freedom fighters'.

There is a strong view in the United States, led by the Reagan administration, that sees Cuba as the primary source for a revolutionary disease, spreading through the Caribbean and Central America, which every day gets closer to American borders. In a March 1985 document entitled *The Soviet–Cuban Connection in Central America and the Caribbean*, the US State Department and the Department of Defense pointed out:

> Since 1975 Castro has sent military forces and/or advisers to Angola, Mozambique, South Yemen, Congo, Ghana, Mali, Guinea-Bissau as well as Grenada and Nicaragua. Although the propaganda focus is on such ideals as 'socialist solidarity', Castro is known to charge many of these countries for Cuban troops, 'construction workers' and other 'internationalists', draining scarce foreign exchange from local economies. According to reliable sources, recipient governments must pay Cuba a fixed sum per month for each Cuban soldier and each civilian technician. Thus, Castro is simultaneously playing the world revolutionary role he has always desired, supporting Soviet foreign policy goals, and acquiring hard currency.

17

Castro is no doubt doing all he can to bring about change, often through the use of violence, in countries unsympathetic to the United States, and these changes are usually of considerable benefit to the Soviet Union. However, this does not mean that Castro is actually the mastermind behind the spread of revolution.

In Africa, too, Cuba is attempting to influence events. In November 1975, the Cuban government sent its first contingent of troops to bolster the Angolan government and fight against the South African- and CIA-supported UNITA* rebels attacking Angola's territory from Namibia. The 20,000 Cuban troops at present based in the country are now the most significant obstacle to a peace settlement between South Africa, the Angolan government and SWAPO, the Angolan-backed guerrilla movement operating in Namibia. The United States government insists that any agreement must include the withdrawal of the Cuban troops from the country, even though the South Africans do not consider the Cuban soldiers a real threat and would make a deal which included allowing the Cubans to stay.

Such overseas adventures have been costly for Castro as well as remarkably unsuccessful – in Angola, for example, the government of President José Santos is increasingly beleaguered, with UNITA occupying nearly half the country – and the Soviet Union's efforts have also met with less than success. In Mozambique and Rhodesia (now Zimbabwe), Soviet-backed guerrilla forces overthrew pro-Western governments but neither of the current governments can be described as faithful friends of the USSR. The president of Mozambique has become pro-West after finding that the Soviets refused to supply the economic aid he needed, and Zimbabwe remains firmly tied to the West. Further north, the Soviet Union was expelled from Egypt, and in Iran, the pro-Communist Tudeh party has been banned and its leaders jailed or executed. Even in Central and South America, there is little evidence to suggest that the USSR will necessarily emerge from the current drama any more powerful.

Cuba's failures at revolutionary attempts abroad could possibly be attributed to the United States government's skill and intransigence in opposing Castro propaganda, but the evidence points in another direction. Cuba's incompetence as a world revolutionary power, and the

* For the full names of all groups mentioned in this book, as well as some details about their make-up and history, see 'A glossary of terrorism', pp. 247–257.

generally low quality of its training of international terrorists, is as responsible for its failures as anything the United States has done.

The Soviet Union currently subsidises the Cuban economy to the tune of $4 billion a year, and while there is no evidence of direct Cuban subsidies being passed on to terrorist groups, Cuba does help train terrorists from around the world. The military base of Guanabo, in the rolling hills along Cuba's northern coast, is Cuba's terrorist training centre. Trainees from Nicaragua, Colombia, El Salvador, the Middle East, Angola and many other countries have passed through there on their way to becoming fully trained terrorists.

In addition, a 1981 US State Department report, which suggests prominent Cuban involvement in promoting armed insurgencies, stated that, since 1978, Cuba has:

★ Worked to unite traditionally splintered radical groups behind a commitment to armed struggle with Cuban advice and material assistance.
★ Trained ideologically committed cadres in urban and rural guerrilla warfare.
★ Supplied or arranged for the supply of weapons to support the Cuban-trained cadres' efforts to assume power by force.
★ Encouraged terrorism in the hope of provoking indiscriminate violence and repression, in order to weaken government legitimacy and attract new converts to armed struggle.
★ Used military aid and advisers to gain influence over guerrilla fronts and radical governments through armed pro-Cuban Marxists.

Western democratic governments view these activities with some alarm, but are in a quandary as to what action to take. A passive response leaves the initiative firmly in the hands of a Castro-supported terrorist movement, while a more active one, involving the support of right-wing groups favourable to the West and possible pre-emptive strikes against the terrorists, offers the opportunity to dictate the terms under which the war against terrorism is fought. However, with such a robust response, the objective observer may find it difficult to distinguish between the behaviour of the terrorists and those governments that are countering the threat.

Alone among the Western nations, the United States, particularly since the arrival of the Reagan administration, has chosen to take a series of active steps against terrorism and those efforts that aim to undermine pro-Western governments. Currently, the United States supports guerrilla operations in Libya, Afghanistan, Iran, Nicaragua, Kampuchea (Cambodia) and Chad. In addition, South Africa's support for the MNR in Mozambique and for UNITA in Angola has come about with US backing, as has Israel's support for the Christians in the Lebanon. According to the CIA's own definition of terrorism (*see* p. 6), the US government has been guilty of financing, training and, to a large extent, controlling terrorists (although under my own definition, they, like the Soviets, have largely restricted their support to guerrilla forces).

In 1984, the Reagan administration officially authorised $24 million in aid to support a 12,000-man army of Contras, dedicated to the overthrow of the left-wing Sandinista regime in Nicaragua. (Given the CIA's involvement, the real amount of cash 'unofficially' allocated to the Contras will be much higher.) Publicly, the Reagan administration has described the Contras' fight against the Nicaraguan government as something approaching a holy war – which has as its aim the halting of the spread of Communism in Central and South America. In early 1986, Reagan asked for $100 million in aid to be given to the Contras. While he may not get the full amount, Congress seems certain to authorise a substantial increase.

To justify this hardline policy, the Reagan government has made a number of allegations which are often unsupported by the facts. In July 1985, for example, the US Defense Department alleged that hundreds of West Europeans are being trained in terrorist tactics by Cuban and Palestinian instructors in Nicaragua.

These allegations are weakened somewhat by the public's awareness of a CIA-written manual entitled *Psychological Operations in Guerrilla Wars*, the Spanish edition of which had surfaced in October 1984. In its way, it is as much of a terrorist handbook as Carlos Marighella's famous mini-manual which became the bible of the terrorist movement in the late 1960s and 1970s. The eight chapters of the CIA manual cover 'armed propaganda teams', 'massive in-depth support' and 'psychological operations', and the most controversial section actually instructs the reader on how to 'neutralise' selected individuals. 'Neutralise' in this context is a euphemism for assassination, and the discovery of the manual was greeted with outrage in the press, in the US Congress and by the public at large. Congress declared the document illegal, and there was almost universal condemnation of the administration and of the CIA for allowing such a document to be written. However, the fact remains that it was widely circulated and the decision for its release to the Contras must have been taken at the highest level. It is important to look at the manual in some detail as its contents counter-balance western propaganda which suggests that terrorism is supported by communists. The manual highlights the lengths to which western governments will go to counter what they see as leftist subversion.

In Chapter 4 of the manual, entitled 'Armed Propaganda', Section 5 addresses itself to 'Selective use of violence for propagandistic effects':

> It is possible to neutralize carefully selected and planned targets, such as court judges, police and State Security officials, CDS chiefs, etc. For psychological purposes, it is necessary to take extreme precautions, and it is absolutely necessary to gather together the population affected, so that they will be present, take part in the act, and formulate accusations against the oppressor.
>
> The target or person should be chosen on the basis of the spontaneous hostility that the majority of the population feels toward the target.
>
> Use rejection or potential hatred by the majority of the population affected toward the target, stirring up the population and making them see all the negative and hostile actions of the individual against the people.
>
> If the majority of the people give their support or backing to the target or subject, do not try to change these sentiments through provocation.

> *Relative difficulty of controlling the person who will replace the target.*
> The person who will replace the target must be chosen carefully, based on:
> – Degree of violence necessary to carry out the change.
> – Degree of violence acceptable to the population affected.
> – Degree of violence possible without causing damage or danger to other individuals in the area of the target.
> – Degree of predictable reprisal by the enemy on the population affected or other individuals in the area of the target.
> The mission to replace the individual should be followed by:
> – Extensive explanation within the population affected of the reason why it was necessary for the good of the people.
> – Explain that Sandinista retaliation is unjust, indiscriminate and, above all, a justification for the execution of this mission.
> – Carefully test the reaction of the people toward the mission, as well as control this reaction making sure that the population's reaction is beneficial toward the Freedom Commandos.

The section entitled 'Guerrilla weapons are the strength of the people over an illegal government' provides the guerrilla forces with justifications for any actions they may have to take against local people, including shooting villagers.

21

The armed propaganda in populated areas does not give the impression that weapons are the power of the guerrillas over the people, but rather that the weapons are the strength of the people against a regime of repression. Whenever it is necessary to use armed force in an occupation or visit to a town or village, guerrillas should emphasize this making sure that they:
– Explain to the population that in the first place this is being done to protect them, the people, and not themselves.
– Admit frankly and publicly that this is an 'act of the democratic guerrilla movement' with appropriate explanations.
– Explain that this action, though it is not desirable, is necessary because the final objective of the insurrection is a free and democratic society, where acts of force are not necessary.

If, for example, it should be necessary for one of the advanced posts to fire on a citizen who was trying to leave the town or city the following is recommended:
– Explain that if the citizen had managed to escape, he would have alerted the enemy and they would carry out acts of reprisal in this way terrorizing the inhabitants of the place for having given attention and hospitalities to the guerrillas.
– If a guerrilla fires at an individual, make the town see that he was an enemy of the people, and that they shot him because the guerrillas recognized as their first duty the protection of citizens.
– The commando tried to detain the informant without firing because he, like all Christian guerrillas, espouses non-violence. Having fired at the Sandinista informant, although it is against his own will, it was necessary to prevent the repression of the Sandinista government against innocent people.
– Make the population see that it was the repressive system of the regime that was the cause of this situation, what really killed the informer, and that the weapon fired was one recovered in combat against the Sandinista regime.
– Make the population see that if the Sandinista regime ends the repression, the corruption backed by foreign powers, etc., the Freedom Commandos would not have had to brandish arms against brother Nicaraguans, which goes against our Christian sentiments. If the informant hadn't tried to escape, he would be enjoying life together with the rest of the population, because he would not have tried to inform the enemy. This death would have been avoided, if justice and freedom existed in Nicaragua, which is exactly the objective of the democratic guerrilla.

A week after the CIA manual surfaced, US Secretary of State, George Shultz, gave a hard-hitting speech asking the American public to accept that attempts to counter international terrorism should go beyond passive defence and could include active prevention and retaliation. 'What will be required, however, is public understanding before the fact of the risks involved in combating terrorism with overt power,' he said. 'The public must understand before the fact that there is potential for loss of life of some of our fighting men and the loss of life of some innocent people.'

There is some evidence that this rhetoric has been translated into a firmer behind-the-scenes stand against international terrorists. In September 1985, for example, the US State Department claimed that it had, over the previous twelve months, successfully prevented ninety terrorist incidents where the West was the target. However, the US is not generally renowned for its expertise in clandestine warfare and those forays that have actually become public have not proved very successful.

For instance on 8 March 1985, a massive car bomb exploded in Beirut destroying buildings and killing ninety-two people. What made this attack different from the daily carnage in the Lebanon was that the CIA had been involved in training the men who set the bomb. Their target had been Sheikh Muhammed Hussein Fadlallah, one of the spiritual leaders of the Shi'ite Muslims who owe their allegiance to Ayatollah Khomeini in Iran and who were responsible for the bombing that killed 241 Americans in Beirut in 1983.

In December 1984, President Reagan, at the insistence of George Shultz, signed an order which allowed the CIA to become involved in a mission in Lebanon. The task was to train two counter-terrorist units which would operate under the Lebanese army's intelligence section. The units were supposed to operate for specific pre-emptive strikes against terrorists or to intervene in a crisis, but the recruits were mostly hoodlums and they interpreted their orders liberally. Reagan subsequently cancelled the CIA operation, but the training had been done and ninety-two people died. The Sheikh escaped injury.

However, in the autumn of 1985, the US government finally succeeded in using force to demonstrate America's ability to counter terrorism. At the beginning of October, the Italian cruise liner the *Achille Lauro*, was hijacked by four members of the Palestine Liberation Front, an organisation that is part of the PLO. As Americans were among the passengers who had, until then, been enjoying a holiday cruise in the Mediterranean, the Reagan government placed the élite counter-terrorist unit, Delta Force, on immediate alert and a team was flown to Sicily. However, negotiations between the Italian government, the Syrians (who were acting as intermediaries) and the hijackers were successfully concluded and the vessel docked at the Egyptian port of Alexandria.

The leader of the PLF, Mohamed (Abu) Abbas, who had flown from Tunis to Cairo to help in the negotiations, had arranged for a safe passage for him and his terrorists. President Hosni Mubarak of Egypt had agreed to this under the mistaken impression that no one on board the *Achille Lauro* had been killed during the hijack. In fact, a sixty-nine-year-old American Jew, Leon Klinghoffer, who was confined to a wheelchair, had been shot by the hijackers and dumped overboard while the vessel was off the Syrian coast. When the freed passengers of the *Achille Lauro* spoke of the brutal killing, there was an immediate decision in Washington to try and bring the terrorists to trial.

When the EgyptAir Boeing 737 carrying the terrorists left Cairo for Tunis, President Reagan had already authorised its interception by F14 Tomcat fighters based on the aircraft carrier, USS *Saratoga*, that was cruising in the Mediterranean. The interception was successful and the Boeing was forced to land at Sigonella, a NATO base in Sicily controlled by the US government. The hijackers were placed under immediate arrest, although their leader, Abu Abbas, was allowed to leave the country, much to the disgust of the US administration. Abbas fled first to Yugoslavia, which refused to extradite him; he was eventually given sanctuary by Iraq, which is currently trying to persuade the PLO leadership to move their headquarters from Tunis to Baghdad. The Italians did finally issue a warrant for his arrest, although there appears to be little chance of his being brought back for trial in Italy.

The hijacking of the terrorists by the US government caused considerable strain in the latter's relations with the Italians. Before the Boeing airliner landed at Sigonella, a US Air Force C130 transport, loaded with a Delta Force team, had arrived and the troops were positioned around the airfield. As soon as the Boeing came to a halt, it was surrounded by Delta Force, who were in turn surrounded by armed men of the Italian counter-terrorist force. Officials from the US State Department, who had been flown in from Washington, listened to the conversations between Delta Force officers from the security of the Rome Embassy. 'It was a crazy situation,' said one of the official eavesdroppers. 'At one time, we heard the Texas drawl of the Delta commander discussing whether he should order his men to open fire on the Italians. That would have been very embarrassing.' In the event, cooler heads prevailed, although the Italian government resented what they saw as US military action on their territory.

The firm action of the United States in hijacking the terrorists, while undoubtedly illegal, was hailed around the world as a model of the use of controlled force. However, at the time of writing, it is not clear if the terrorists will be brought to trial by the Italians. If they are and they are then found guilty, and if America's actions are to have any long-term effect, it will be necessary for the terrorists to receive exemplary sentences. It is likely, however, that before a trial can take place, the terrorists' colleagues will carry out a series of attacks against Italian and US targets to try to get them either quietly released or very light prison sentences. If history is anything to go by, that campaign is likely to be successful.

The interception of the jets was an immediate response to a volatile situation. However, the planning for a more thorough lesson for those countries which support terrorism began in July 1984, some months before the *Achille Lauro* hijacking. A White House meeting of the National Security Planning Group that month agreed that a target for counter-terrorist action should be chosen. Vice President George Bush set up a committee of fourteen senior government officials called the Task Force to Combat Terrorism.

There was broad agreement among the Task Force that Libya would be a popular and logical target for counter terrorist action. (Two other countries which are both bigger sponsors of terrorism, Syria and Iran, were ruled out, the former because of its close ties with the Soviet Union and the latter because of the difficulties of carrying out a limited military action.) A meeting in December 1985 of terrorist experts drawn from the CIA, National Security Council, the State Department and the military at Bolling Air Force base outside Washington DC, agreed a common strategy on how the action against Libya should be carried out. Although the conference had no formal powers to dictate policy, every major government policy-maker either attended the conference or knew of its findings.

The conference scenario went something like this: For some months prior to an actual attack a major propaganda effort should be launched to convince the American public and international opinion that the target nation was a threat to the world and beyond rational control. This softening-up period would be followed by a swift and decisive military action which would be portrayed as having been forced on a reluctant United States. After the action, a further bout of propaganda would emphasise the necessity for the military action and America's determination to combat terrorism, by force if necessary.

The reality worked almost exactly to the script which the terrorist experts had agreed was logical at the December conference. Early 1986 saw a steep rise in anti-Libya propaganda: In January, President Reagan announced economic sanctions against Libya and the State Department issued special report number 138 which detailed Gadaffi's alleged support of terrorist groups. At the same time the US began 'Operation Prairie Fire' which was to have its climax at the end of March at the Line of Death, Gadaffi's arbitrarily imposed border in the Gulf of Sirte, off the Libyan Coast.

For many years the US Sixth Fleet has exercised in the Mediterranean, including the Gulf of Sirte, and the US government decided that this exercise would provide the perfect cover for giving Gadaffi a bloody nose. Operation Prairie Fire envisaged a softening-up period to raise the tension in the Libyan armed forces, to be followed by an overt move over the Line of Death. Gadaffi would attack and be beaten off.

For thirty-two days prior to Monday 24 March, US pilots based with the Sixth Fleet had been regularly invading Libyan air space, forcing Gadaffi's pilots to scramble and intercept. The aim was to keep Libya's armed forces constantly on alert. Then, on that Monday, with a Sixth Fleet reinforced by the addition of two extra carriers, the USS *Yorktown* and its escorts crossed the Line of Death. Gadaffi reacted exactly as planned, launching missiles and ordering patrol boats to attack the fleet. Over the next forty-eight hours the US sank two naval vessels and destroyed a third, as well as attacking shore-based radar stations and missile sites.

Just over a week after Operation Prairie Fire, Libya retaliated by planting a bomb in a West German discotheque which exploded, killing one American serviceman, Sergeant Kenneth Ford, and injuring 230 others. Intercepted radio, telephone and telex traffic between Tripoli and the Libyan People's Bureau in East Berlin gave the US government clear evidence of Gadaffi's involvement in the bombing. GCHQ, the British government's top-secret spy centre in Cheltenham, played a key role in the affair. The highly sophisticated computers there were able to decode the Libyan messages and, as is usual, all the information was shared with the United States. 'We automatically have access to ninety-five per cent of everything that comes out of GCHQ,' said one State Department source.

The first message from Tripoli came the day after Operation Prairie

Fire, and among other things, said: 'Prepare to carry out the plan.' The Reagan administration was so convinced by this and other intelligence that an attack was imminent that it decided to inform the Russians. The Soviet minister counsellor in Washington, Oleg M. Sokolov, was summoned to the State Department and told of the US evidence. The same message was passed to the Russians in East Berlin. US officials hoped that the Russians and East Germans would step up their surveillance of the People's Bureau in East Berlin, instruct the Libyans to call off their attack and threaten to close down the People's Bureau if it went ahead. Instead, the Russians apparently did nothing.

The second key intercept was made on 4 April, when the People's Bureau in East Berlin alerted Tripoli that the attack would be carried out the following morning. The second message read: 'It will happen soon. The bomb will blow. American soldiers must be hit.' Hours later, after the attack on the discotheque, the Bureau reported that the plan had been carried out. The message said: 'Action carried out. No trail left.' Then on 6 April came a final message congratulating the Bureau on its success and exhorting it and other Bureaux in Western Europe to carry out further 'heroic acts'.

The intercepts provided the first clear and detailed evidence of Libyan complicity in a terrorist attack and marked a new departure for the Gadaffi regime which in the past had confined its terrorist efforts to attacks on Libyan dissidents or other Arab governments. Initially, the State Department, with the full agreement of the President, had little thought of military retaliation. Instead, they planned to show the Western allies the evidence of Libyan guilt to persuade them to take strong action, including economic and political sanctions, against the Gadaffi regime. If the Europeans refused to follow the American line, then the details of the message interceptions and Europe's refusal to act would be leaked to the world's press. It was hoped that fear of embarrassment and the political fallout that would result from such apparently feeble behaviour would unite Europe for the first time in its fight against terrorism. This subtle plan was completely undermined by the US ambassador to Bonn, Richard Burt, who leaked the details of Libya's involvement. 'Once he had done that we really had no choice but to go for a military strike,' said one State Department source.

On the evening of Tuesday 8 April, President Reagan decided in principle to go ahead with a retaliatory strike. The next day, Reagan and his senior advisers made a definite decision to go ahead, whether or not they got allied co-operation. Several factors influenced Reagan's decision: growing frustration at being unable to persuade American allies to join in economic sanctions against Libya; an intense personal dislike of Gadaffi who Reagan was determined to make pay for his support of terrorism; growing evidence of a change in Gadaffi's terrorist activities, including increasing evidence of new plans to attack American targets; and an emerging consensus among his senior staff, especially those closest to him in the White House (particularly John Poindexter, the national security advisor, Colonel Oliver North and Don Fortea). Apart from those in the White House, other senior figures – Edwin Meese, the Attorney General; William Casey, the CIA chief; and George Shultz, the Secretary of State – all favoured tough action. Shultz had long been urging a military response to terrorism and in this instance he had little opposition to overcome. Caspar Weinberger, the Defense Secretary, had in the past opposed military action (earning himself the nickname 'the minister for procurement and pacifism') and so, to a lesser extent, had George Bush, the Vice President. However, during the critical planning, Weinberger was in Australia and Bush in the Middle East. Both returned the weekend before the strike in time to influence last minute planning, but neither – realising they had been outmanoeuvred – argued against the attack.

Britain was the first of the allies to be informed of the planned attack, in a coded telex over a secure line to the Prime Minister's office at No 10 Downing Street. Mrs Thatcher was in the middle of a dinner for President Chun of South Korea when the message arrived, and as soon as the meal was over she called a meeting with the Defence Secretary, George Younger, and the Foreign Secretary, Sir Geoffrey Howe. The following day she brought in Lord Whitelaw to complete the inner cabinet team which was to discuss and would eventually authorise the use of British bases for the attack. The full Cabinet was not involved until after the attack had been carried out.

The Prime Minister's initial reaction to the plan was cautious. Britain's own experience in Northern Ireland had shown that overwhelming use of force plays into the hands of the terrorist and is always counter-productive. She was concerned that any attack would hit civilian targets; would, in the short term, probably cause the deaths of a number of hostages being held by terrorist groups in the Middle East; and in the longer term, would cause an increase in terrorism. Perhaps more than President Reagan, Mrs Thatcher had clear evidence of Libyan involvement in terrorism against her own people. Recent intelligence showed that the IRA had received more than £2 million

($3 million) in cash and gold bullion since 1982 and that two British teachers, John Douglas and Philip Padfield, were being held by Libyan-backed terrorists in Lebanon. Despite this evidence, in a number of secure telephone conversations, Mrs Thatcher tried to dissuade President Reagan from military action.

In the end, the key argument was not Britain's debt because of US support in the 1982 Falklands War, which was never even mentioned in conversation, but a need to keep the casualties down. If the retaliatory action had to be carried out by the Sixth Fleet alone it would be much messier than if F111 fighters based in England were used. There is really no such thing as a surgical strike – 'like carrying out a heart operation with a bayonet' as one Pentagon official put it – but the F111s stood the best chance of carrying out precision bombing. The Ministry of Defence in London supported the Pentagon argument. Agreement in principle was reached on Thursday but there remained two points of issue between the allies: how the action should be justified to the world and exactly what targets would be hit. Thatcher was determined that any action had to be justifiable under Article 51 of the UN Charter which allows for an act of self-defence. It could not be justified as retaliation, revenge or deterrence. After some argument this was agreed.

From this discussion evolved the British position on targetting: all the targets must be terrorist-related and there must be minimum collateral damage, so all targets where there might be a high risk of civilian casualties must be avoided. As the attack was to take place at night, alleged terrorist camps were also to be avoided and only military targets should be hit. The list which was eventually agreed was kept to five – two military airfields, a barracks, a training centre for frogmen, and Gadaffi's headquarters, in the hope of killing the Libyan leader who was known to be in residence. Once the details had been sorted out, Mrs Thatcher agreed that British bases could be used to launch the strike. The US was not so successful with two other allies, France and Spain, who both refused to allow their bases to be used or to allow the US planes to overfly their territory.

The attack, codenamed 'Operation El Dorado Canyon', began on Monday 14 April. Twenty-four F111s from the 48th Tactical Fighter Wing at Lakenheath, five EF111 electronic counter measure aircraft from Upper Heyford, and twenty-eight KC10 and KC135 transport aircraft (for air-to-air refuelling) from Fairford and Mildenhall, all gathered off Britain's south coast and headed towards the Mediterranean and the rendezvous with the Sixth Fleet.

Five hours later and after a 2,800 mile flight, the aircraft, now reduced to thirteen fighters and three radar-jamming planes, began their attack on Tripoli. At the same time, an assortment of aircraft from the Sixth Fleet, including Hornet and Tomcat fighters, Corsair light attack jets and Hawkeye command planes, began an assault on the port of Benghazi. The rules of engagement for the fighters were strict. Each plane was allowed to make only one bombing run to reduce the chances of it being hit, and before releasing his bombs or missiles the weapons officer had to have a double 'lock on' to the target. This meant that he had to fix the target with his Flir (forward looking infra red) night-sight and also with his PAVE TACK radar. The orders specified that any crew failing to get a double 'lock on' should simply leave the target area and jettison its weapons in the sea.

Early warnings that a surgical strike was likely to be only partly successful proved all too accurate. While all the agreed targets were hit, several others came under fire as well, especially in the Tripoli suburb of Bin Ashur, which was a residential area not on the agreed target list. The apparent target, the Libyan Bureau for State Security, the country's equivalent of the CIA, escaped with a few broken windows, but the nearby French and Swiss embassies were hit as well as several houses, a park and a children's playground. Six men, three women and two children — including Gadaffi's fifteen-month-old adopted daughter — were killed and sixty civilians were injured, including two more of the Libyan ruler's children. The Libyans were to turn these casualties to great political advantage, allowing the world's press to visit hospitals and the civilian areas affected and allowing photographers to take pictures of dead children. These were duly spread across the television screens and newspapers of the world to great effect.

All except one F111, which had been hit by anti-aircraft fire and exploded while heading out to sea, returned safely to their bases. Even though much of the equipment used by the aircraft failed to work properly and there was far more collateral damage than had been allowed for, the mission, viewed in strictly military terms, was a success. However, the political fallout that resulted from the raid far outweighed the military dimension.

The Prime Minister, Mrs Thatcher, first heard the details of the strike on the BBC early morning news, by which time the fighters were almost back in England. According to sources at No 10 she was 'appalled' by the civilian casualties. Later that morning the full Cabinet met for the first time to discuss the affair and a large number of Ministers, including such loyal allies as the Home Secretary, Douglas Hurd; the Chancellor, Nigel Lawson; the Leader of the House of Commons, John Biffen; and Norman Tebbit, Chairman of the Conservative party, all opposed the action and the Prime Minister's support for it. As the day wore on, Thatcher faced a storm of protest from opposition parties, and opinion polls taken later in the week showed an average of seventy per cent of those questioned were opposed to the action. This view was mirrored elsewhere in Europe and directly contrasted with polls in the United States which showed overwhelming support for President Reagan's tough new stand.

More practically, the immediate results of the raid seemed to confirm the fears of the critics. Terrorists in Lebanon killed two British and one American hostage whom they had been holding for some months; in Beirut the British ambassador's residence was shelled; also in the Lebanon, a British journalist was kidnapped and another is thought to have been hanged; a US embassy employee was shot in Khartoum; and bomb attacks were foiled at London's Heathrow airport and in Istanbul. While alarming, these attacks may well have been little more than an instant reaction to the raid. A sophisticated terrorist attack takes weeks, often months, to set in motion, so the true response to the American attack has yet to be seen. There is little doubt, however, that the US attack will act as a catalyst for terrorists worldwide and a substantial increase in terrorism will follow.

Politically, too, the real reaction to the raid will only be apparent in the longer term. For Mrs Thatcher, there could be a high political price to pay at the next election. She will lose the votes of those who feel she agreed too easily to the American request for support, and her opponents will develop the image of her as a lackey of the US. In Nato, the threatening rift between Europe and the United States has been exacerbated by the attack. America is becoming increasingly frustrated by what it sees as European weakness, and there is a growing feeling that if the US cannot rely on its close allies in the face of the common threat of terrorism, then there is little economic or political justification for basing 365,000 American troops in Europe to defend the feeble and weak-willed Nato allies.

Given the high cost of the raid, was it really worth it? The answer must be no. Politically, militarily and morally it was a serious mistake. The result will be an increase in terrorism, new strains on an already shaky

Nato alliance and for many a blurring of the distinction between democratic nations and terrorists. The bombing was based on a fundamental misunderstanding of the nature of modern terrorism and the effective methods of countering the threat.

In 1985 there were 690 terrorist incidents around the world. This year it is predicted there will be 800, a fifteen per cent increase which is expected to continue for the foreseeable future. Far ahead of any other country, the United States has borne the brunt of them: 217 attacks last year, twice as many as in 1984.

The American government has, understandably, become frustrated by its apparent inability to strike back and by the lack of co-operation it has received from its allies in devising methods to restrict the movement and actions of terrorists. For too long the initiative has been left with the terrorists who choose when, where and with what weapon to hit their targets, often at a high cost in civilian casualties.

But striking back is not as easy as it sounds. Actually identifying terrorists and their bases is very difficult. Intelligence is usually poor – much worse, certainly, than the various agencies would have us believe – and directly apportioning blame for a particular act immediately after the event is often impossible, the only evidence being the customary claim of responsibility made over the telephone. To the politicians an easier option appears to be to attack those who sponsor terrorists; and by his own admission Gadaffi is certainly one of that band.

But, by attacking Libya, the US has chosen to take at face value the rhetoric of a man of little credibility who is despised in the West as a bombastic dictator. The Americans have also ignored the view of their own counter-terrorist professionals. The fact is that state sponsorship – the funding, training and arming – of terrorist groups plays a very small part in the current growth of terrorism.

In the late 1960s and early 1970s, when modern terrorism first emerged to threaten the developed world, a number of countries, led by Libya, believed they could use terrorist groups to spread their own particular brand of revolution. Since he deposed King Idris in 1969 Gadaffi has practised three main types of terrorism: killing Libyan exiles opposed to his regime, destabilising the governments of neighbouring Arab countries, and supporting violence, particularly by funding and arming small, extremely violent, groups which might otherwise be unable to survive. In addition, Gadaffi's rhetoric, which received wide coverage around the world, consistently mocked the West and his Arab enemies and made much of his support for revolutionary movements. He raised his profile to a level where he became the most obvious target for punishment.

But all this should be kept in perspective. Although Gadaffi has sponsored more than thirty terrorist groups in the past, from the Red Brigade to the IRA and Abu Nidal, none of his protégés have ever been wholly dependent on him for their survival. Eliminating Gadaffi's influence on world terrorism would not significantly affect the current level of activity. A secret twenty-nine page 'vulnerability assessment' written about Libya by the CIA in June 1984, looked at the problem of getting rid of Gadaffi, and concluded that he was not the madman people believed him to be. Instead, the report described him as a 'judicious political calculator' and concluded that 'no course of action short of stimulating Gadaffi's fall will bring any significant and enduring change in Libyan policies.' Although the death of Gadaffi would have provided an incidental bonus to Operation El Dorado Canyon, the US government has not yet reached the stage where it is planning the actual assassination of the Libyan leader. But intelligence assessments made in the first few months of 1986, which suggest Gadaffi has stepped up his involvement in terrorism, may change that.

The US administration believes that the Berlin bombing in April came after a string of other Libyan-sponsored acts of terrorism, and that more are planned. The CIA take a different view, arguing that the actual evidence against Gadaffi is thin. But, following a series of arguments with the White House, the Reagan view seems to have prevailed and much of the new wave of terrorism expected in 1986 will be laid at Gadaffi's door.

But while Gadaffi, in an attempt to regain some lost credibility, may step up his involvement in terrorism (thus apparently justifying American action), in the longer term the growth of terrorism will continue without any encouragement from Libya, and no use of military force by the United States, against any country, is likely to alter that.

Terrorists, far from relying on state sponsors, have increasingly moved towards self-sufficiency. They have found over the past decade that sponsors are unreliable allies who attach too many strings to each Kalashnikov machine-gun and so groups have developed their own resources. For example, the Palestine Liberation Organisation, including its subsidiary groups, has assets of around $5 billion and a substantial investment income. State sponsorship amounts to no more than $100 million a year – an insignificant sum out of its total resources. The IRA, too, has changed so that today, out of an annual income of £5 million (£7.5 million) less than £150,000 ($200,000) comes from its supporters in the US, with the balance being raised from a wide range of criminal activities including protection rackets, smuggling and kidnap for ransom.

While the US has been so obsessed with state-sponsored terrorism, the enemy has been gathering recruits and committing new atrocities.

In Europe in 1985, for example, a new anti-Nato alliance, composed of terrorist groups from France, West Germany, Belgium and Portugal, carried out bombings and assassinations, many of them against Nato targets. And as the massive US counter-terrorist effort has concentrated on Libya for the past eight months, this very effective group has been able to flourish.

If state sponsorship does not account for the current growth in terrorism, what can be done effectively to counter the growing threat?

In the early 1970s, the British government responded to that question by endorsing the active use of covert forces against the IRA. The government decided to fight terror with terror and the results played into the hands of the IRA. It gained recruits and sympathy in the face of London's tough policy.

Today, the British believe that countering terrorism means a long war, one which requires considerable investment of money, time and intelligence. Given the success of this policy, Mrs Thatcher's decision to support the US is all the more extraordinary.

However sensible such a policy may be, the politicians who are ultimately responsible for counter-terrorism will always favour the quick and easy method which gives instant reassurance to a worried electorate. This plays into the hands of the terrorists, one of whose aims is to provoke a strong reaction and repressive measures from the society it sets out to overthrow. But the very strength of democracies is their ability to absorb punishment – no modern terrorist group, after all, has achieved its political aims.

Responding to terrorism with terror is completely counter-productive: it brings new recruits flooding to the terrorist banner and gives terrorist groups around the world, usually split by different political philosophies, a focus for their activities.

The US, as the world's strongest democracy, has taken the lead in countering terrorism in the world. It is a role it rightly assumes, but with the duty comes a responsibility for a more coherent counter-terrorist policy. There is no quick and easy solution to the terrorist problem. Occasional short-term gains, while politically satisfying, must be sacrificed to achieve longer-term benefits which will do more to undercut the structure of international terrorism.

The key is not military action but better intelligence gathering, including the infiltration of terrorist groups, the sharing of information among the Western allies and a common policy to counter the growing threat.

The Western alliance has so far demonstrated a striking lack of united resolve in the face of terrorism. Rather than co-ordinating policy to meet the threat, it has continued to try to counter terrorism on national lines. Terrorists can flee France to find sanctuary across the border in Belgium, leave Ulster and find a home in the United States. Even when agreements have been reached, their implementation has been arbitrary. At the same time, those nations which support terrorism, such as Libya, Iran and Syria, can do so without the allies reaching an agreement which would make such support of terrorism too expensive to bear, both economically and politically. It remains to be seen how effective the agreement on a wide range of counter-terrorist measures reached at the May 1986 Tokyo summit of Western leaders, will be.

Much of the blame for this sorry state of affairs must lie with the intelligence services who are responsible for generating the information on which the politicians can act. Not only are their systems of gathering intelligence unsuitable to meet the threat – relying increasingly, as they do, on signals intelligence rather than old-fashioned spying – but they are also overly concerned with chauvinistic protection of data.

In the face of a common threat, such behaviour is ridiculous. But without firm political leadership, little will change in the search for a solution to this growing problem. One of the benefits that has flowed from the US strikes on Libya has been a new allied resolve to do something about terrorism and adopt a common policy on countering the threat. Within days of Operation El Dorado Canyon several European countries, including Britain, Italy, France and Spain, had expelled or curtailed the activities of Libyans in their countries, and in a series of meetings there was broad agreement that a new counter-terrorist policy should be formulated urgently. In part this new initiative is driven by a fear bordering on terror that the US will strike Libya or

35

another country once again. For their part, the US believe that after a brief flurry of activity the Europeans will slump back into their usual do-nothing lethargy. To stop that happening the US intends to use its economic muscle by continuing to discourage American citizens from travelling to Europe in the face of the terrorist threat. It is hoped that the allies, faced with the loss of billions of dollars in revenue from tourism, will then continue to address the problem of terrorism. If that does not work the US will once again use military force.

But, even if the allies were to unite to face the common enemy, there is no evidence that they understand the nature of modern terrorism, which has evolved significantly from the heady idealism of the 1970s to produce a more pragmatic and skilful protagonist. It is time for Western political leaders to realise that 'kill counts', are not enough in the fight against terrorism. What is needed is a coherent long-term strategy which would use democracy's strengths to undermine the bomber and assassin and show him that terrorism does not pay. Counter-terrorism continues to concentrate on preventing the act of terrorism rather than attacking the terrorists' resources; meanwhile, the terrorists have quietly taken care of their own business, expanding and getting rich in the process. No organisation illustrates this better than the PLO, which began its assault on the world's consciousness in 1970 at Dawson's Field in Jordan.

2

An international conspiracy?

THE DATE 6 September 1970, has become known in terrorist folklore as
Skyjack Sunday. By the end of that day, the Popular Front for the
Liberation of Palestine (PFLP) had hijacked four airlines: one each in
West Germany and Switzerland and two in the Netherlands. The events
of that day were the most spectacular demonstration of co-ordinated
terrorist attack in modern times.

TWA Flight 741, hijacked in West Germany, and a Swissair DC8
were ordered to Dawson's Field, an old British flying station outside
Amman, the capital of Jordan. Renamed Revolution Airfield, it was
surrounded by the terrorists' well-armed forces to keep out both the
Jordanian army and interested onlookers. Explosives were placed in
position around the aircraft, after which the PFLP demanded the release
of prisoners held in West Germany, Switzerland and Britain and the
freeing of an unspecified number of Palestinians held in Israeli jails.

Meanwhile, during a stopover in Amsterdam, two PFLP members
boarded an El Al Boeing *en route* from Tel Aviv to New York. (Two
others, due to join them, were unable to board the aircraft which was
overbooked.) The two who did board were Leila Khaled, a young
Palestinian woman with a successful hijacking behind her, and Patrick
Arguello, a Nicaraguan leftist. Immediately following takeoff, after
Khaled announced the hijack, security guards travelling incognito shot
and killed Arguello and overpowered Khaled. Both hijackers had pulled
the pins of grenades (Khaled had hidden two in her bra) but neither
exploded: one had not been properly primed and the other was rusted
solid. The aircraft returned to London's Heathrow airport, and Khaled
was arrested.

The two who had been bumped from that El Al flight boarded and
seized a PanAm 747 bound for New York, with 170 people on board,

and ordered it to the Middle East. After refuelling at Beirut, they ordered the plane to Cairo where they blew it up.

At Dawson's Field, negotiations with the hijackers of the TWA and Swissair planes lasted four days. Three days into negotiations, a British aircraft was added to the two on the airfield. The PFLP high command had decided that British hostages were needed to persuade London to release Khaled, so BOAC flight 775 from Bombay to London had been hijacked by three PFLP members while refuelling in Bahrain.

By 15 September, 375 hostages had been released, with fifty-five still in custody. These last were then removed from the three aircraft, which the PFLP feared would be attacked at any moment by Israeli commandos, and the aircraft were blown up in full view of the television cameras.

The Jordanian government, unable to tolerate such anarchic behaviour on its territory, authorised an armed strike against the Palestinian terrorist groups in Jordan, and in seven days of fighting, during what came to be known as Black September, 7000 Palestinians died. Negotiations for the release of the hostages continued throughout the fighting and all were eventually freed when each government – with the exception of Israel – met the PFLP demands to release all the Palestinians held in their jails. The Israeli hostages were freed by Jordanian army commandos.

The Dawson's Field episode served notice on the world that international terrorism had arrived and could, if not win the war, certainly achieve some notable victories. Skyjack Sunday marked the beginning of a new militancy among the various Palestinian groups that were committed to re-establishing their homeland in territory which they believed Israel had taken from them by force in 1948, when the Jewish state was established. The Palestinians had tried conventional force in two Arab–Israeli wars, in 1948 and 1967, as well as diplomatic persuasion to convince the world of the justice of their cause, but both had failed to interest world opinion.

To understand the evolution of the terrorist movements that operate under the umbrella of the Palestine Liberation Organisation, it is necessary to go back to 1948. In that year, the British abandoned Palestine and the Arabs launched an attack on the Jewish settlers who intended to establish the State of Israel. The short and bloody war that followed ended in the defeat of the Arab armies. After the establishment of Israel, the Arab Higher Committee (AHC), led by the ex-Grand Mufti of Jerusalem, Haj Amin Al Hussaini, was formed to continue the fight on behalf of the Palestinians who argued that they had been expelled from their homeland.

Then, as now, the Palestinians were used by different Arab leaders, with the AHC primarily a front organisation for the Egyptians with other Arab nations jockeying for influence. It became apparent to the more radical Palestinians that the AHC could not unite the different Palestinian factions: while it was so much a servant of other masters, it could never be a strong voice for the Palestinian people. However, a 1964 conference of the Arab League in Jerusalem gave the Palestinians an 'entity and personality' by bringing together Palestinians from all over the Middle East for the first time, and the Palestine Liberation Organisation was formed under the chairmanship of Ahmed Shukairy, the Palestinian representative at the Arab League.

At the same meeting, a National Covenant was drawn up which declared that Palestine is an Arab homeland, and condemned Israel in the following terms:

> Zionism is an Imperialist movement in its development; aggressive and expansionist in its aims; racist and fanatical in its formation; and fascist in its means. Israel, which is the front line of this destructive movement and a stanchion of Imperialism, is an endless source of trouble and annoyance for the Middle East and the international community.

(The Covenant was amended and expanded in 1968, but the basic aims remained the same: the elimination of the State of Israel and the establishment of a Palestinian homeland in Israel, on the West Bank of the Jordan and in Gaza.)

Following the Arab League meeting, a formative meeting of the Palestinian Congress was called which all those who were influential in the movement at the time attended, by invitation only. The Congress agreed to form the Palestine National Council, which is now commonly regarded as the Palestinian Parliament-in-exile. In addition, a fifteen-man Executive Committee, generally considered to be the real power of the organisation, was formed. A Palestine National Fund was established to 'draw contributions from all Palestinians', and a Palestine Liberation Army was to be formed under the control of the PLO.

The PLO had been established with the enthusiastic support of President Gamal Abdel Nasser of Egypt, who thought the Palestinian cause was a way to unite the Arab world under his leadership. He also hoped to develop a militant and more united Palestinian movement to replace the discredited AHC. Inevitably, Nasser's ambitions for control of the PLO provoked other Arab leaders who had similar ideas for influencing the movement. Syria became the first to try to undermine Nasser's control of the PLO, by sponsoring a young man named Yasser Arafat, then aged thirty-five, who had emerged as leader of a small militant group (formed in 1961) called the Palestine National Liberation Movement (more commonly known as Al-Fatah).

Al-Fatah had been backed financially by Syria and had received some training in guerrilla warfare in Algeria which, after a long and bloody guerrilla war against the French colonialists, had received independence in 1962. (Ahmed Ben Bella, the country's new leader, identified strongly with the PLO cause, and today Algeria remains one of the PLO's staunchest allies.) In 1964, Al-Fatah embarked on a campaign of sabotage in Israel because Arafat believed that, contrary to the current philosophy of the PLO, armed revolution was the only way to achieve results. Its attacks on Israel were amateurish and largely unsuccessful: poorly trained and armed with ancient weapons, Al-Fatah was no match for the Israelis and lost large numbers of men. With their Arab backers apparently not prepared to give them better weapons and training, Al-Fatah seemed to be condemned to remain on the fringes of Middle East politics.

In 1967, convinced that the Egyptians, in concert with the Syrians, were planning to attack Israel, the Israelis launched a pre-emptive strike against both countries. Israeli forces reached the Suez Canal in two days and, a day later, the banks of the Jordan river, taking total control of Jerusalem. Egypt and Jordan (which entered the war later) accepted a ceasefire on 8 June, three days after war broke out. In the north, the Israeli forces had similar successes against the Syrians, who agreed to a ceasefire on 10 June, thus ending the Six Day War and giving Israel total victory and, with it, a great deal of territory.

In a new mood of militancy after the 1967 war, the PLO welcomed Al-Fatah into its midst. A year later, Arafat's group had emerged as the most powerful and best-organised under the PLO umbrella, and Arafat was elected PLO chairman, a position he has held ever since.

Despite Arafat's leadership of the PLO, there have been political differences within the movement, and the organisation has been wracked by factionalism. Disagreements over the best way to achieve PLO aims have arisen between moderates who favour negotiation and extremists who support vicious terrorism. Outside influences have also prevented Arafat from being master in his own house. Every major

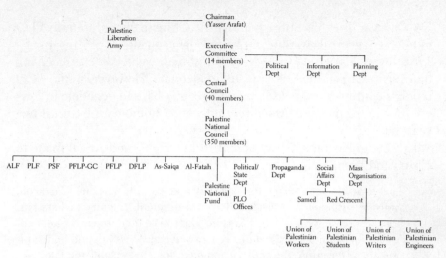

country in the Middle East, including Syria, Jordan, Libya, Iraq and Algeria, have their own terrorist groups which, although officially owing allegiance to Arafat, respond more commonly to the demands of the Arab sponsors who are their paymasters. With each group in the PLO owing allegiance to an outside sponsor as well as to the PLO high command, the organisation has never been truly united with a coherent common policy. However, despite considerable difficulties, the PLO has remained the umbrella organisation that shelters eight major terrorist groups and fifteen social and educational associations.

Initially, the Soviets appeared to accept the existence of Israel and had argued to every Arab leader that the solution to the Palestinian issue should come through negotiation. By the early 1960s, they seem to have concluded that the Arab nations could unite as the USSR had united all its different nations under one leadership, and they preferred to talk of Arab 'peoples' and not the states then in existence. But the PLO did not fit into this scheme, concerned as they were with achieving their own individual state.

The People's Republic of China's dealings with the PLO differ sharply. Arafat had first visited China in 1964, with the result that the PLO opened an office in Peking the following year, and in 1966 the Palestinian representative was accorded the full status of ambassador (with the organisation's embassy in the Chinese capital and the ambassador's car flying the Palestinian flag). Arafat visited China again in that year, and according to Abu Iyad, Arafat's deputy in the PLO, this resulted in a promise of material aid, which eventually arrived after the

Six Day war of 1967. Subsequently, the Chinese offered to train PLO followers in guerrilla warfare, and supply large quantities of arms, but by 1968, even though a number of Palestinian fighters were receiving training in China, the help was still inadequate. However, senior PLO officials continued to visit China on a regular basis to negotiate follow-on arms deliveries, but Arafat did not return to the country until two years later.

In his autobiography, Iyad described the trip he and Arafat made to China and Vietnam in February 1970:

> The trip was kept secret for political and security reasons. To avoid arousing suspicion, we each followed a different itinerary to Pakistan, from where we were to take the same plane. We tried to pass unnoticed. Arafat, for example, dressed in a conservative business suit and traded his usual head covering, the *kaffiyeh* and *agal*, for a respectable felt hat.

Such precautions were unnecessary. On the same aircraft was Abdal Salam Jallud, a close confidante of Muammar al-Gadaffi, Libya's new ruler who had overthrown the monarchy of King Idris I on 1 September 1969. Both parties had the same mission: to win support from China. Landing in Peking, the Palestinian delegation was lodged in the old French embassy and were, for a revolutionary group, given unprecedented access, having several meetings with Chou Enlai (Iyad was impressed by 'his profound sympathy for the Palestinian people, but also his extraordinary knowledge of the problem in its regional and international context').

Hedging their bets, the PLO had already been making overtures for cash and arms to the Soviets who by then were proving to be more willing to listen, having learned that uniting Arab nations divided by centuries of enmity was more difficult than expected. However, the PLO were concerned that relations with the USSR could jeopardise their growing friendship with China, which was fiercely opposed to Moscow. In fact, Chou Enlai could not have been more accommodating. 'You represent a national liberation movement,' he told Iyad, 'and it is normal that you should try to get help wherever you can find it.'

The informal agreements made during the visit resulted in the placement of Hani al Hassan, a senior PLO figure and confidant of Arafat, as head of PLO–China relations, a position he held for ten years. In 1971, Hassan visited Peking and negotiated a formal agreement between the PLO and China that allowed the Chinese to supply arms regularly to the PLO. When a Chinese foreign ministry official attempted to write in a clause restricting PLO–Soviet relations, Hassan went direct to Chou Enlai, and in the first written agreement between China and the PLO, the PLO were allowed the freedom to have relations with both China and the Soviet Union.

Since 1973, the Chinese have given the PLO enough war material to equip a batallion. However, the great distances between China and the Palestinian bases in the Lebanon have limited supplies to the more portable weapons such as rifles, mortars, ammunition and some Katyusha rocket systems. China has never asked for payment for any of the goods delivered and, according to PLO sources, has always been prepared to supply more than the PLO asked. Relations between the two remain good, and China has helped fill the gaps in the PLO's armoury following the 1982 Israeli invasion of the Lebanon. As one senior PLO source has pointed out: 'The Soviets never give us anything for free but the Chinese are real friends.' In addition, the Soviets never fail to announce their support for the PLO while the Chinese tend to keep a much lower profile. By the end of 1972, according to the head of the PLO mission to China, 'More than seventy-five per cent of the arms used by the Palestinian revolutionary groups have been given to us from China.'

It was not until June 1976 that the PLO's office in Moscow opened, two years after an agreement for its establishment had been reached. Its opening was delayed as officials from both sides discussed its exact status. Depending on the status of the person or organisation concerned, offices of foreign representatives in Moscow can be on an inter-party, government-to-government or popular level. The PLO office in Moscow is 'unofficial' and is classed below the three 'official' categories and is the minimum that can be granted. In addition, the PLO is accredited by the Soviet Committee of Solidarity with the Countries of Asia and Africa rather than by the Foreign Ministry, again an indication of the organisation's lowly status.

By the end of the 1960s, the Soviets had given up on their grand idea of Arab nationalism. The PLO was gaining international significance, and the Soviets thought the organisation might be a useful tool for them to gain influence in the region. They were anxious, too, to counter the growing influence of the Chinese.

The PLO had begun sounding out the USSR again at the beginning of the 1970s and had received some encouraging noises but no cash or guns and very little in the way of propaganda support. However, their relationship was boosted by the 1973 Arab–Israeli war. Israel, although taken by surprise in an Egyptian attack across the Suez Canal, again emerged victorious; Egypt and Syria suffered serious defeats; and the Soviet Union which had supplied large quantities of arms to the Arabs, did not come out of the war well either. Henry Kissinger, then US Secretary of State, played a prominent part in the negotiations leading to peace, and as a result of his efforts, relations between Egypt and the United States improved. Three years later, President Sadat expelled several hundred Soviet advisers from Egypt, dealing a severe blow to Soviet influence in the region.

Anxious to retain and expand its influence, the USSR stepped up supplies of arms, aid and propaganda support to the PLO. On the other hand, the Soviets have consistently qualified their support for the PLO cause, referring to Palestinian 'statehood' but without making clear what exactly that means. Nor have they subscribed to the PLO view that Israel should not exist and that it should be replaced by a Palestinian state. They have generally urged moderation by the PLO, and have sought to maintain their influence by stoking terrorist fires and hoping to profit from the instability that results. Their conditional support has caused considerable resentment against the Soviets inside the PLO, and indeed, whenever the PLO came under attack – by Jordan in 1970 and Israel in 1982 – the Soviet Union stood by and did nothing. However, the PLO realise that even the qualified support of the USSR is essential to give the organisation some credibility in international forums such as the United Nations. They are, therefore, prepared to tolerate what they believe to be public support from the Soviets, even if the talk is never matched by arms and cash.

When the Israeli government launched 'Operation Peace for Galilee' in June 1982, the Israeli cabinet and the Americans had been told by Prime Minister Menachem Begin and Defence Minister Ariel Sharon that it would be a strictly limited exercise, lasting no more than forty-eight hours, which would create a *cordon sanitaire* forty kilometres north of Israel's border with the Lebanon. This would have put Israel's northern settlements out of range of the PLO's rockets.

Israel's attack took the PLO completely by surprise. Since the PLO had been expecting one for several months, the surprise element in the attack was all the more extraordinary and a tribute to the efficiency of the Israeli military. In fact, the PLO knew the Israeli operational plan for the Lebanon in considerable detail. Weeks before the Israelis moved north, Arafat told the Americans and anyone else who would listen that their target would be Beirut, and he even passed on details of how the attack would be carried out, more detail than was made available to the Israeli cabinet by Ariel Sharon.

The Israeli attack met only light opposition from the PLO, and within a week, the Israelis had taken control of Sidon, one of the principal headquarters of the PLO. In a series of underground tunnels in and around the city, they discovered documents relating to the activities of the PLO and its various organisations, and several truckloads were taken south for analysis. Among these documents was a transcript of a meeting in Moscow on 13 November 1979 between Soviet Foreign Minister Andrei Gromyko and Yasser Arafat. The conversation provides a graphic insight into Soviet–PLO relations:

GROMYKO:
First of all, I will speak of the main problems of international politics, and about our position concerning these problems.

The USSR continues its principled policy regarding the Middle East as it did in the past. We are in favour of Israel's withdrawal from the occupied territories and in favour of granting the Palestinians their legitimate rights and the establishment of their independent state, together with the right of all states in the region to be sovereign. This is the essence of our position regarding problems of the Middle East . . .

We are now just prior to the presentation of the Palestinian issue in the UN. This matter is very important to us and to yourselves. We will no doubt support and assist the Palestinian and Arab position, and we will back every proposal and every plan that you submit to the UN. This support also applies to our socialist comrades. The last question is, and it is only a question: it is known that America – when it talks with us about the Palestinian problem – its delegates tell us: how is it possible for us to recognise the PLO and the establishment of an independent Palestinian state when the PLO does not recognise Israel?

Are you considering certain tactical concessions in return for getting recognition from the hostile camp? And are you also considering recognising Israel's right to exist as an independent sovereign state?

During the discussions with the Americans, we felt we were at a dead end. Here I would like to know what your opinion is and please regard it as a question only . . .

ARAFAT: Knowing that we are the victim, we raised many possible solutions, while none of our enemies presented any. We said: A democratic state where Jews and Arabs will live. They said: This means the destruction of Israel. In 1974, we said we will establish the Palestinian state on every part of land that Israel withdraws from, or which will be liberated, and this is our right.

We have proposed all these things and they have offered nothing.

GROMYKO: If there is a change in your position, I ask you to notify us, since one cannot escape this issue. In every statement, the Americans say: How can we recognise an organisation while they are not ready to recognise anything? This is demagoguery, but we have to know how to deal with it. I ask you to think about it and make your comments.

I thank you for the useful discussion. We think that we march with you on the same path concerning the Middle East problem. The Soviet Union is a friend of the Arabs and does not tend to change its friends. We hope that the Arabs and the PLO feel the same way.

ARAFAT: The PLO has no doubts.

This conversation does not reflect a radicalism that might have been expected from the USSR, the sponsor of worldwide terrorism, and a revolutionary organisation like the PLO. In fact, the PLO have consistently complained that they have never received adequate support from the Soviet Union. 'They always make a big show of supporting us and other revolutionary groups in public,' one member of the PLO central committee has said. 'But in private, the reality is very different and they give us the bare minimum in terms of concrete support.'

Israeli propaganda suggests that one of the key areas in which the Soviets are most active in their support of the PLO, is the supply of arms. When the Israelis had completed Operation Peace for Galilee and had expelled the PLO fighters from the country, an enormous quantity of arms was captured from the PLO. The Israeli Defence Force claims to have seized:

* 4670 tons of artillery and small arms ammunition
* 1077 combat vehicles, including eighty tanks
* 28,304 small arms including rifles and pistols
* 1352 anti-tank weapons, including 1099 RPGs, twenty-seven anti-tank missile launchers, 138 recoilless rifles and eighty-eight major anti-tank guns
* 202 mortars
* Fifty-six Katyusha rocket launchers, from 106 mm to 122 mm
* Seventy heavy artillery pieces, from 122 mm to 155 mm
* 158 anti-aircraft weapons
* 1916 field communication pieces

The general assumption, encouraged by Israeli propaganda, was that the arms were supplied by the Soviet Union as a gesture of solidarity with the PLO. In fact, the PLO has had to pay cash for every bullet, rocket and tank received from the Soviets since the struggle for Palestinian independence began.

Similar misconceptions have grown up around the question of Soviet involvement in the support and training of Palestinian terrorists. Those who see a Soviet hand behind every aspect of the PLO, suggest that the USSR has set up a number of camps specifically to train Palestinians, who are provided with excellent facilities as part of the USSR's policy of encouraging destabilisation in the West.

In testimony before Senator Jeremiah Denton's sub-committee on security and terrorism, Robert Moss, a British journalist based in New York and an active proponent of the grand terror conspiracy theory, stated:

> The total number of Palestinians who have been trained in Soviet-bloc camps cannot be precisely gauged. West European intelligence sources currently estimate that between 2000 and 3000 Palestinians have received military training in the Soviet Union over the past two years.
>
> There are many dozens of training establishments in the Soviet bloc for the Palestinians. Some of the biggest are the military academy at Sanprobal, Simferopol in the Crimea, the military academy at Odessa, a large camp outside Moscow – where one of the Palestinians involved in the massacre of Israeli civilians at Hebron last year was trained, according to his own confession – and so on.
>
> One defector to whom I have had access has stated that the Odessa higher infantry school was a place where Soviet officers were trained until 1965 when the intake from Arab and African groups became so large that the Russian officers themselves had to be moved on to another place – to Kiev – so that the entire facility could be given over to training these Third World terrorists.

On the face of it, such information appears damning, but Moss received much of his information from Israeli intelligence who, while wishing to make use of such a sympathetic voice, privately scoff at the links between the Soviet Union and international terrorism. They point out that it is not unusual for a country selling arms to provide training in the use of those arms. 'There is no doubt that Russia does provide some help and training to the PLO,' one senior Israeli intelligence officer said. 'However, I personally am not prepared to make the enormous leap in logic to say that the Soviets are backing or masterminding international terrorism. The whole international terrorism operation is much more chaotic than people seem to realise.'

47

PLO sources confirm that in any arms purchases they have consistently made it a subject of formal agreements that the Soviet Union will provide the training for Palestinian fighters in the use of Soviet-supplied arms. In this, the PLO merely requests that the USSR follow standard practice in the arms business. Britain, for example, trains Iraqis and Libyans in the use of arms which have been sold to the respective countries.

However, even when the Soviets do provide training, the idea of a stream of highly skilled guerrillas emerging from secret special warfare schools in the Soviet Union is very wide of the mark. Another report captured by the Israelis in the Lebanon, dated 22 January 1981, of a PLO military training mission to the Soviet Union, illustrates the discipline problems produced by the reciprocal training arrangements between the PLO and the Soviet Union:

> On 1 September 1980, the delegation arrived in Simferopol in the USSR. The number of the delegates: 194 officers. Factions represented:
>
> 1. The Fatah
> 2. The Palestine Liberation Army
> 3. The Armed Uprising
> 4. The PFLP
> 5. The DFLP
> 6. The PFLP-GC
> 7. Saiqa
> 8. The Arab Front
> 9. The Popular Struggle Front
> 10. The Front for the Liberation of Palestine

Later in the report, the commander, Colonel Rashad Ahmed, detailed a series of problems which he encountered on the training course:

> The participants in the courses did not correctly understand the political aspects of sending military delegations abroad. As a result, the upper echelon of the delegation, namely the participants in the battalion officer course, refused to study and asked to return, using all sorts of illogical excuses.

A number of other officers were also sent home from the training course for a wide variety of offences, including passing counterfeit money, indecency, perversion, drunkenness and general disobedience. Colonel Ahmed also said in his report that, if he had strictly followed the code of conduct, he would have been forced to send back more than half of the PLO delegates for misbehaviour, instead of the thirteen eventually returned. He asked that, in future, a higher calibre of trainee be sent to the Soviet Union.

The PLO have consistently had a problem with the standard of their recruits and the low standard of training they receive in the Soviet Union. This has always been a major difficulty for aspiring terrorist and guerrilla forces. Even in their own army, the Soviets have a hard time encouraging initiative and individual enterprise with even senior officers having to refer to higher authority for the smallest change in battle orders. In addition, while Soviet battle tactics have evolved and today a greater emphasis is placed on battlefield decisions, they still have not adjusted to the idea of guerrilla warfare. Trainees who have gone through the Soviet courses complain of too many political lectures and not enough training in field tactics.

This was illustrated during Operation Peace for Galilee. While some Israeli soldiers were impressed with the fighting qualities of a small minority of the Palestinians, the latter did not fight as an army but as a disorganised group of individuals. The Palestinians' tactical skills and their use of the sophisticated weaponry at their disposal was poor. Tanks, for example, were almost invariably employed in fixed positions as artillery rather than as a highly mobile force which could have inflicted considerable damage on the Israelis.

(There was a similar problem in the Rhodesian war where many of the guerrillas had been trained by the Soviet Union: the army could rely on a 30–1 kill ratio in favour of the government. And in Namibia, where the South African government fight the Soviet-backed South-West African People's Organisation (SWAPO), the kill ratio is even higher.)

The Soviet Union may not have been particularly successful in its campaign to win new friends through the support of armed revolution, but the level of support it does provide is enough to ensure that international terrorism has gained a firm place in modern society.

A briefing paper issued by the Israeli Defence Force in March 1981 suggests that the PLO co-operates to some degree with twenty-two different international terrorist groups, including the Black Panthers in the United States, MIR in Chile and the IRA in Northern Ireland. The Palestinians also allegedly run training schemes for international terrorists, charging between $5000 and $10,000 for a six-week course. Sources in Al-Fatah strongly deny this, and it is possible that another group, such as the DFLP or the PFLP, run such schemes as a way of making money. Those groups that are alleged to have been trained in this way all suffer similar deficiencies, unsurprisingly given the low fighting ability and poor tactical skills of the PLO members. Irrespective of nationality, the average terrorist is not skilled in unconventional warfare.

The PLO denials that they run terrorist training camps become more credible when the quality of the evidence supplied by the Israelis to back up their propaganda becomes apparent. When Israeli troops searched through the debris of the Rashadiye refugee camp outside Tyre in June 1982, they allegedly came across the service card of a young IRA member who had been training with the PLO. Stephen Robert Howe, whose Arabic cover name was Kassem Muhammed Salim, was born in Northern Ireland in 1955, and on 24 November 1980, he joined Al-Fatah. The card gives no details of his service in that organisation, but Israeli intelligence sources insist that he was trained by the PLO and then shipped back to fight for the IRA. As well as listing his place of birth as Northern Ireland, the service card named Howe's mother as Charlotte, his marital status as bachelor, his education as academic and his profession as construction worker. His height was listed as 191 cm, his complexion fair, hair blond and eyes blue. His rank in Al-Fatah was that of *mukatal*, or fighter. According to Israeli intelligence, he was one of many hundreds of recruits to pass through the PLO's hands in the last decade, but British intelligence claim that they have no knowledge of Howe or any other IRA member trained by the PLO.

'We have always been very doubtful about the PLO training element,' one British counter-intelligence officer said.

> All sorts of claims have been made but we have never been able to find a single person who has been trained by them. In all the years we have been operating in Northern Ireland and the hundreds of people we have picked up, there is no doubt that we would have found at least one person who had been trained by them if there was any truth in it.

Of course, politically sympathetic foreigners have joined the PLO as well as other terrorist groups – at various times the PLO has had American, British, Japanese and West German nationals in its ranks. However, these, like Ian Davidson, the young British citizen who was involved in the assassination of three Israelis in Cyprus in 1985, join such organisations because they approve of their aims, and that is very different from being seconded from other terrorist groups.

Despite this, there undoubtedly are links between different terrorist groups. Those who believe in an international terrorist conspiracy see a common hand – generally the KGB's – manipulating behind the scenes, but there is insufficient evidence to justify such a conclusion. More accurately, terrorism can be compared, in some respects, to a multi-national corporation with different divisions dotted around the world, all of which act in an essentially independent manner. When the head of another operation comes to town, generally he or she will have the use of the company apartment, may get an advance against expenses and will probably be given access to local equipment if required.

The PLO can be compared to the headquarters of the multi-national corporation but with one essential difference: there is no chief executive officer of world terrorism and no world budget produced by the terrorist accountants. However, the PLO is the one international terrorist organisation that can operate with the support of different governments, and before it was driven out of the Lebanon, it effectively ran a state within a state. It is understandable, therefore, that other, less fortunate groups from around the world should come to visit the PLO.

Western intelligence believes that, between 1970 and 1984, twenty-eight meetings involving different terrorist groups have been held around the world. The meetings were generally convened to discuss co-operation rather than the co-ordination of a revolutionary master-plan for the overthrow of established order. The meetings are listed opposite (for a more detailed explanation of each group, see 'A glossary of terrorism' on pp. 247–257).

PLO policy welcomes links with revolutionaries from around the world. This helps spread the word about the Palestinian cause and provides the basis of a support structure outside the Middle East. The policy has been immensely successful and the PLO has become the true godfather of international terrorism. However, it owes its success not to the support of the Soviet Union and its allies, but to its own survival skills. The Soviets are used whenever possible, but far from the PLO being a tool of the Soviet machine, the relationship is often reversed, the PLO's pivotal position in Middle East politics giving them a strong bargaining position.

Neither side trusts the other, and the PLO, while it may be useful on occasion to the Soviet Union in providing some valuable foreign exchange, has had to turn elsewhere for money to finance its long-term survival. The Palestinians have traditionally held very strong positions in Middle East countries, as teachers, bankers and advisers. It was a happy coincidence that the boom in oil revenues occurred at the same time as the PLO were in the greatest need of capital to finance their bases

51

in the Lebanon and their worldwide propaganda campaign. The organisation found allies in the Middle East who provided the backing to allow it to develop into the multinational corporation it is today. And while the PLO grew in influence, other terrorist groups sprang up in their wake.

October 1971	Firenze, Italy	IRA, ETA, ERP, PLO, 12 other groups
May 1972	Baddawi, Lebanon	PFLP (organiser), IRA, Iranians, TPLA, JRA, ETA, BR, Tupamaros, Baader–Meinhof, Abu Iyad
1973	London, England	IRA, FLB, ETA, BR
July 1973	Tripoli, Libya	PFLP, TPLA, Baader–Meinhof, Iranians, IRA, Tupamaros, JRA
December 1973	Dublin, Ireland	ETA, IRA, FLNC, FLB, Quebecois, BR, AD
January 1974	Dublin, Ireland	As above + PLO
1974	Belfast, Northern Ireland	IRA, ETA, PLO, Frelimo, Tupamaros
Summer 1977	Spain	PIRA, FLB, Baader–Meinhof, FLNC, Welsh, RZ, June 2, BR, Grappo, PLO
April 1978	Havana, Cuba	PLO, Baader–Meinhof, JRA, BR.
September 1978	Beirut, Lebanon	PLO, BR, IRA, Baader–Meinhof, Montoneros, ETA, JRA, ASALA
October 1978	Frankfurt, West Germany	PFLP, KGB, BR, IRA, Baader–Meinhof, JRA
October 1978	Portugal	ETA-M PIRA
January 1979	Benghazi, Libya	FSLN, Tupamaros, Montoneros, MIL, JCR, Al-Fatah, M19, representatives from Costa Rica, Bolivia, Mexico, Brazil
February 1979	Sardinia	21 organisations
April 1979	Puerto Hero, Spain	ETA-M, Al-Fatah, Montoneros
Summer 1979	Belfast, Northern Ireland	PLO, IRA
October 1979	Milan, Italy	PLO, BR, IRA, Baader–Meinhof, ETA, JRA, Montoneros
November 1979	Lisbon, Portugal	PLO, World Peace Council
July 1980	Nicaragua	Unknown
April 1981	Athens, Greece	Cypriots, Kurds, ASLA, PLO
Summer 1981	Lausanne, Switzerland	PFLP, Baader–Meinhof, BR, IRA, ETA
August 1981	Ottawa, Canada	PLO, SWAPO, ANC, FMLN, IRA
September 1981	Managua, Nicaragua	Nicaraguans, Salvadorans, Cubans
November 1981	Caracas, Venezuela	Unknown
16 November 1981	Tripoli, Libya	PLO, rest unknown
February 1982	Southern Lebanon	PLO, BR, Baader–Meinhof, JRA, Cubans, Libyans, Pakistanis, Salvadorans
6/7 August 1982	Corsica	PLO, IRA, ETA, Polisario, FLNC
June 1984	Lisbon, Portugal	ETA, BR, AD, FP25, CCC, RAF

3

The oil incendiary

ASPIRING REVOLUTIONARIES usually start with little more than enthusiasm for their cause. All terrorist groups have begun with a few dedicated idealists, no money, no training and few concrete ideas. In the progression from fringe radicals to recognised terrorists, all groups first have to acquire some income; second, they have to buy some arms; and third, they have to achieve the international recognition that will help gather donations from supporters outside the organisation. Many terrorist groups have achieved the first two aims but have failed to gather the international support necessary to build up an infrastructure that can survive the activities of counter-terrorist forces.

In order for terrorism to succeed, a friendly border or safe haven must be adjacent to the area of operations. Without such a bolthole, terrorists have nowhere to run and no direct conduit for arms and cash. If the terrorists have no safe haven, their prospects will be slim.

While the Eastern Bloc and Cuba may have armed and, to some extent, trained many terrorists, the countries of the Middle East have contributed most of the cash and arms that are given to the different terrorist groups and have ensured their growth.

Early support for the PLO by the Arab nations from the mid-1960s coincided with a period of revolution and instability in the Middle East. Those countries which benefited from the oil bonanza found they had more money than they could possibly absorb internally. The PLO and other terrorist groups around the world then also benefited from the oil revenue windfall, which contributed to the establishment of terrorism as a permanent feature of international politics.

As in so many other areas of terrorism, such as financing, training and weapons, it is the PLO that has set the pace in developing independence and in gathering support from friendly countries. Given the nature of the Palestinian diaspora, with large numbers concentrated throughout the Gulf, Arab leaders were, not surprisingly the first to give cash to the PLO. However, over the years, the motivation for this support has varied from country to country, and in the last five years Arab aid has decreased to such a level that the PLO has had to rely more and more on its own resources. This is partly the impact of reduced oil surpluses in the Gulf States, and partly because Arab nations feel that the PLO has failed to deliver a Palestinian state and doubt that it ever will.

The Arabs and the Palestinians have always been wary of each other. The Palestinians distrust the Arabs and, in particular, despise the backwardness of the Gulf Arabs who did not begin to develop as nations until the discovery of oil. The Arabs, on the other hand, have reservations about the Palestinians, who they view as a source of potential dissent and disaffection within their own countries, as well as envying their business acumen.

Palestinian mistrust of the Arabs was cemented during the 1948 war which established the State of Israel. On 29 November 1947, the UN General Assembly passed a resolution which allowed the establishment of a Jewish state in Palestine. Although the resolution was passed, neither the Palestinians nor the Arab states supported the vote. Less than six months later, on 15 May 1948, the State of Israel was proclaimed, and immediately the armies of Jordan, Egypt, Syria, Iraq, Saudi Arabia, the Lebanon and Sudan, and a contingent of Palestinians, attacked Israel. Israel turned the Arab armies back, and in the peace agreement that followed, Israel was allowed to keep a central section of what had been Palestine, while Egypt took the Gaza Strip in the south-west and Jordan was given control of the West Bank.

At the time of the 1948 war, more than 500,000 Palestinians fled from their country to seek refuge with Arab neighbours. Their expectation was that the Israelis would be swiftly defeated and they would soon return to their rightful homeland. However, the Arabs carved up their land between them and the Palestinians took up permanent status as refugees in camps in the Lebanon, Jordan and Syria.

In every Arab country where the Palestinians landed, they were treated as second-class citizens, confined to ghettos specially created for them and banned from voting or holding certain jobs, such as company directorships, which might have given them influence.

In an abortive attempt to preserve something of their heritage, the Palestinians formed a provisional government in Gaza in September 1948. This declared the borders of Palestine to be 'between Syria and

Lebanon in the north, Syria and Trans-Jordan in the east, the Mediterranean in the west and Egypt in the south'. This bid for international recognition failed when no Arab government supported them, and Egypt moved swiftly to dissolve the government and declare all its decisions invalid. As the Gaza Strip was now under Egyptian military control, the Palestinians had little choice but to comply. The unfortunate experience of the 1948 war gave rise to the Palestinian saying: 'All revolutions conceived in Palestine abort in the Arab capitals.' And as Abu Iyad has pointed out in his autobiography: 'Experience has shown that, when the chips are down, all the Arab regimes, whether progressive or reactionary, act in the same way, sacrificing the Palestinian cause to their own parochial interests.'

Funding for the PLO and its offshoots has been mainly the result of blackmail by the PLO or political opportunism by Arab leaders. As terrorists, the PLO have considerable power over vulnerable Arab leaders: the threat of terrorist attacks against Arab countries who refuse to support the PLO with hard cash or arms is a powerful weapon which the PLO has not hesitated to use. Also, for countries such as Syria and Saudi Arabia, having a friendly PLO faction can provide useful leverage in the melting pot of Middle East politics. For example, sponsorship of the PLO and support for the organisation's activities in the Lebanon has kept President Hafez al-Assad of Syria at the centre of all negotiations on a possible Middle East peace settlement.

Originally, Al-Fatah swore independence from Arab influence, relying on individual donations from committed Palestinians around the world. However, as the organisation grew, the need for funds grew, too, and independence had to be sacrificed to ensure its survival. Arafat's decision to join the PLO in 1968 also forced him to revise his ideas of political independence. The PLO had been formed by Arab nations and survived with their support. Arafat could not have become the organisation's leader without some compromise over the question of financial support.

The PLO's early efforts to raise money from Arab governments such as Kuwait, Egypt, Saudi Arabia and Syria were greeted with some suspicion by the conservative Arab states, who viewed Arafat and his followers as young radicals who might want to spread revolution to all the countries in the region. However, Nasser's Egypt, King Faisal's Saudi Arabia and King Idris's Libya were early sympathisers, donating small amounts of money that enabled the PLO to buy arms for its terrorist attacks.

September 1970 – Black September – was a humiliating defeat for the PLO in Jordan, when it was unable to put up any serious resistance against the army of King Hussein, and this setback led to a sharp fall in the amount of aid flowing to the PLO from other countries. At a meeting of the Palestine National Council in Cairo on 5 July 1971, it was revealed that the only income received so far that year was $40,000 from Qatar; $10 million promised by other Arab states had not been delivered. A desperate search for more money began, with more pressure being put on Arab leaders and wealthy Palestinians. The organisation also decided to carry out a series of spectacular terrorist actions designed to show a sceptical Arab world that the PLO was still capable of successful military action against Israel and other Jewish targets around the world, and therefore worthy of Arab support.

The increasing success of the PLO as a terrorist organisation gave it heightened credibility in the Arab world. Other circumstances also helped Arafat's cause. In 1973, Egypt and Syria launched a surprise attack against Israel on Yom Kippur, the Jewish holy day, but despite early successes, the Arabs were eventually defeated. This setback to their military ambitions helped convince the Arabs that they should use other methods to undermine Israel's position. The most logical candidate for their support was the PLO who were pledged to the destruction of the State of Israel and had terrorist forces willing to launch attacks against Israel.

The PLO gained a reputation as a major force in their own right after a series of armed clashes with Christian forces and the Lebanese army in 1973 and 1974. The Lebanese had become increasingly concerned by the PLO's control of large parts of Lebanon and their use of the refugee camps in the south as a base for expansion north towards Beirut. However, the PLO successfully fought off a number of attempts to curb their powers and were left in virtual control of large sections of southern Lebanon from where they could continue to launch terrorist attacks against Israel.

Even in those auspicious circumstances, the Palestinians were still struggling financially. The PLO discovered that Arab countries, including Saudi Arabia and Kuwait, were selling arms to the PLO's enemies, the Phalangists in the Lebanon, simply to make money; they were also promising the PLO large sums of money but were not delivering the cash. Short of money and lacking in wholehearted Arab support, the PLO leaders were anxious to persuade the Arab leaders to be more consistent. A meeting of senior PLO leaders at the end of 1974 resulted in a decision to launch a fund-raising drive that, it was hoped, would bring with it increased political support.

In early 1975, Abu Iyad toured the Gulf States to raise money for the PLO. He began in Kuwait, which is more left-wing than others in the area and has a large Palestinian population (300,000 out of 1.37 million). The Kuwaiti government has welcomed the PLO's continued confrontations with Israel but is concerned that instability will spread within its own borders. Abu Iyad gave a series of speeches in Kuwait aimed at both the rich Palestinians and the government, which warned that 'whether they like it or not, they will pay'. Such an overt threat to the Kuwaitis had the desired effect, and the next day, a meeting of millionaires agreed to increase their donations – as did the government.

The momentum was only temporary, however. By the end of 1977 King Hassan of Morocco was able to say: 'The PLO will tell you that, since 1971, only Saudi Arabia and Morocco have continued to provide it with money. Libya no longer funds the PLO, nor does Algeria. So it is only our two countries which contribute, each according to its means.' (This was a slight exaggeration as Kuwait and the United Arab Emirates had both contributed to the PLO since 1970.)

The signing of the Camp David agreement between Egypt and Israel in September 1978 shocked many of the Arab leaders. They were suspicious of the agreement and viewed President Anwar Sadat's actions as a betrayal of their united stand against Israel; they also feared that an Israel without Egypt to worry about posed a far greater threat. The Arabs decided to use their hired muscle, the PLO, to keep the Israelis busy.

In November 1978, in Baghdad, ten Arab heads of state agreed to provide $3.5 billion a year in aid to nations such as Jordan, Syria and the Lebanon and to the PLO, all of which were in confrontation with Israel. Contributors to the Baghdad aid programme included Saudi Arabia, Libya, Kuwait, Iraq, the United Arab Emirates, Algeria and Qatar. The bulk of the money would go to Syria, with $800 million to Jordan, $250 million for the PLO and $150 million to the occupied territories – the West Bank and Gaza – that had been taken by Israel in either the 1967 or 1973 Arab–Israeli wars. This latter sum was to be administered by a joint Jordanian–PLO committee but, in reality, was completely controlled by Jordan.

The actual distribution of the $250 million earmarked for the PLO was a matter of some debate. Yasser Arafat and his organisation, Al-Fatah, were opposed to the distribution of the money proportionately among the terrorist groups: the other factions, believing they would be

57

short-changed by Arafat, wanted a quota system where each group would get a share of the cash proportionate to its size. The Arab states, wishing to spread their donation among as many terrorist groups as possible, sided against Arafat. Of the $250 million for the PLO, $50 million would go into the reserves, $50 million into the overall budget of the PLO and $10 million for the 'families of the martyrs'. The remaining $140 million would be distributed as follows: fifty-eight per cent to Al-Fatah; ten per cent to Saiqa; seven per cent each for the DFLP, PFLP, PFLP-GC and the Arab Liberation Front; and two per cent each for the PLF and the Popular Struggle Front.

However, the Arabs largely failed to deliver. Algeria and Libya never honoured the agreement, and of all the other donor countries, only Saudi Arabia has consistently kept up a high level of cash transfers. Even that has only been maintained by the constant prodding of the PLO Central Committee, who privately always complain that their Arab neighbours are unreliable and untrustworthy.

For example, in 1979 the forty-two-member Islamic Conference Organisation, which is based in Jeddah and was formed in 1971 to promote Islamic solidarity all over the world, announced the formation of the Jerusalem Fund, which was to generate funds for Palestinians in Jerusalem and the West Bank. $100 million was promised but, after three years, no more than $26 million had been raised from grants and contributions.

At the same time, individuals – who generally have a far better record of commitment – were giving large sums every 29 November, the UN-designated 'Day of Solidarity with the Palestinian People'. The Day of Solidarity has become a symbolic time for all Palestinian supporters in the same way as May Day commemorates the struggle of the labour movement. For example, according to a story in the *Middle East Reporter*, in 1982 Saudi Arabian Defence Minister, Prince Sultan Ben Abdel Aziz, began one series of royal contributions by donating two million Saudi riyals ($582,000). Prince Salman, the Emir of Riyadh in Saudi Arabia, followed with a donation of one million riyals ($291,000), and Prince Sattam, the Deputy Emir of Riyadh, also contributed half a million Riyals ($145,000). In addition, the report said that Lebanese businessman Rafik Hariri, whose Beirut-based business interests to a large extent relied on the good will of the PLO, donated three million riyals ($873,000). The Saudi Ojjeh Company, which owns the luxury cruise liner *France*, gave $291,000 and other Saudi businessmen contributed over $500,000.

However, even though some individuals contributed to the PLO cause with no thought of an immediate return on their investments, donations from Arab countries usually came with strings attached. In December 1982, after Yasser Arafat was evacuated from Tripoli in the Lebanon, he was scheduled to stop at Jeddah in Saudi Arabia. This was an opportunity for the Saudis to show the other Arab leaders that they were loyal to the Palestinians and also that they were the most important among them, which was why Arafat had chosen Jeddah as his first stopping point. There was considerable unhappiness among the Saudis, therefore, when Arafat stopped in Cairo *en route* to see President Mubarak. Egypt had been ostracised in the Arab world since the Camp David treaty, and this unscheduled meeting was downgrading Saudi support. Consequently, the Saudis banned the Jeddah visit and told Arafat that the quarterly $28.5 million payment to the PLO would be stopped. However, three months later, in March, Arafat was allowed back to Saudi and was also promised the overdue cash.

In the same way as Abu Iyad had to use blackmail to raise cash from friendly Arab countries, so today's leaders of the PLO use the same tactic to try and keep the funds flowing in. In October 1985, Jamal Sawrani, the head of the Palestinian Lawyers Organisation, claimed that the PLO was heavily in debt, and had an annual income of $250 million, with only $30 million from individual donations and minimal contributions from Arab states. His account was interesting on two levels: it gave a figure for the PLO's annual income which is one-fifth of its real size, and it was a none-too-subtle attempt to play on the sympathies of the Arab leaders for more cash donations. These have not been forthcoming.

Despite the constant problems with funding, since 1973 the PLO has never received less than $100 million a year from the Arab states, and generally has close to $250 million. However, the organisation currently needs in excess of $500 million a year simply to meet its running expenses. This largely accounts for the PLO's drive towards self-finance in the last decade – an effort that has proved exceptionally successful.

While grateful for any cash handed down from the main organisation, the individual groups under the PLO umbrella have always relied on additional donations from the principal radical Arab countries: Iraq, Syria, Libya and Iran. This measure of independence from central control allows for the expression of the widely different political and military philosophies that abound in the movement, and for the donating country, cash is a way of imposing some loyalty on a terrorist group that can influence Middle East affairs considerably.

President Hafez al-Assad seized control of Syria in 1970 in a military coup, and with his brother, Rifaat, he has ruthlessly held on to power ever since. Assad rules a country that is bankrupt and supported entirely by donations from other Arab nations, particularly Saudi Arabia, because of Syria's pivotal role in the Arab conflict with Israel. In the Arab–Israeli wars of 1967 and 1973, Syria played an important part by harrying Israel's northern flank via the strategically important Beka'a valley, which covers an area including the Lebanon's border with Israel to the south and its border with Syria in the east. Assad never fails to point out his contribution to the Arab–Israeli conflict to those Arab leaders, in countries such as Saudi Arabia or Kuwait, who are less directly involved as their borders do not abut Israel's. Assad sees himself as occupying the centre stage in the Middle East, and he tries to preserve that position of importance.

Assad has been liberal with his support for different terrorist groups, including Saiqa and the PFLP-GC. Syria's financial assistance to such terrorist groups varies from year to year, but is generally between $50 and $100 million. Saiqa and the PFLP-GC favour a military solution to the Palestinian issue and provide a useful weapon to maintain Syria's place in the Middle East conflict. Both groups also make a formidable bargaining counter in any negotiations either among Arabs or with the United States.

The presence of over 50,000 Syrian troops in the Lebanon can be expected to have some impact on the region, but Assad has backed this up with more covert support, which resulted in the 1982 assassination of Bashir Gemayal, the Lebanon's president-elect, and which was also responsible for the partial coup organised against Yasser Arafat by Abu Musa that same year. At that time, Assad hoped that Musa would take control of the PLO following the expulsion of Arafat.

However, Arafat has held on to the organisation, and in negotiations in mid-1984, Arafat and Assad re-opened discussions using intermediaries, although, as usual, Arafat has been hedging his bets. In 1985 he had several talks with President Saddam Hussein of Iraq to persuade him to allow the PLO headquarters to move to Baghdad. It seems likely that Arafat will shortly be back in the mainstream with a base in Syria, and Assad will once again be playing a pivotal role in Palestinian affairs. Certainly Assad's crucial involvement in June 1985 in the successful freeing of the American hostages held on TWA flight 847 has increased his credibility in the eyes of the US government: it was Assad's role as intermediary that helped free the hostages. The US may see Assad playing a similar role in their delicate attempt to bring the Palestinians and the Israelis to the negotiating table.

Arafat has been a regular target of political machinations because of his control of the PLO, but he and his organisation, Al-Fatah, are only one part of the PLO, and each of the groups that fall under the PLO umbrella is a regular target for intrigue and bribery. There are also the breakaway groups, in particular, Black June, which was formed in 1976 to protest against the involvement of Syrian troops in the Lebanese civil war in June of that year, and has come to symbolise the most extreme of the terrorist groups. In 1976, President Saddam Hussein of Iraq allocated $50 million per annum to Black June, which had announced as its aim a series of attacks on Syrian targets. As Iraq and Syria are traditional enemies, Black June's policies happily coincided with Hussein's.

The organisation is led by a renegade Palestinian called Sabri al-Banna, also known as Abu Nidal, who has been responsible single-handedly for the most savage terrorist attacks to have outraged the world. His political fervour was born in the late 1940s during the establishment of Israel and the beginning of the Palestinian diaspora. Trained as a teacher, Nidal (whose name means 'Father of The Struggle') joined Al-Fatah in the late 1960s, and by 1969 was its representative in Khartoum, Sudan, and then, in 1970, the representative in Baghdad. Nidal was sent for military training to North Korea, and he later visited China where he was taught guerrilla warfare tactics and the use of explosives, and received a thorough grounding in Maoist theory. In the same contingent to North Korea was Abu Daoud, who later was one of the planners behind the massacre of Israeli athletes at the Munich Olympics.

Under the influence of the Iraqis, Nidal came to believe that any policy which combined military force with political negotiation was unacceptable, and that violence was the only way to establish a Palestinian state. The disagreements between Nidal and Arafat, who saw some virtue in a compromise between violence and negotiation, became so serious that in 1974 Nidal sent an assassination squad to kill Arafat in Damascus. The assassins were captured and Nidal was sentenced to death by a PLO court, which heard evidence from Arafat and others.

There followed a bitter underground war between Arafat's followers and Black June. PLO representatives in Kuwait, Paris and London were killed and there were several further assassination attempts on Arafat himself. Al-Fatah also succeeded in killing a number of Black June supporters. Finally, in 1978 a truce was called and Black June switched its attention away from the PLO.

Since then, Nidal and his 100 followers have acted as 'guns for hire' around the world. Uniquely among terrorist groups, Nidal has been able to ally himself to different paymasters. Thus, even though his organisation was originally set up to attack Syria, as he moved on to attack the PLO and then to concentrate on Jewish targets, so he was able to alternate between Syria and Iraq, and for many years he maintained offices in both Damascus and Baghdad.

In the opinion of senior PLO officials and intelligence sources, Nidal is the closest thing to a psychopath currently on the international terrorist scene. This makes him especially difficult to control and his group particularly deadly.

Black June has been responsible for a string of assassinations of PLO representatives, including Said Hammami who was gunned down in his London office in 1978, and Issam Sartawi who was shot in Portugal in 1983, after Nidal unilaterally went back on the 1978 ceasefire agreement. Both men were prime movers within the PLO in opening up a dialogue with moderate Israelis. In addition, with the support of the Iraqi government, a three-man hit squad was sent by Abu Nidal to London, where they attempted, in 1982, to assassinate the Israeli ambassador to Britain, Shlomo Argov. The ambassador was seriously wounded and the three men were captured and are now in British jails. Three days later, the Israelis used the assassination attempt as an excuse to launch Operation Peace for Galilee.

Initially, it was thought that one possible reason for Iraq's encouraging the attack may have been that an Israeli invasion into the Lebanon would give Iraq an excuse to sue for peace in the Iran/Iraq war. However, it was later revealed that the attempted assassination of Argov had not, in fact, been guided by the Baghdad government. When the British police raided the flat used by the hit team, they found a long list of potential targets including: Jewish schools and synagogues; the Kuwaiti ambassador; Sir Immanuel Jacobovitz, the Chief Rabbi in England; and Nabil Ramlawi, the then London representative of the PLO. The decision to attack Argov appears to have been made on the spur of the moment.

'You have to remember that Nidal is simply a gun for hire,' explains one intelligence source. 'The problem with him and his band is that you have to give them a home while you are paying them but most of the time you have no control over him or his henchmen.'

This view seems finally to have reached Saddam Hussein in Baghdad. In November 1983, Iraqi security police arrested Nidal at his comfortable villa provided courtesy of the Iraqi government in a Baghdad suburb. Hussein, wishing to win new allies in his war with Iran, and responding to diplomatic pressure from the United States, had finally decided to expel Nidal. (The United States was in the early stages of negotiations about re-opening diplomatic relations with Iraq – having previously severed them in protest at Iraq's support of terrorism – but was insisting that a formal agreement would be impossible while Hussein was playing host to one of the world's most notorious terrorists. Diplomatic relations were re-established at the end of 1984.) Under heavy guard, Nidal and his immediate entourage were driven in a convoy of trucks to the border with Syria. From there, Nidal was taken to a heavily fortified building in the Shaalan suburb of Damascus.

Having Abu Nidal under his wing proved a double-edged sword for Assad in Syria. Happy as Assad may have been to have a willing assassin at his beck and call, Nidal has always been somewhat indiscriminate in his attacks – for example, he was responsible for at least fifty in the first six months of 1984.

Assad evidently found Nidal too hot to handle for, in the middle of 1985, the latter moved on to Libya. US intelligence sources claim that they monitored Nidal in Tripoli for some months prior to his re-emergence on the world scene – with the spectacular hijacking of EgyptAir flight 648 *en route* from Athens to Cairo. The aircraft landed in Malta, and after the terrorists began to kill the passengers, Egyptian commandos stormed the plane. In the fighting that followed, sixty people died, including four of the five hijackers. US State Department and CIA sources state categorically that it was Nidal's men who carried out the hijacking. Certainly the savagery involved had all Nidal's style, but hijacking is not usually in his repertoire; he prefers assassinations and bombing to make his political points.

Supporting Nidal represents a new and radical step for Colonel Muammar al-Gadaffi. The EgyptAir hijacking very nearly escalated into a more widespread war, for as soon as it began, the Egyptian government called Washington to tell them that the hijacking was simply a diversion to distract Egypt from a major attack by Libya. The United States was requested to use its aerial surveillance systems – particularly the AWACS and ECZA Hawkeyes based in the Mediterranean – to monitor Libyan troop movements. In addition, if Egypt were to launch an attack on the hijacked aircraft, the US was asked for US fighters to guard the plane carrying Egyptian commandos. The Americans readily agreed to both requests.

As always, details of Nidal's current whereabouts are sketchy, with reports that he is now based either in Tripoli or Damascus. Wherever he is, more attacks can be expected, especially against the United States. As Nidal himself said in a rare interview: 'You will see that we will stage operations against the Americans, and the billions of dollars their forces have will not be enough to protect them. You will see proof of what we are saying in the next few months.'

Support for Nidal will confirm to many people that Gadaffi is 'Mr Terrorism', the man with the money who will bankroll any extremist group with no questions asked and no political dividend expected. However, a rationale does exist behind Gadaffi's seemingly random support of international terrorism.

He came to power in 1969 in a country that was still feudal. Now one of the longest-serving Middle East rulers, he has brought his country into the twentieth century while at the same time holding on to the loyalty and affection of the vast majority of his people. His style is a mixture of bribes, beatings and charisma, and his support of terrorism comes from personal conviction and from a need to stage-manage his role as a world revolutionary and to promote Libya as the little Arab nation leading the world.

'You have to remember that he is very street-smart. He may not be particularly brilliant intellectually but he has the pulse of his people and they love a showman,' explained one Middle East expert who knows him well. 'Of course, he is interested in spreading the thoughts of his Green Book [the Gadaffi bible] but he is most interested in his own survival.'

In addition to supporting Palestinian groups such as the PFLP, the DFLP and the PFLP-GC with approximately $100 million a year, Gadaffi has given money to, or helped in other ways, the IRA, ETA, the Baader–Meinhof gang, the Red Brigade, the Japanese Red Army, the Tupamaros in Uruguay and the Moros in the Philippines. However, his largesse seems to depend greatly on whim, and among terrorists there has been consistent frustration with his level of support. He has always promised a great deal to world terrorism in terms of cash and arms – his propaganda, for example, makes much of his role as 'father of the world revolution' – but, groups such as the IRA who have visited him to request money and arms, have almost invariably departed with little more than promises.

Gadaffi's global ambitions have been fuelled by the fabulous oil wealth that has given him considerably more power than would other-wise accrue to a dictator of a small and previously insignificant country. As the cash supply increased, Gadaffi began influencing small terrorist groups outside his territory and relished the role of international maverick. Then, when he became more secure, his plans for the world grew more aggressive and expansionist. However, Gadaffi's image as the terrorists' patron, constantly doling out gold and guns to anyone who asks, however lunatic their cause, is incorrect. Instead, he uses his support as a selfish political tool rather than as a philanthropic extension of his personal philosophy.

In a speech marking the twelfth anniversary of the Libyan revolution of 1 September 1981, Gadaffi said:

> We welcome Arafat as one of us and not as a guest . . . We are duty-bound, because of world solidarity with the Palestinian people, to mobilise all our means on behalf of the revolution against Zionist racism . . . We wish to tell the Israeli settlers: Do not expect to live in security for ever, for you are occupying Palestinian cities. The fact that you have lived in security for 30 years does not mean that such a situation will persist. Indeed, Palestinian missile and cannon fire reached you this year. Those missiles and cannons will not be withdrawn until all the land of Palestine has been liberated. We stand behind them and so do the Arab people. We will keep on fighting until the final liberation. The liberation of Palestine will be achieved with blood.

This kind of flowing rhetoric is exactly what a budding terrorist wants to hear, and listening to it, one could get the impression that Gadaffi is solidly behind the PLO in its fight for a state. However, only three months later, Gadaffi cut off all funds to the PLO with little prospect of resumption.

According to senior sources within the PLO, Gadaffi was responding to US pressure to reduce his funding for terrorists. Even though five senior PLO leaders were summoned to Tripoli in January 1983 and, after the usual speeches, promised a large donation of cash, that money has yet to appear, and the PLO no longer regard Gadaffi as a bankroller of the organisation. 'He has always been vastly overrated as a supporter of terrorism,' says one PLO official. 'Even when the Israelis invaded in 1982 he only gave us a tiny amount of cash.' While the United States has been at the head of international criticism of Gadaffi, and the United States Embassy is no longer open in Tripoli, US oil companies still operate in Libya – despite a trade embargo – and more than 1000 US citizens currently work in the country.

From the outset, Gadaffi's relations with the Palestinians have been uneasy. Although he is allegedly at the forefront of the Arab supporters of the organisation, he has been the most mercurial of all the backers and the least popular with the PLO. As Arafat's deputy, Abu Iyad, pointed out in 1979:

> We have had a long history of quarrels with Gadaffi since 1975 . . . Gadaffi advocated the view that a Palestinian leader may move only when he orders him to. He always wants us to toe his line fully. We must be the friends of his friends and the foes of his foes . . . What he wants is a paid revolution, and he treats us like paid mercenaries. He never abided by the decisions made in the different Arab summit conferences to give us financial support. He is moody. If you do not satisfy him, you get a kick. He owes us contributions to the amount of between $80 and $90 million. Yet we are not prepared to submit to any Arab capital.

Even so, Gadaffi's role in international terrorism is not small. In the early 1970s when he appeared to discover terrorism as a new toy and a way of keeping his name in the headlines, the reputation he got for using his huge oil surpluses to finance terrorist attacks was quite justified. Israeli intelligence believe that Gadiffi paid a $5 million bonus to the Black September terrorists who took part in the massacre at the Munich Olympics in 1972. They also say that the international terrorist and 'gun for hire', 'Carlos', received a bonus from Gadaffi of nearly $2 million after the seizure of the OPEC oil ministers in Vienna in December 1975, and other reports suggest that he took a cut out of the $5 million ransom paid by Saudi Arabia and Iran for the release of their ministers. Another of the terrorists involved in that incident, Hans-Joachim Klein, was shot in the stomach during the attack and received $100,000 for his discomfort. However, such largesse has been tempered by time and falling oil revenues. For a terrorist killed in action while operating on Libya's behalf, Gadaffi will now pay his family only between $10,000 and $30,000, a considerable reduction in ten years.

The most extraordinary long-term arrangement that Gadaffi established during the 1970s was with two ex-CIA men, Edwin Wilson and Frank Terpil. Wilson is now fifty-six and Terpil ten years younger, and both share a chequered past that includes considerable involvement with CIA covert operations: Terpil in the Middle East and Bangladesh; Wilson from the Bay of Pigs to Vietnam.

Terpil was fired from the CIA in 1971 after his cavalier attitude to orders proved too much even for them. He immediately put his expertise to use by forming a company called Oceanic International Corporation which dealt in various ordnance for President Idi Amin of Uganda. Terpil's contacts in the underworld of the illegal arms business and his ability to supply items ranging from torture equipment to exploding briefcases swiftly endeared him to Amin, who in turn recommended him to Gadaffi. (Gadaffi had by then been joined by Amin on the lunatic fringe of international politics.) Newspaper reporters and FBI detectives subsequently discovered a contract for $3.2 million between Terpil and Amin's State Research Bureau, Uganda's dreaded secret police.

Wilson left the CIA at the same time as Terpil but under more favourable circumstances and apparently on assignment for the US government. He joined Task Force 157, a secret US Navy spy group involved in covert operations around the world and, presumably with the US government's full knowledge, he also became involved in the export of arms products.

According to the Los Angeles Times (29 September 1981), Wilson cultivated congressional and White House contacts at his 1500-acre estate in Upperville, Virginia. Eventually, his vigorous lobbying cost him his job after he had made a business proposition to Admiral Bobby Ray Inman, then director of naval intelligence. Wilson apparently wanted Inman to help push a contract his way in return for Wilson's influence with the Navy's budget in Congress. Instead, Inman disbanded Task Force 157 and Wilson was fired in 1976.

Terpil contacted Wilson and the two men teamed up to form a terrorism advisory service that not only trained terrorists for Gadaffi, but also provided the terrorists with the arms necessary to execute particular tasks. In the early days, they concentrated on selling the Libyan army weapons and equipment that they purchased for low prices in the United States surplus market. For example, in the late 1970s they sold to Gadaffi for $900,000 one US military vehicle equipped with night surveillance equipment that they had bought for $60,000. However, Wilson and Terpil soon began supplying and training terrorists.

In 1977, they recruited ten former Green Berets to work for the Libyan government. Each recruit, who had been interviewed outside Fort Bragg, was given $1000 in cash and an airline ticket from Washington to Zurich via New York, where they were met by Wilson. The leader of the group was offered and accepted (under the impression that this was a US government-sanctioned contract) a payment of $140,000, and the other team members were each paid $100,000. Health care would be provided in Europe, and insurance coverage for each man would be $250,000 for loss of life and $125,000 for loss of limb. The money would be paid in any currency and to any bank that the men requested.

Part of the team's task was to train terrorists in the use of high explosives, and Wilson and Terpil amassed a stock of 20 tons of C4, a particularly powerful and stable type of explosive, at a cost of $300,000; this was later airlifted to Tripoli from Houston, Texas in a chartered DC-8 in boxes labelled 'drilling mud'.

Intelligence sources believe that Wilson and Terpil were personally responsible, via their former trainees, for the murder of a Libyan lawyer in London in 1979, an attempted coup in Chad in 1978, a $1 million contract to assassinate Umar Abdullah Muhayshi, a senior Libyan defector, in 1976, which was never carried out, and the 1978 assassination of Bruce Mackenzie, a close confidant of the late Jomo Kenyatta of Kenya. In addition, Wilson and Terpil established a number of terrorist camps in Libya that are thought to have trained hundreds of local people, and dozens of potential terrorists recruited from abroad, in assassination and bomb-making.

While the recruiting of terrorists internationally has fallen off in recent years, as Gadaffi has shown less interest in sponsoring the world revolution, there are still training camps in Libya and an established salary structure: $400 a month to every trainee from Africa or the Arab world, and $1000 a month for all other foreigners. All personal needs, such as housing and food, are taken care of in the camps, but after graduation, the terrorists are allowed to take only fifty per cent of their earnings abroad with them.

Wilson and Terpil have made a fortune from their association with Gadaffi. Federal agents have traced property in the US and Europe, belonging to both men, worth in excess of $4 million and the US Internal Revenue Service filed a civil suit in 1980 claiming that Terpil owes $2.4 million in taxes and fines. According to the suit, Terpil bought forty cashiers' cheques from Barclays Bank in denominations of $100,000 each. For both men, terrorism has simply been a matter of selling their expertise to the highest bidder – with no questions asked. In one undercover operation, two New York detectives, posing as South American revolutionaries, asked Terpil for guns and poisons. Terpil simply noted: 'If you're knocking off Americans, it'll cost you forty per cent more.'

Wilson was eventually arrested, tried in New York and convicted of illegally sending guns to Colonel Gadaffi. Wilson always maintained that he had been acting on behalf of the CIA and that he had passed regular intelligence back to the United States. None of the ex-Green Berets who helped train terrorists in Libya was charged, and they also claimed to have been working for the US government. Given Wilson's access to Gadaffi, the CIA certainly would have benefited from having an agent so closely involved in the training and supply of international terrorists. For this reason, there may be some logic – if not proof – in Wilson's defence.

Terpil remains free although a number of outstanding warrants for his arrest still exist. The last confirmed sighting of him occurred in August 1982 when he and an associate, Jim Boyd, were staying as guests of the PLO in the Hotel Tahiti in Beirut. The CIA requested that Israeli intelligence try and capture Terpil and Boyd, but when the special commando team detailed for the job broke down the door of Room 302, the two men had fled, and neither has been seen since.

As the mood of the 1970s, when terrorism was seen as the precursor of worldwide revolution, appears to have gone for ever, Gadaffi has adapted his role to changing circumstances. He still regularly dispatches assassination squads to liquidate his enemies, and he still contributes to his pet Palestinian organisations. But now, instead of just dealing in donations to small terrorist groups, Gadaffi attempts to change governments.

For example, in 1973, Gadaffi occupied the Aozou Strip in the north of Chad, the only part of the country that is rich in manganese and uranium, and for ten years he financed various factions in the country in an attempt to establish a pro-Libyan government. However, the intervention of French troops in 1983 brought some stability back to the country and has temporarily frustrated Gadaffi's expansionist aims.

Gadaffi has also talked of establishing a Saharan Republic, led by Libya, which would include Niger, Chad, Algeria, Tunisia, Mauritania and Western Sahara (a country which would be formed by Polisario guerrillas fighting in Morocco). Although he has not achieved his goal, Gadaffi either finances dissidents or organises attacks on all of the countries that might come under the Republic's umbrella.

In the name of pan-Islamic unity, Gadaffi, who sees himself as the 'Guardian of the Faithful' and 'Keeper of Muhammad's Word', has supported other Islamic countries such as Pakistan and Turkey in confrontations with Western nations, as well as providing guns and money to the Moro insurgents fighting in the Philippines. Libya also has been supplying arms and training to the Sandinistas in Nicaragua and the guerrillas in Colombia. Both groups have paid for this aid, but it follows Gadaffi's philosophy of supporting anti-imperialist movements wherever they may be.

However, the fall in oil prices since 1980 has radically altered Libya's position in the world. This reduction in income – from $22 billion in 1980 to $8.5 billion in 1985 (the anticipated income for 1986 is $5.5 billion) – and the results of the People's Revolution (Gadaffi's version of a totalitarian state) have created such chaos in the country that many staple goods are no longer available. For the supply of arms, Gadaffi owes the Soviet Union approximately $5 billion which he appears to be unable to pay, and this has not pleased his friends in the Politburo. He is having to turn his attention inward as the pressures of a failing revolution and a declining economy give added currency to those who wish to overthrow the Colonel. Despite support for acts of terrorism against opponents of this regime abroad and for isolated groups, such as Abu Nidal's, Gadaffi's role as the terrorists' main godfather is over, perhaps for ever.

In the cycle of international terrorism, as one prime supporter falls away, another always rises to take its place. As Libya moves off centre stage, Iran's Ayatollah Ruhollah Khomeini has emerged as the world's leading patron of terrorism, and his brand of terror is more extreme and potentially far more damaging than anything the world has yet seen.

The Iranian revolution in 1979, which overthrew the Shah, brought to power the fundamentalist style of Ayatollah Khomeini. Where Gadaffi helped spread the terrorist word with liberal donations of cash, Khomeini relies on religious fervour to ensure the loyalty of the terrorists he recruits to the flag of Islam. To the Westerner, the idea that, in the twentieth century, Khomeini can command followers who are prepared to commit suicidal acts of terrorism in his name is extraordinary, even beyond the comprehension of modern thinking. However, for the Iranians such religious devotion is part of a long heritage that reaches back over 900 years to the time when Al-Hasan ibn-al-Sabbah was a power in the country.

Sabbah, a leader of the dissident Muslim Ismaili group (which in turn is one of the two divisions of the Shi'ite sect) was born in Iran in the eleventh century. For his time, he was exceptionally well travelled and educated, moving around the Middle East spreading the word and his particular interpretation of Islam. At the age of forty, Sabbah stumbled across a hidden valley at Alamut in northern Iran and, in about 1090, decided to make it his base, giving rise to the legend of the 'Old Man of the Mountains'.

Finding that peaceful persuasion had failed to bring people in line with his personal philosophy, Sabbah decided on a campaign of terror.

He began recruiting a number of followers who believed absolutely in his creed and were prepared to die for their beliefs. To ensure the loyalty of his followers, Sabbah constructed a beautiful garden complete with streams, waterfalls and delicately scented flowers. Sabbah would bring his potential killers, who had been smoking hashish, to the garden where they would be plied with food and women in an attempt to bring to life the Koranic descriptions of Paradise. Two days later, the followers, having again smoked hashish, would be taken back to their hovels. The next day, Sabbah would summon them and explain that Allah had given them a vision of Paradise and that they had been specially chosen for a dangerous mission from which they might not return. But Allah had shown them that, if they were killed, they would go straight to Paradise.

Sabbah's methods of political indoctrination were so effective that, by the time of his death in 1124, his empire extended from the Persian Gulf to the Mediterranean. The devotees' alleged use of hashish to increase their courage to extraordinary levels led to the name that struck terror into the hearts of those who came into contact with them – *Assassins*. No medieval dignitary travelling in the region would move without a coat of chain-mail and a troop of guards to protect himself from the Assassin's knife. Sabbah himself called his followers *fedai*, or *fedayeen* – 'adventurers' or, according to the PLO, 'men of sacrifice' – another name that has passed down into terrorist folklore and has been adopted by PLO soldiers as their *nom de guerre*.

The legacy of Al-Hasan ibn-al-Sabbah has fallen on the shoulders of the Ayatollah Khomeini who, like Sabbah, believes that his mission is to spread the pure word of Allah through his particular interpretation of Islam. And, like Sabbah, Khomeini, who also spent most of his years as a wandering prophet trying to change people's religious perceptions through sermonising, has achieved influence only through the violent acts of his followers.

Iran is the home of the Shi'ite branch of Islam that has opposed the majority Sunni branch for centuries. The Shi'ites believe that Muhammad's son-in-law, Ali, was the first true Caliph and they firmly reject the three Caliphs recognised by the orthodox Sunni Muslims as Muhammad's heirs. To Christians in the West, this difference appears to be a peripheral footnote to religious history, just as the importance of the difference between Protestant and Catholics is difficult for Arabs to understand. However, in the same way as Europe has had its religious wars, the distinction between the Shi'ites and the Sunnis has been at the heart of many Middle East conflicts. This is evident in the current Iran/Iraq war, where Khomeini, a Shi'ite, views President Saddam Hussein of Iraq, a Sunni, as a heretic.

The Shi'ites believe that they have been unjustly treated for a millennium by other countries in the Middle East. With a religious leader such as Khomeini, who has come to power through armed revolution and who has combined religious fervour with nationalism, the Shi'ites now feel they have a prospect of redressing what they see as centuries of persecution. Khomeini appears convinced that his duty is to combat the Sunni or any other heretic branch of Islam and to undermine the seductive and unhealthy influences from the West and East.

Immediately after Khomeini came to power in Iran in February 1979, the first rumblings of discontent were heard among the Shi'ites living elsewhere in the Middle East. The first country to suffer was Bahrain, an island state lying just off the east coast of Saudi Arabia, which is the centre for communications and foreign investment in the Middle East. Unlike many other countries in the Gulf, Bahrain has become almost entirely Westernised, with alcohol readily available and a nightlife comparable with that of many European capitals – a contradiction of Khomeini's interpretation of a true Islamic way of life. The native population, estimated at 280,000, is generally agreed to comprise seventy-five per cent Shi'ites, but in government, Sunnis hold twelve out of seventeen cabinet posts as well as most of the top jobs in industry and commerce.

The first signs of trouble came in the middle of June 1979, when the Shi'ite community presented a petition to the Emir of Bahrain demanding an Islamic government, alteration of the liquor laws, more conservative clothing for women, separate facilities for men and women in hospitals and a curtailing of nightclubs. Although these demands were largely ignored, during Ramadan (the month when the Koran calls on all good Muslims to fast during the hours of daylight) the liquor stores were shut down for the first time and hotel bars opened only after sundown.

When a series of speeches by a local Shi'ite leader resulted in his imprisonment for preaching treason, the Iranian Ayatollah Rouhani accused the Emir of 'chaining religious leaders who had called for the implementation of the principles of Islam' and warned the Emir that his would be the same fate as the Shah's unless he released all imprisoned Shi'ite religious leaders. This incident was followed by a series of violent demonstrations.

The oil incendiary

The Saudis' turn came next: on 20 November 1979, 200 armed men attacked and took over a part of the Great Mosque at Mecca, the object of pilgrimage for Muslims all over the world. In the furious gun battle that followed, dozens of Saudi soldiers and seventy-five of the rebels were killed, and two weeks later, 170 rebels surrendered after the Saudi government called in French counter-terrorist experts to advise the Saudi security forces who had been unable to clear the Mosque. Of those arrested, sixty-three were executed in January the following year: forty-one Saudis, ten Egyptians, six South Yemenis, three Kuwaitis, and one each from North Yemen, the Sudan and Iraq.

What was subsequently described as 'intensive interrogation' failed to reveal who was behind the well-armed and well-trained attackers. In their proclamations, made through loud hailers from the Mosque before their capture, they had called for a return to Islamic fundamentalism and criticised the growing Western influence in the country. There were allegations by senior Saudi officials and Western intelligence that the rebels had been backed by Khomeini, who claimed that the modern ways of Saudi Arabia had disqualified its government from being the guardians of Islam's most holy place, Mecca.

Some doubt remains about Iran's involvement in the Mecca attack, but the origins of a series of demonstrations in Saudi's eastern province of Hasa, which includes the vital oil-producing region of Dhahran, are more certain. Shi'ites, who form a substantial minority numbering approximately 275,000 people in Saudi Arabia as a whole, make up the majority around Dhahran, an area that faces Iran across the waters of the Gulf. Since the Iranian revolution, a series of violent demonstrations and sabotage attacks have caused considerable alarm among the Sunni rulers of Saudi Arabia. A number of attacks have also occurred against oil installations and government buildings in Kuwait and the United Arab Emirates.

In March 1982, 380 clergy and leaders of Shi'ite revolutionary movements arrived in Tehran from all over the Arab and Western world. At this meeting, they agreed that the Iranian government would have to do more to spread the true word of Islam to the unfaithful and the unbelievers around the world, and, to that end, a number of terrorist training camps would be set up in Iran. In addition, $100 million was immediately allocated as a fighting fund to support worldwide terrorism, and a further $50 million was to be spent each year for an unspecified period to fund specific acts of terrorism.

This cash allocation has been used effectively. It has paid for the

73

formation of powerful terrorist groups in the Lebanon, a series of extremely damaging bomb attacks in Kuwait, a rapid rise in Islamic fundamentalism in southern Asia, the dispatching of hit squads to Europe and the setting up of a global network of clergy-dominated religious groups designed to mastermind further terrorism and recruit twentieth-century versions of Al-Hasan ibn-al-Sabbah's assassins.

Since November 1981, Shi'ites have performed thirty-two terrorist attacks, six of them perpetrated by assassins who committed suicide during the execution of their tasks. Recently, Iran has increased its recruitment of assassins by spreading out from the Middle East into Europe. These moves are being organised by the Iranian Foreign Ministry's Department for Liberation Movements (informally known as the Department for the Export of the Revolution).

According to documents supplied by the Iranian opposition in London, Khomeini gave permission on 14 May 1984 for a recruitment drive to find more Iranians willing to commit acts of terrorism. According to the minutes of a meeting held twelve days later, chaired by Ayatollah Muhammed Khatami, the Minister of Islamic Guidance, Khomeini gave his permission for the setting up of new suicide squads by saying: 'Whatever is necessary to destroy them [the unbelievers] must be done.' The meeting agreed that the armed forces would be asked to supply instructors to train between 1500 and 2000 men under the age of thirty, preferably bachelors. 'They must be completely committed to martyrdom,' Khatami told the meeting. It was expected that the men would be fully trained by the summer of 1985 and they would then be sent abroad, often in the guise of military attachés, to attack targets in Saudi Arabia, Kuwait, the United Arab Emirates, Jordan and France, the latter being singled out because the French government currently plays host to many Iranians who oppose Khomeini's government.

The basic training for today's Assassins takes place in three centres scattered around Iran and lasts three months. Under the guidance of revolutionary guards helped by Palestinians, Libyans, North Koreans, Pakistanis and South Yemenis, the recruits are taken to either Tehran, a base in Ahwaz Shiraz or a camp near the Busheir naval base. The recruits – who are distinguished from other trainees by the Iranian emblems embroidered on the left breast of their sweatshirts and the red bandanas tied around their foreheads – learn not only basic rifle training but also the use of explosives and grenade launchers.

The single most devastating example of Iranian fanaticism came on 23 October 1983 when a truck loaded with explosives drove past the US

Marine guards at the American camp in Beirut. By the time the Marines on duty were able to fire shots at the driver of the truck, the vehicle had exploded. In the devastation that followed, 241 Marines were killed and many more were injured. The driver of the truck (described by witnesses as smiling happily as he drove to his target) was blown to pieces by the explosion.

The man thought to have been behind all the attacks on US personnel in Beirut is Husain Mussawi, a Shi'ite of Lebanese–Iranian extraction, based in the Beka'a valley in the Lebanon, who is head of Islamic Jihad, a terrorist group based in the Lebanon and supported by the Iranian government. After the attack on the US Marines, Mussawi, though denying any direct involvement, said: 'I salute this good act and I consider it a good deed and a legitimate right, and I bow to the spirits of the martyrs who carried out this operation.' As a reward for his successes in the Lebanon, Mussawi has been placed in charge of the training of the new suicide squads being established in Iran.

His cousin, Mohsen Mussawi, is the first secretary at the Iranian embassy in Beirut, and another cousin, Abu Haydar Mussawi, organised the truck used in the bombing of the Marines' camp. In Tehran, distant relatives include Mir Hossein Mussawi, the Prime Minister, and even Khomeini himself. However, most of Husain Mussawi's business is conducted with Seyyed Mehdi Hashemi, a cleric who is in charge of the Department for the Export of the Revolution. Hashemi supervises the ideological and military training of foreign Muslim militants, and has established secret fundamentalist organisations in many countries, including the Liberation Organisation of Islamic Tunisia and the Unity and Holy Struggle Organisation in Egypt.

A close friend of Husain Mussawi, Hassan Hamiz, handled a $50,000 cheque that could be cashed only at the Iranian embassies in Beirut or Damascus, to buy both the explosives and the trucks used in the American attack and the subsequent assault on the French contingent in the Lebanon. In addition to Hamiz, a wide range of people of various Middle East nationalities and groups have been united behind Iranian money and political inspiration. For instance, intelligence sources have identified a Syrian intelligence colonel, a former PLO security officer, Syrian members of Saiqa and various veterans of other terrorist acts in the Middle East.

As Iran has achieved notable terrorist coups, so it has come to dominate the fanatical end of the terrorist scene in the Middle East. In April 1985, Khomeini sent a special emissary to the Lebanon with

$7 million in cash to be spent on uniting the militant Islamic terrorist groups under one banner. On 14 July, at a secret meeting in Tripoli in the Lebanon, seven leading fundamentalists, both Sunni and Shi'ite, agreed to the formation of the Islamic Liberation Organisation. The ILO now acts as a controlling force for a number of different Lebanese terrorist groups in exactly the same way as the PLO is an umbrella organisation for Palestinian groups.

Since the capture of the United States embassy in Tehran in 1979, the Khomeini government seems to have made a particular target of American nationals. Not only have a number of them been kidnapped in the Lebanon where Iranian-sponsored terrorists are most prominent, but the Khomeini government's hand has also stretched out into Europe. In April 1985, a bomb exploded in the El Descanso Rib House, a restaurant popular with American servicemen stationed at nearby Torrejon air base in Spain. Eighteen people were killed in the blast – fourteen of them women – and eighty-two more were injured.

Initially, police believed the bomb had been planted by European terrorists who had launched a co-ordinated campaign against NATO targets earlier that year. However, an analysis of samples of the bomb and other intelligence suggests that it was actually planted by Islamic Jihad. This bombing marked a disturbing escalation of Iranian-supported terrorist violence that had previously been confined to the Middle East.

Further evidence of Iran's antagonism towards the US came with the hijacking of TWA Flight 847 in June 1985. The aircraft, with 145 passengers and eight crew, was on its way to Rome on 14 June when it made a scheduled stopover at Athens airport. Two Arabs, carrying Moroccan passports in the names of Ahmed Karbia and Ali Yunes, boarded the aircraft there. A third Arab, Atoua Ali Tourenda, was not allowed to board the flight as it was full. In the men's hand luggage were a 9 mm machine pistol and at least two hand grenades, wrapped in glass fibre which successfully concealed them from the airport's security system.

Shortly after take-off, the two twenty-one-year-old Arabs took control of the aircraft, forcing it to fly to Beirut where it was allowed to land. There, nineteen of the hostages were freed before the aircraft took off again, this time heading for Algiers. The aircraft stayed a day and a night in the Algerian capital before heading back once again to Beirut. At the beginning of the negotiations at Beirut, the terrorists executed a twenty-four-year-old US Navy diver, Robert Stethem, whose body was unceremoniously dumped on the airport tarmac. Obviously fearing an assault by US commandos (who were, in fact, poised to attack), the aircraft flew once again to Algiers and then back to Beirut in the course of a weekend.

Although the hostages were eventually released, after the intervention of President Assad of Syria and after a secret deal was struck between the US and Israeli governments for the release of several hundred Shi'ite prisoners held in Israeli jails, the hijacking was a chilling demonstration of American impotence to respond with force in such a crisis.

Within hours of the hijack, members of America's élite counter-terrorist unit, Delta Force, had left their headquarters in Fort Bragg, North Carolina, for Europe. Delta is trained to deal with terrorists holding hostages on aircraft, but, from the outset, the terrorists appeared to be one jump ahead of any action planned against them. Until the hijacking of TWA Flight 847, it had been generally accepted that terrorists, once they have begun negotiations, tend to remain in one place and eventually surrender – in other words, once dialogue has begun, a peaceful end to the hijack is in sight. It was also accepted that once the killings begin, it is time to launch an assault to release the hostages as the terrorists no longer have anything to lose and will continue to kill until their demands are met. In fact, the terrorists on board the TWA flight conformed to none of the usual patterns.

In both Beirut and Algiers, negotiations were well under way; hostages were released and food taken on board. However, just as the negotiators were beginning to feel confident that a solution was near, or when Delta Force was in a position to storm the aircraft, the terrorists would move on to another airfield. At every stage in the hijack, the terrorists held the initiative, and what is perhaps most disturbing about that hijack is the sophisticated understanding of counter-terrorist methods demonstrated by the hijackers.

It is now acknowledged that they were Shi'ite Muslims, followers of Khomeini and from the same stable as planted the bomb in the restaurant in Spain and killed the US Marines in Beirut. The final plans for the hijacking had been agreed at a meeting in Baalbeck in the Lebanon on 8 June between the chief of staff of the Iranian Revolutionary Guards, Muhammad Awai, and Islamic Jihad. Given the success rate of Iranian-sponsored terrorists so far, there is every reason to suppose that, in the future, there will be many more such attacks, with the United States as the prime target.

For the US, too, the TWA hijack was a salutary experience. Much to the chagrin of the American administration, it was discovered that a major superpower such as the United States is largely impotent at the hands of a few, very highly motivated terrorists. Not only was President Reagan forced to negotiate – while denying that he was doing so – but the administration also appeared, after the event, incapable of exacting any punishment on those involved. The attempt to introduce some form of sanctions against Athens airport for their poor security failed, airlines refused to boycott Beirut airport as demanded by the US, and the Pentagon and US State Department combined could find no credible way of using force to attack the terrorists in the Lebanese camps. The hijacking of the Italian cruise liner, *Achille Lauro*, and the subsequent hijacking by US fighters of the aircraft taking the terrorists concerned to freedom, did do much to restore American pride. However, it remains to be seen what price Italy and the United States will be forced to pay in bombings and killings if the terrorists are successfully tried and jailed.

The Iranian government is now trying to expand its sphere of influence beyond simple terrorist training and support. For example, it is estimated it gives more financial aid, primarily through the supply of oil, to the Syrian government than does Saudi Arabia, the Assad government's traditional backer. Iran provides Syria daily with 150,000 to 160,000 barrels of light crude at $3 below the official price. In addition, one million of the annual total of 7.6 million tons of crude is provided free.

The *quid pro quo* in the arrangement is Syrian support in Iran's war with Iraq, through regular shipments of arms from Syria to help the ailing Iranian war effort, and evidently some shared sponsorship of international terrorism. In many respects, this is an unnatural alliance between two countries which are opposed on political and religious grounds. Syria follows a largely socialist Ba'ath line that includes a distinct separation between church and state, while Khomeini believes in unity of the two.

The growth of Iranian militancy is particularly alarming because it is broad in its complexion and carried out by fanatics for whom the Western notion of the sanctity of human life carries little weight. Previously, all terrorists (with the possible exception of the Japanese Red Army, now defunct) had a healthy regard for their own lives, and this naturally placed some limitation on the terrorists' *modus operandi* since they also planned to survive each attack. With Iran, such logical rules do not apply. In fact, the reverse is the case in that some Shi'ite revolutionaries embrace death and welcome entry into· Paradise in exchange for an early existence marred by contact with Muslim heretics and dissolute Western unbelievers.

Also, unlike most terrorist groups who have a narrow focus – the overthrow or changing of their particular society – the Iranians sweep most of humanity into two categories: enemies of Islam or enemies of Iran, which, in Khomeini's eyes, amount to the same thing.

The result of this broad-brush approach has been an attack on French troops because the French had been shipping arms to Iraq; attacks on US troops because the US had not opposed that French action; a series of attacks in Kuwait to demonstrate Iran's disapproval of that country's support of Iraq; demonstrations in Saudi Arabia and other Gulf countries against Western influence in the region; support for Moroccan revolutionaries; and the recruitment of terrorists in Italy, France, Britain and the United States both to keep Iranian exiles in line and to act against foreign governments who are seen as enemies of the Iranian revolution.

Western society is ill-equipped to deal with the twentieth-century brand of Iranian terrorism which draws heavily on its eleventh-century heritage. Suicidal fanatics and religious fundamentalism are alien to our way of life, and yet Khomeini's brand of revolution offers real hope to Shi'ites around the world who feel at last that they have a chance to influence their own lives.

Iran has placed such a rigid interpretation on what constitutes an enemy of the state that it is difficult to see the steps that can be taken to counter the threat that Khomeini poses. The Gulf countries have reacted by introducing some curbs on Western dress and behaviour as a gesture of appeasement which is unlikely to have any effect. For the West, the solution is not so readily to hand.

In the past, counter-terrorism has relied on good intelligence and the ability to predict, with some degree of accuracy, likely targets of terrorist action. However, little is predictable about Iran, and the motives for some attacks have been so labyrinthine as almost to defy logical analysis. In addition, Iran's leaders are prepared to allow the more militant revolutionaries great freedom of action while at the same time generously funding terrorist training and attacks.

The Speaker of the Iranian Parliament, Hashemi Rafsanjani, has warned the United States that if it attempted 'any adventurism in Lebanon, Syria, the Gulf or other places, then its interests would be threatened everywhere.' The United States would be engulfed, not just in another Vietnam, but in 'a sea of fire'. This could be dismissed as simple blood-thirsty rhetoric were it not for the fact that nearly 300 Americans have already been killed and a large number of terrorist acts have already been committed in the Middle East and Europe.

In recent years, other Middle East countries have used terrorism as a foreign policy tool to ensure for themselves a place in the intricate political game constantly played in the region, but Iran's ambitions have been even larger. The current Iranian government came to power through a violent revolution. In the first flush of post-revolutionary fervour, they believe, like Gadaffi, that their example will incite terrorist groups all over the world. Therefore, the Khomeini regime thinks that Shi'ite revolution will help bring revisionist Arab leaders back to the path of pure Islam. Realising the threat that Khomeini poses, all the Arab countries, with the exception of Syria, have been supporting Iraq in its war with Iran. This particular form of opposition has not proved successful so far, and Iran seems able both to fight a costly war and devote considerable energy fomenting revolution abroad.

The revolution may run out of energy and Khomeini's ambitions for a world Islamic revival may fade, but there has been no sign of that happening. To thousands of Islamic fundamentalists around the world, Iran remains a symbol of hope, and Khomeini's brand of revolution will undoubtedly provide the focus for international terrorism for some years to come.

While the fanaticism of Khomeini's followers will continue to grab the headlines, the significance of Iran's contribution, or indeed of any other Middle East country, to the sum total of international terrorism, is diminishing. The state sponsor plays an important role in the establishment of a terrorist group, but once the foundation has been laid, the successful terrorist is increasingly able to go his or her own independent way.

To understand the modern terrorist, it is necessary to look behind the headlines and beyond the simple solution which suggests that terrorism would wither and die without the support of countries such as the Soviet Union, Libya and Iran. Ten years ago, that might have been true, but today's terrorists are hybrids. They have learned that state support is unreliable, and if they and their groups are to survive, they have to look to their own resources. Because terrorism operates outside society's normal constraints of laws and taxes, it is uniquely well-placed to use the established order to its own advantage. The terrorists have been quick to realise this and have skilfully turned the capitalist system – which they nearly all despise – to their own advantage. Once again, the PLO has led the way.

Part Two

THE PLO

4

Criminal capital

THE FOUNDING of the State of Israel in 1948 propelled more than 200,000 Palestinians north into the Lebanon. Huddled in refugee camps, they were to become pawns in a political game that today shows no sign of ending. Although the PLO and their Arab supporters have more than enough capital to provide decent housing and a living wage for every single Palestinian in the Lebanon, the refugee camps remain – as a symbol of what the PLO claim the Israelis have done to their nation.

The Lebanese did not welcome the arrival of the Palestinians, whom they viewed as foreigners with little or no understanding of local customs or traditions. Lebanese laws actually discriminated against Palestinians, who were seen in much the same way as many Jews had been in Europe earlier in the century. Palestinians were not allowed to own banks or shops or even to drive taxis. They were restricted to the role of employee, in positions where their skills and business expertise could be used, but where they posed no real threat to the established order.

The Palestinians, who regarded the Lebanese as unsophisticated and poorly educated, reciprocated this distrust and, consequently, the tension between the two sides resulted in large sections of the country being partitioned, with the Palestinians banding together in sprawling refugee camps and making no effort to integrate into the local society.

This division could have led to the total suppression of the refugees by the already established Lebanese. In fact, the reverse happened: the Palestinians used their business skills, their intense sense of family and their racial ambitions, as a ladder to a dominant position in the local society. This left the elected government in Beirut powerless and gave the PLO control over much of the country's industrial base.

The camps were crucial to the growth in influence of the Palestinians in Lebanon. They provided a pool of motivated young people who could be trained in business skills, and they acted as a focus for aid and assistance from Arab countries sympathetic to their plight.

Education has always played a prominent role in the life of a Palestinian family, and living in the camps did nothing to alter its importance. Each family did everything possible to provide a broad education for their children, which in many cases included higher education. In the 1950s, a large number of Palestinians went to university on the West Bank and in Cairo, and as money became more readily available, increasing numbers travelled to Europe and the United States. Because formal work was difficult to find in the camps, many of those who returned became teachers, which led to the emergence of a new, well-educated generation of Palestinians with a sophistication that had little to do with their background or apparent poverty. These highly educated Palestinians were able to use their knowledge to compete with the comparatively poorly educated local business community that relied more on tradition than professional expertise in business affairs.

At the same time as young Palestinians were being sent to universities and business schools in Cairo, London and New York, the Arab world was going through a period of instability brought on by the heavy influx of oil money. Revolution was in the air and many of the traditional leaders in the Middle East were overthrown: Libya, Iraq, Iran, South Yemen, Syria and others all suffered changes of leadership. This instability created a certain amount of nervousness among all Middle East leaders and the leading merchant families. All began to hide a little money abroad, and most chose what was then the most stable business centre in the region: the Lebanon. The country's capital was aptly called the 'Paris of the Middle East', with its casinos and *laissez-faire* attitude to banking and business.

This influx of cash created boom conditions in the Lebanese economy as a whole, and the Palestinians benefited. But the Palestinians in the camps received an additional bonus from the creation of the PLO. The organisation and its various offshoots became a focus for Arab aid and that aid was channelled either into their bases, then in Jordan, or directly into the businesses run from the camps in southern Lebanon. When the PLO were expelled from Jordan by King Hussein in 'Black September' 1970, an additional 150,000 Palestinians fled to the camps in the Lebanon. In future, all PLO aid came direct to the Lebanon, and the organisation concentrated on developing a strong financial base there.

The consolidation of the PLO in the Lebanon coincided with the boom in the country's economy and the return of ever larger numbers of Palestinian students from abroad. These students had been taught many Western values and had been a part of the anti-Vietnam era that had radicalised a whole generation. They were natural and willing recruits to the PLO.

With all the various PLO groups operating in the Lebanon, each commander inevitably attempted to carve out his own turf in order to provide income from the territory under his control and credibility for his group. These conditions left the Lebanese as mere incidentals to the power plays going on around them. While the Palestinians' expertise in business would eventually have led to a high degree of self-sufficiency, the PLO changed all that. The terrorist achieves results through the regular use of force, whereas the businessman must conform to certain social standards, one of which is not to use a Kalashnikov machine-gun to eliminate the competition. Unfortunately, the various terrorist offshoots that make up the PLO signally failed to make the distinction between legitimacy, which they constantly proclaimed, and terrorism, which they disavowed.

As first set up, the camps were controlled by the Lebanese police force, but as their power waned, the terrorists took charge. In the early days, their leaders lived in luxury apartment blocks outside the camps, but later set up headquarters in the camps themselves so that different parts – often only a street or a small section – were controlled by particular groups.

For the terrorist leaders, the members in their groups were crucial because Arafat based the allocation of funds on the number of members a group could claim. Recruiting was therefore fierce and only a membership card from another organisation prevented recruitment at the point of a gun.

Any Palestinian man who joined a PLO group received an income of between 700 and 1000 Lebanese pounds a month – the equivalent of the average monthly wage of a local agricultural worker. In addition, his wife received 650 pounds a month for herself and twenty-five pounds for each child under the age of sixteen. At that age, a child joined the PLO Ashbal youth movement, when he or she would receive 650 pounds a month.

The loyalty of the fedayeen was always uncertain. There was a great deal of poaching by one organisation from another, and loyalty had its price: those groups that refused to tolerate any resignations or punished disloyalty had to pay the highest wages. Numerous incidents have been reported of fighters being advanced as much as three months' salary to prevent their defection to another group. Such straight cash bribery to ensure the continued loyalty of recruits established a disciplinary standard that has had a debilitating effect throughout the PLO and shaped the attitudes of even the lowliest recruit towards the way day-to-day life should be conducted. Bribery and corruption became the normal way of doing business.

To join an organisation, the recruit merely had to sign the membership form, go through an elementary training course and fight with the group when the Israelis invaded. They were left with ample time to pursue their own individual businesses, which many did.

At its most basic level, the PLO were able to force local landowners to pay above the market price for Palestinian labourers to work in their fields, which resulted in the landowners complaining of having to pay high wages for little work. However, once the PLO became truly established in the country, the business projects became far more ambitious.

Building on the Palestinians' natural entrepreneurial skills, Yasser Arafat was the first to recognise that a strong financial base was essential if his organisation were to flourish. Arafat's concern was twofold: he needed the Palestinians to see the PLO as a humanitarian organisation while, at the same time, maintaining his personal control over the PLO's military muscle. This would enable the increasingly fragmented PLO to continue to be viewed seriously in Israel and elsewhere.

To give the PLO some direction in its business development, in 1970 the organisation established Samed – the Palestine Martyrs Work Society – under the direct control of Arafat's Al-Fatah. Samed was designed to take advantage of the large workforce in the refugee camps and to build a social and industrial infrastructure. It was originally based in Beirut but quickly mushroomed to embrace all the refugee camps.

Arafat's control of Samed gave him enormous power within the PLO and, in some measure, accounts for his survival over such a long period. Since Samed is responsible for the employment, education and welfare of large numbers of Palestinians, Arafat has been able to ensure the loyalty of successive generations of Palestinians.

According to its own literature, Samed has seven main objectives:

1. To provide skills and the possibility of work for the children of martyrs of the Palestinian revolution.

2. To offer the possibility of work to all Palestinians wherever they live and to develop their technical and scientific competency.
3. To create the material basis for the survival of the Palestinian people to enable them to continue the resistance struggle both inside and outside occupied Palestine.
4. To provide Palestinian communities with basic necessities at prices corresponding to their material means.
5. To preserve and advance Palestinian cultural traditions.
6. To create the nucleus for a Palestinian revolutionary economy; to develop economic self-sufficiency for the Revolution and the masses; and to lay the foundation for the economic structure of the future Palestinian society in the land of Palestine.
7. To develop economic, commercial and industrial relations with fraternal parties, democratic forces and friendly countries.

Samed acts as the economic arm of the military forces. Its ultimate goal is to make the PLO independent of the donations from Arab countries that, in the 1960s and early 1970s, formed the staple source of its income. In this, Arafat has been so successful that today the PLO is self-funding and no longer dependent on outside donations for its survival.

Samed's operating principles were aimed at extensive worker participation in what was originally designed as a welfare operation. Among them were:

1. Samed adopts modern scientific methods in management and production aimed at organising production for the benefit of the workers and in the service of the revolution.
2. Samed follows democratic procedures to ensure the right of worker participation in the responsibilities of organising production.
3. Samed assists its employees in developing their skills and administrative capabilities and in defending their cultural and union rights.
4. Samed follows revolutionary principles with regard to bonuses and workers' discipline with a view to developing a militant, revolutionary and productive workforce.

Ahmed Abu Ala, the general manager and chairman of Samed has pointed out: 'We started with ready-made clothes; our revolution needs uniforms for the fighters, our camps need clothes for the children, women and men. We find that blankets are necessary, for fighters and the masses in the camps. We produced them. We started in a small way in textiles, and then we found that shoes are necessary for both civilians and the military so we produced them too.' (Abu Ala, now based in Amman, is often criticised by PLO purists, who claim he is 'one of the fat cats of Fatah', having made a fortune from Samed, and that he 'lives like a Pasha'. His children have been sent to both American and Soviet universities, a sign of some status within the movement.)

In the early days, Samed received donations from various sympathetic governments: knitting machines from East Germany; cotton for clothes from the Soviet Union; and timber from Romania for a furniture workshop. With a willing workforce and almost unlimited funds, Samed quickly expanded to cover a wide area of industrial production. According to a senior official in Samed, by 1982 the organisation had a turnover of $45 million with thirty-five factories operating in the Lebanon, a number of businesses located abroad and a regular flow of exports to Eastern Bloc and Arab countries.

'I can't tell you which was profitable,' says the Samed official. 'Profit is not one of its aims as it is a non-profit institution. But our profit is calculated at the end of each year by how many workers we were able to add to the number we already have. Therefore, any profit is reinvested to extend the workshops or to send some of the workers abroad for training and education.'

Samed is divided into four main sections: industrial, cinematography and information, agricultural, and general commercial. The industrial section includes: the manufacture of clothing for men, women and children; textile production, fabrics and blankets; the plastics industry, mainly kitchen ware; production of leather shoes, military boots, bags and suitcases; woodwork, production of office furniture and items for the home; food processing, halawa and halkum (sweets); handicraft manufacture; a folklore and embroidery branch manufacturing Palestinian national costumes; the knitting of summer and winter sweaters. This produced a turnover of around $18 million per annum before the 1982 Israeli invasion of the Lebanon.

The cinematography and information section is responsible for the production of documentary and other films, and has a modern studio for film developing and printing and one for colour film developing, as well as a technical section for the production and printing of propaganda. This area produced around $5 million a year.

The agricultural section is responsible for producing food of all types, with the aim of making the camps self-sufficient with some products remaining for export. For instance, in Africa, Samed ran six huge farms, one each in Uganda, Congo-Brazzaville, Guinea-Bissau, Somalia, the

Sudan and Guinea-Conakry. But the Ugandan farm has now been abandoned because instability in that country made it impossible to run the business with any guarantee of success. In addition, two farms outside Damascus in Syria produce enough milk, butter and eggs to satisfy most of the needs of the Lebanese camps. The agricultural section produces an income of $16 million per annum, and will most likely prove to be the most enduring and the most profitable in the long term.

The general commercial section is responsible for: importing raw materials for the Samed factories; all exports; organising and mounting thirty-six travelling exhibitions of Palestinian art, pottery and propaganda as well as staffing the permanent exhibitions in South Yemen, North Yemen, the United Arab Emirates, Iraq, Libya, Algeria, Uganda, Djibouti and the Congo.

Prior to the 1982 invasion, Samed employed approximately 5000 people in the Lebanon, 200 in Syria and 1800 in Africa. Another 6000 worked part-time in the Lebanon, mostly from home, and 12,000 passed through the Samed workshops and then set up businesses of their own.

Although much of Samed in the Lebanon was destroyed by the Israeli invasion, and the organisation has since relocated to Algeria, Tunisia and Syria, the basic structure has remained the same. The Samed-run farms continue to provide increasing income and new factories have already been built in Tunis and Algiers. PLO leaders are quite confident that Samed will have established itself as a major economic force in the Middle East by the end of this decade. With their access to cheap, highly motivated labour and a market that allows all Samed goods to be imported free of taxes, they may well manage to take advantage of the good will evident in the Gulf and the Eastern Bloc to develop their markets and build a major industrial enterprise.

Aside from the general business operation of Samed, the PLO has also sponsored a vigorous 'hearts-and-minds' campaign in the camps that has ensured that each successive generation born and brought up in the Lebanon has been firmly imbued with a sense of Palestinian solidarity and a strong loyalty to the PLO. The PLO evolved a large and successful social welfare system which not only included free schooling and free medical care but also generous compensation to the families of anyone killed or injured in the fight against Israel. Because the PLO had so much capital at its disposal, it was able to fund the services of local doctors and to construct its own superbly equipped hospitals.

The PLO had developed a perfectly sensible infrastructure which gave the organisation some credibility among the local Lebanese. However, the anarchic nature of the groups operating under the PLO umbrella – though making many terrorists rich – led to widespread abuse of both the Palestinians and the Lebanese.

With the 'hearts-and-minds' campaign well under way with the formation of Samed, in the early 1970s, Arafat secretly formed the Black September Organisation (BSO), one of the most extreme and feared bodies in or outside the Palestinian movement.

The BSO was the result of the bloody battles in September 1970, when King Hussein's Jordanian army moved against the Palestinian forces in his country, killing more than 7000 of them in a few days of exceptionally savage fighting. To commemorate this defeat, Al-Fatah's intelligence organisation, Jihaz ar-Rasd, authorised the formation of Black September, which from 1971 to 1974 was responsible for some of the most brutal attacks on Israeli and Jordanian targets. The organisation's top officers had all been trained in terrorist tactics in Cairo, and as a result, the BSO had an effective cell structure of around sixty highly motivated terrorists.

Abu Iyad, Arafat's right-hand man, was in charge of the BSO, and Abu Yussuf was the strategist. Arafat formed the BSO as part of a deliberate strategy to have a secret terrorist arm operating alongside the more pragmatic image of the PLO he wished to project, and throughout its operations, he undoubtedly remained in close control of the BSO.

The BSO first appeared on the world scene with the assassination of the Prime Minister of Jordan, Wasfi Tell, in Cairo on 28 November 1971. Three gunmen, who waited for Tell to return from a meeting of the Arab Defence Council, shot him in the lobby of the Sheraton Hotel. Israeli reports of the incident describe one of the assassins kneeling over Tell's body and drinking his blood. In fact, the assassin shouted, 'I have drunk his blood,' as a symbolic statement of victory. None the less, the sentence, which was widely misinterpreted, caused great revulsion in the West, and contributed to the terrifying image of the BSO.

The BSO members were arrested by the Egyptian police who, from the start, were ambivalent about the case. The killing of Tell was greeted with enthusiasm in the Arab world, and when the preliminary examination of the terrorists took place in a Cairo court, forensic evidence was produced to show that Tell could not have been killed by bullets fired from the gun found in the terrorists' possession. They were released on bail and, at the expense of Colonel Gadaffi, were given rooms in a luxury Cairo hotel as well as lavish expense accounts. In the end, all of the assassins left the country without being put on trial.

After the assassination in Cairo, a number of other BSO attacks followed, culminating in the assault on the Israeli athletes at the Munich Olympics on 5 September 1972. Abu Hassan Salameh, known as 'The Red Prince' and in charge of BSO operations, was responsible for the planning and logistics of the massacre, although he was safely across the border in East Germany when it actually occurred. Ten Israelis were killed during the episode, which, more than any other single incident, brought the PLO and their cause to the attention of a world audience.

Salameh was the son of a Palestinian militant, Sheikh Hassan Salameh, who had been at the forefront of local resistance against the formation of an Israeli state. During the 1948 Arab–Israeli war, Sheikh Hassan was blown up by an Israeli bomb, a fate which was to be shared by his son nearly thirty years later.

Coming from a rich family, the younger Salameh did not fall into the category of the poor Palestinian refugee. Educated in Cairo, at Bir Zeit University on the West Bank and in West Germany, where he studied engineering, Salameh developed a European style that was criticised by his more moral and principled Muslim colleagues in the PLO. He acquired a taste for fashionable designer clothes, fast cars and attractive women, and took up karate to help his muscle tone. His slim figure, dark good looks and sensuous mouth made him many conquests, and he had a reputation as a womaniser. He also liked to gamble, and the tables in the South of France were an easy drive from his villa in Geneva.

Although Salameh controlled some of the most militant and ruthless terrorists of the PLO, he also had a pragmatic side. This led him regularly to seek diplomatic contacts with the United States and to argue within the organisation for a more moderate policy worldwide.

In 1973, a secret meeting in Rabat, Morocco, between a senior member of the PLO and General Vernon Walters, then a deputy director of the CIA, resulted in an agreement that the PLO would not attack American targets. Salameh was responsible for enforcing the agreement, and at the end of 1973, he warned Henry Kissinger that an attempt would be made to shoot down his plane when it arrived in Beirut. (This was during Kissinger's Middle East tour, when he was trying to arrange an acceptable agreement on territorial boundaries in the wake of Israel's victory in the war earlier that year.) The aircraft was diverted and Salameh provided armed men to look after Kissinger during his trip. He continued this policy with warnings to the US ambassador in Egypt of an assassination plot against him, of a planned attack on the US embassy in Rome, of a proposed plot against President Sadat of Egypt, and he also helped various Western intelligence agencies with details about extremists operating in their own countries.

This policy had obvious advantages for the PLO. While continuing his acts of terrorism on behalf of Black September, Salameh was able to advance the idea of the PLO, maintaining Yasser Arafat as a voice of moderation. The channels of communication between the Western countries and the PLO were thus opened on an unofficial basis. Arafat and his advisers hoped that these informal contacts might blossom into more public discussion, which would give the PLO the legitimacy it desperately wanted.

By the end of 1973, Arafat believed that the BSO had outlived its usefulness, the extreme terrorist acts of his followers no longer suiting the more moderate image he now wished to project. At the same time, the need for a terrorist group committed to such ruthless violence had all but passed. The world, which at the end of the previous decade had never really heard of the Palestinians or their problems, now knew what the PLO was, who it claimed to represent and what they wanted. Arafat had achieved a great deal by the skilful use of the bullet, the bomb and the olive branch. It was a lesson that other terrorist groups were to follow effectively.

Even though Arafat disbanded the BSO, he appointed Salameh (who, PLO insiders say, was like a son to him) head of Force 17. This group had 3700 members, a budget of $1.5 million a month and was responsible for the personal security of Al-Fatah's leaders. Salameh was also responsible for any unorthodox operations that Arafat might want carried out, and the Lebanese civil war, which laid the foundations for the effective partitioning of Lebanon between Christians and Muslims, gave him the perfect cover to pull off the greatest financial coup in the PLO's history.

Beginning in April 1975, the civil war lasted nearly two years and caused the deaths of more than 60,000 people and more than 100,000 casualties. It began when a group of Palestinians attacked some Christians, members of a prominent and powerful local group, the Phalange, who then retaliated by opening fire on a bus, killing all the Palestinian passengers. Intercommunal fighting quickly spread to other religions and political factions until the whole country was consumed by violence. The largely Muslim Palestinians, who had made huge inroads into business and regions previously controlled by Christian Phalangists, some of whom had been virtual warlords for generations, remained at the heart of the fighting.

In eighteen months, more than fifty ceasefires were declared, most of which lasted for no more than a few hours. However, at the height of the fighting, on 20 January 1976, the Palestinians and the Phalange struck an extraordinary deal which resulted in forty-eight hours of peace in the financial district of Beirut. The deal brought together two unlikely allies – Bashir Gemayal, the leader of the Israeli-backed Christian Militia, and Salameh – and was responsible for the biggest robbery of all time.

At the time, Beirut's financial district, which housed the majority of the nation's major banks as well as some diplomatic residences in and around the Place de Martyr, was controlled to the south by the Phalange and to the north by Al-Fatah. This was the centre for business in the Middle East. With extremely relaxed tax and currency laws, as well as an ineffective police force, virtually every bank – legitimate and those that were less so – was represented in Beirut. In many respects, it resembled Zurich as a financial centre, with the major difference being that the Swiss tend to cloak their more fringe business deals behind a veil of legitimacy while the Lebanese have no such qualms.

Therefore, the financial centre was the hub of the Middle East business world and home for much of the hot money that came from drugs, gold smuggling and arms deals, as well as from the substantial 'commissions' regularly paid to the many Middle East entrepreneurs who had sprung up to take advantage of the oil boom.

The Bank of America, the Bank of Beirut and Riyadh, the Commercial Bank of Lebanon, the New Syrian Bank, the Lebanese Investment Bank and the Bank Intra are all located in the financial district, appropriately on the Street of Banks. On the corner of the street was the main Beirut branch of the British Bank of the Middle East, one of the oldest and most reputable in the region. Next to the BBME was a Catholic Capuchin church, which marked the northern and southern border of the district.

That 20 January, armed militia from the PLO and the Phalange advised workers in offices and residences around the district not to show up for work two days later. Those who insisted on coming to work on 22 January found the area cordoned off, with guards turning away both workers and visitors.

Behind the cordon, a team of PLO and Phalange terrorists were trying to break through the wall of the Capuchin church into the BBME. Instead of simply dynamiting a hole in the wall, the terrorists worked all day using pick axes and shovels, trying to keep the damage to the church to a minimum, it being something of a landmark in the city. Once through to the bank, the delicacies of a subtle piece of safe-breaking proved too daunting, and to help them out, they called on the services of a small team sent over from Italy. (The origin of the Italian team is not known but one of the Palestinians who took part in the robbery believes they were from the Mafia.) Even the safe-breakers were eventually forced to use dynamite to open the safe, and so much explosive was used that investigators who appeared on the scene later were astonished that the whole building had not collapsed around the thieves. However, while the explosion brought down ceilings and filled the vault area with rubble and clouds of dust, it also burst open the doors of the safes.

The robbery was a major success. As well as the safes, the robbers rifled safe deposits, and they also reportedly stole the BBME's gold stocks and took away all the financial records stored in the vaults. The haul was loaded into trucks under heavy guard, and the small convoy was allowed through the roadblocks. The most valuable of the loot was taken by ship to Cyprus, where it was divided up into equal shares for the three major participants.

In all, a fortune in cash, gold and jewels was stolen. Former Lebanese finance minister Lucien Dahadah estimated that $50 million was stolen, while others closer to the robbery say that $100 million vanished. If the figure of $100 million is accurate, the PLO, the Phalange and the safe-breakers each received $33 million. The Phalange spent their money on arms, and the PLO invested their proceeds abroad; one PLO member reports that senior members went on a spending spree in Monte Carlo and gambled a large part of the loot on the casino tables of the Riviera. Whatever the truth, the robbery was large enough to earn a place in the *Guinness Book of Records* as the biggest bank robbery of all time.

Even without the cash, the financial records taken from the BBME, which must have detailed the hidden dealings of some of the most prominent men in the Middle East, gave the terrorists a useful source of blackmail for many years.

Taking advantage of the freedom provided by their cordon, the two gangs then moved along the street down from the ABC supermarket (another local landmark) and cleaned out shops and houses as they went, including the Greek and Canadian official residences.

While robberies and looting were commonplace at this time, the BBME attack was unique because it united two groups who were deadly enemies. Although the PLO exercised such control over very large areas of the Lebanon that there was usually no need to co-operate with anybody if they wished to carry out attacks, the exceptional financial rewards from the robbery caused both sides to bury their political differences for forty-eight hours. And after the robbery, Gemayel and Salameh remained, if not friends, certainly well known to each other and were regularly in touch.

Arafat was naturally pleased with the robbery's contribution to the growing wealth and status of his organisation, but the Israelis were less content. And they saw Salameh, whom they had not forgotten for his role in the Munich massacre, as a major factor in the PLO's growth. To many senior Israelis, Salameh had become a symbol of PLO terrorism through his close association with the massacre, as well as a dangerously moderate voice within the PLO who had regular contact with the West. They determined on revenge. Various attempts to assassinate him failed before a hit team, equipped with false Canadian and British passports, arrived in Beirut at the beginning of 1979.

The plot had actually begun the previous November when Erika Mary Chambers, a thirty-year-old British citizen, who was apparently an eccentric cat lover and artist, moved into an apartment with an entrance in the fashionable Rue Verdun in downtown Beirut. Her flat overlooked Rue Madame Curie, which was part of the route Salameh took every day from the house where he lived with his wife – the former Miss Universe, Georgina Rizak – to Al-Fatah headquarters.

Marriage to Rizak appears to have dulled Salameh's highly developed survival instincts, and Chambers was able to report that, instead of varying his route each day, he followed exactly the same routine, making him an easy target. In January 1979, the hit team arrived in Beirut. They rented a Volkswagen from a local agency and parked it on the Rue Madame Curie within sight of Chambers' flat. As Salameh was driven by in his tan Chevrolet estate car, sandwiched between his two bodyguards, Chambers detonated the explosives hidden in the Volkswagen – blowing it, the Chevrolet and Salameh to pieces.

At a single stroke, the Israelis had avenged themselves on a man they considered to be one of the most ruthless terrorists in the PLO as well as the main contact between Western intelligence services and the Palestinians.

*   *   *

At every stage in the history of the Lebanon since the foundation of Israel in 1948, the Palestinians and particularly the PLO have been able to consolidate their political and financial structure.

The key to the Lebanese economy was the control of ports through which the vast majority of their raw materials were imported. Once they arrived in force, after their expulsion from Jordan in 1970, the PLO swiftly took these over and by the time the Israelis invaded in 1982, little could pass through the ports without some form of bribe or tax being paid to the particular PLO faction in charge of the port. This not only helped fill the coffers; the organisation's control of much of the country's economy also brought with it considerable political authority.

For example, Arafat appointed Asmi Zarir, a former Jordanian army officer, as commander of the Tyre area. He joined forces with the head of the Tyre fishermen's association, a known smuggler, and between them, they controlled the import and export of all goods through the port. Zarir's influence gradually spread to the surrounding countryside, which meant that almost all trade that occurred in the area involved some form of tribute paid to Zarir and the PLO.

At the same time as the PLO was receiving these unofficial import –export duties, the organisation was bribing officials at all levels of the Lebanese government. As one senior member of the PLO said: 'Some money has been spent on various people in Lebanon [and Syria]. The PLO couldn't have survived in Lebanon without pay-offs. But as part of the total budget, it is a small sum.'

Indirectly, one of the major people to benefit from PLO largesse was Amin Gemayal, Lebanon's president and the brother of the country's former president-elect, Bashir Gemayal, who was assassinated before he could take office. Between 1969 and 1975, Amin Gemayal was one of the lawyers who regularly interceded on behalf of Palestinians who had been arrested but not yet charged with various offences. Lawyers were also a favourite conduit for pay-offs to local people. Gemayal was a friend of Abu Iyad (Arafat's No. 2), whom he met several times during the civil war and prior to the 1982 evacuation, always in West Beirut and once at the Commodore Hotel.

Some individual PLO groups were effectively able to establish their own fiefdoms and to operate with little central control from PLO headquarters in Beirut. Thus, both the DFLP and the PFLP were the major employers of agricultural workers, and the PFLP became the dominant force in the iron and steel industry.

On the southern outskirts of Sidon, the Modern Mechanical

Establishment, a PFLP front company, established a near monopoly of the supply of iron and steel to the building trades in southern Lebanon. In 1982, the invading Israelis discovered stocks that they valued at between $30 and $40 million. Such a vast inventory gave the PFLP a stranglehold on the local economy. They – along with other PLO groups – imported most of their raw materials from Eastern Bloc countries and, by arguing that the materials were essential to the war effort, were able to get large discounts, thus increasing their profit margins; as they controlled the ports, they were also able to bring in goods duty-free. This substantially undercut their competitors and eventually put the PLO in a pre-eminent position as a supplier of materials to the construction industry.

The PFLP's Modern Mechanical Establishment was equipped with the latest (mostly American) equipment, which had been supplied by supportive Arab countries. Factories, generally run by PLO supporters, and supplied by the PFLP, produced window and door frames as well as gun platforms, all of which were sold on to the highest bidder.

Of all the PLO's groups, the PFLP is one of the most adept at making a reasonable income from terrorist activities. Founded in 1968 by George Habbash as a Marxist organisation, the PFLP has always taken a particularly hard line over compromise with the Israelis. Habbash has disagreed with Arafat over hijackings and operations against other non-Israeli targets, which in Habbash's lexicon are classed as 'imperialist' and therefore fair game. Habbash has accused PLO leaders of co-operating with 'capitulationist Arab régimes' and he firmly maintains his support for the total liberation of Palestine – in other words, for Palestine to exist, Israel must disappear.

In the early days, the PFLP, like all the Palestinian terror groups, had trouble raising money, although Habbash's extremism made him an early favourite of Colonel Gadaffi, who donated $1 million to the PFLP coffers in March 1971. This enabled the PFLP to buy more guns and recruit and equip more soldiers, all of whom soon saw action.

On 22 February 1972, five armed members of the PFLP hijacked a Lufthansa aircraft flying from Tokyo to Frankfurt. On board were 172 passengers, including nineteen-year-old Joseph Kennedy, the son of Robert Kennedy who had been assassinated four years previously. The aircraft was flown to the Marxist state of South Yemen, landing at the old British airbase outside the country's capital, Aden. After a short time, the passengers, including Kennedy, were freed while the terrorists wired the aircraft with explosives.

The next day, a ransom letter demanding $5 million for the freedom of the aircraft crew and the plane arrived at the Lufthansa head office in Cologne. According to the letter, the money was to be flown to Beirut airport where the courier would be met by a car with a portrait of Colonel Gadaffi in the front window and a portrait of President Nasser in the back. The ransom was paid and both the aircraft and crew were released. The South Yemeni government kept $300,000 out of the ransom, which it regarded as a temporary loan; this was repaid to Lufthansa, without interest, some months later.

From such successful and profitable beginnings, Habbash never looked back. Although responsible for some of the bloodiest acts (e.g. he organised the Lod airport massacre in May 1972 when twenty-six Israelis were killed and seventy-six wounded by killers from the Japanese Red Army), Habbash is also a successful terrorist entrepreneur. Besides his building ventures in the Lebanon, his excellent connections with other terrorists around the world have made the PFLP the centre for a profitable network involved in the forging of documents.

With construction playing such an important part in the financing of terrorist groups in the Lebanon, the PLO has made great efforts to expand its influence in that area. Many local firms are either secretly controlled by the PLO or established with Palestinians as the main directors. For example, the Daoud Al Ali construction company, one of the largest in the Lebanon, was originally funded by the PLO. Al Ali, a Palestinian from the Ain Hilwe refugee camp, had done some contracting work in the Gulf, and when he returned to the Lebanon, Al-Fatah provided the money for him to start his own business. He bought a piece of land at Wadi Zeina outside Sidon where he built his first big building; this was profitable and eventually led to other buildings in the same area. (Sidon was remarkable for its large numbers of modern multi-storey buildings, all of which were funded by Palestinian groups.) Once established, Al Ali had to pay the money back to Al-Fatah, and he paid them 'interest' by lending crews and equipment for 'social works' in the camps, such as repairing roads or putting up new schools.

Typically, Al-Fatah's financing was aimed at encouraging the entrepreneurial skills of the Palestinians. This form of social responsibility had the added advantage of demonstrating to the PLO's Arab paymasters that their donations were being used wisely rather than disappearing without trace. Of course, all of this was a shrewd investment for the PLO. A successful business meant employment for Palestinians, which in turn meant increased income for the PLO since each Palestinian 'civilian' is required to give five per cent of his or her salary to the organisation (as distinct from the simple soldier who receives a salary from the organisation).

The Beirut headquarters may have dispensed cash to the different groups located throughout the Lebanon, but each local leader was given considerable local autonomy to raise funds. Thus, every local commander set up his own checkpoints and regularly demanded taxes from all those passing through the area under his control. Robberies and looting were commonplace in the countryside where the only law was Palestinian and the local police made no attempt to investigate crime.

In Beirut, where Arafat was anxious to preserve the image of the PLO as a responsible organisation, some effort was made to disguise the more extreme activities. For example, in downtown Beirut a small group might rob a jewellery store or hi-fi shop and walk straight into a PLO checkpoint. The goods would be confiscated and sold back to the store owner. While this appeared to be a semi-legitimate deal on the surface, the PLO, in fact, both hired the robbers and manned the checkpoint.

Individual leaders were also able to satisfy their particular penchants. For example, Zuhair Mohsen, leader of the pro-Syrian Saiqa, was known as 'The Persian' because of his love of the carpets from that region. He regularly sent his men to steal the finest carpets from private houses to line his luxury apartments in Beirut and Cannes.

For the larger financial institutions, Beirut was a difficult place to do business. Aside from the robbery at the BBME, that same year all the banks, with one exception, were robbed, netting the different terrorist groups involved millions of dollars. In such an anarchic environment, the Christian Phalange, too, had their share of the spoils by committing their own robberies in the areas under their control. In the civil war of 1975–76, for example, they looted the port of Beirut, and government officials estimate they got away with a staggering $715 million in goods, most of which they sold to Iraq.

In all the chaos, one bank on the Street of Banks was never robbed: the Arab Bank emerged unscathed and continued business as usual. However, in 1982 when the Israelis moved north into the Lebanon, it looked as if their luck had run out.

On Wednesday, 9 June 1982, the manager of the Arab Bank in Sidon was visited by three Israelis, who he believed came from the Mossad (Israeli intelligence) in the wake of the Israeli troop invasion. The Israelis wanted to penetrate the PLO's financial structure, and they had started with the bank known – with some justification – throughout the Middle East as the 'PLO Bank'.

The Israelis brought a list of all known Palestinian depositors at the Arab Bank in Sidon and demanded to look into the accounts. They made a similar request at the local branch of the Banque du Liban, the country's central bank. However, the Lebanon's extremely tight bank secrecy laws, which locals argue are even more restrictive than Switzerland's, would not allow the banks to comply with the Israelis' request. The Arab Bank manager managed to persuade the Israelis to leave and made an appointment with them for the following day. In the meantime, he telephoned the bank's governor, Michel Khoury, who in turn contacted the then president-elect of the Lebanon, Bashir Gemayal, who immediately telephoned Menachem Begin. The Israelis didn't return for their appointment.

As the Israelis moved north and the noose tightened on Beirut, the PLO moved their funds from Beirut to Switzerland. As one bank manager commented: 'We were surprised to find out just how many banks had PLO deposits.' Bank estimates, backed up by Israeli sources, suggest that, in the course of a single week, more than $400 million was withdrawn from the Lebanon and shifted to Switzerland, with some other transfers going to Amman in Jordan.

This enormous sum shows how much cash the different terrorist groups operating in the Lebanon had on deposit. Understandably, they feared the Israeli seizure of their assets more than they did a military defeat. Without available money to pay for the loyalty of his soldiers, a leader in the PLO has no power, since all direct funding is based on a membership head-count.

The exodus of the PLO fighters from the Lebanon was an extraordinary period. For those not lucky enough to have organised bank transfers or whose holdings were in a less liquid form, more basic smuggling operations were arranged. Israeli intelligence claims that a large number of PLO fighters boarded the ferry boats to Cyprus with gold bars in their knapsacks. Arafat paid $2.4 million in cash for the ferry boats that made the exodus from Tripoli possible. In addition, he paid a reward of $5000 to every captain and $3000 to every sailor who successfully completed the journey. The battle for Tripoli lasted forty-five days and cost the PLO more than $26 million dollars. Approximately $580,000 flowed out from PLO bank accounts each day to pay for the soldiers who had been somewhat restive, and to purchase spare arms and ammunition to continue the battle.

Even before the 1975 civil war, the PLO groups had become familiar with the technicalities of international financing. When the civil war started on 3 April 1975, at least $1 million a day poured into the Lebanese banking system from Arab supporters and from foreign assets which the PLO had made liquid. This did not include cash earmarked for arms purchases, but simply covered day-to-day living costs and the hire of street-corner gunmen employed at fifty Lebanese pounds for a soldier, with 200 Lebanese pounds extra for an assassination. From 1977 to the present, whenever the PLO appeared to be making substantial diplomatic gains internationally and when many Arabs believed that a settlement of the Palestinian question was possible, the organisation's income doubled to $2 million a day.

The Palestinians learned early that the banks would play a crucial role in their future, and they also learned throughout the various wars to live by the motto often cited in Beirut: 'Never harm the baker, the doctor or the banker.' (The occasional robbery didn't count as all the banks were insured.) Most of the groups tried to remain on good terms with the different banks, even providing armed guards on occasion. The policy paid personal dividends for Yasser Arafat during the siege of Beirut when he hid for five days in the vaults of the Banque Nationale de Paris Internationale in the Piccadilly building near the Rue Hamra.

Despite occasional lapses, however, the different PLO groups were generally loyal only to the Arab Bank. This had been founded before World War II and was originally based in Palestine. When the Palestinian exodus began in 1948, the Arab Bank lost its three branches in Haifa, Jerusalem and Jaffa to the Israelis, but of all the Palestinian banks that suffered such a loss, it was the only one to pay its depositors, loyalty that the Palestinians, and in particular the PLO, never forgot.

When, during the 1967 Arab–Israeli war, the Israelis took over seven more branches of the bank – six on the West Bank and one in Gaza – the Arab Bank transferred all its assets held there to Amman, which remains its headquarters today, and again, all depositors were paid in full. Of all the losses in that war, the Arab Bank must have been among the least damaged. They lost only $75,000 in cash which they were unable to transfer quite fast enough.

The bank's founder, Abdulhameed Shoman, died in 1973, and his son Abdul-Majeed Shoman, remains chairman of the organisation, which has mushroomed to become one of the largest banks in the world, with assets in excess of $10 billion and branches all over the world. Before taking over as chairman of the Arab Bank, Abdul-Majeed

Shoman was chairman of the Palestine National Fund, which was created when the PLO was founded in 1964 as a controlling arm of the organisation's finances (the PNF is distinct from the Palestine National Council, which deals with political policy rather than money). Shoman played a crucial role in formulating the organisation's early financial policies and in laying the foundations for its highly sophisticated investment programme which today brings the PLO many financial rewards. Shoman says he gave up the chairmanship of the PNF because of 'pressure of work', but he has retained his support for and contacts with the PLO.

His concern for the Palestinians was reflected in his message to shareholders at the beginning of the 1983 annual report of the Arab Bank:

> Israeli occupation of southern Lebanon has continued, and the Palestinian question, calling for the return of the Palestinian Arabs to their home country, has remained without solution. The latter has been made even more complicated by increased instability in the Middle East and by continued Israeli expansion through the building of large numbers of new settlements in Palestine [West Bank and Gaza Strip].

Such a highly political statement would be considered extraordinary if it came from Wall Street or from the City of London, but given the Arab Bank's sympathies, the financial community tolerates such views. This is perhaps explained by the fact that the Arab Bank is not an insignificant corner bank with little power or influence; it is a major force on the international scene and can persuade borrowers and other financial institutions to place business in a particular direction. This has been helpful to those Middle East companies that either have Palestinian sympathies or are largely financed by the PLO.

The Arab Bank, aside from its links with the PLO, was ideally positioned to take advantage of the oil money that flooded the market in the 1970s. The bank has a reputation for integrity and conservatism, both attributes that make it attractive to Arab investors. By 1983, the total assets of the Arab bank increased by $860 million and deposits by $840 million, reaching respectively $10.4 billion and $9.9 billion. Shareholders' equity rose from $400 million in 1982 to $445 million in 1983. The bank's conservatism has resulted in its retaining more than seventy per cent of its assets in cash and short-term bank deposits. Around one-third of the bank's assets are in Europe, and about one-quarter in

Jordan. Of the remaining forty-two per cent, thirty per cent are in Saudi Arabia and the Gulf states and the rest mainly in the Lebanon, Egypt and the United States.

The Arab Bank now has a presence in fourteen countries, including Greece, Singapore, Switzerland, the United States and most of the Middle East countries. At its headquarters in Amman, the bank is as big as the Jordanian government and, in many respects, just as powerful. Although King Hussein moved against the PLO and expelled the Palestinians from his country in 1970, he has made no such move against the Arab Bank, nor is he likely to. On the contrary, the bank plays a vital role in Jordan's economy and is a useful asset.

Since Amman acts as the financial centre for the PLO's bank deposits, many of the richer PLO members visibly display their material assets in the town. Rich Palestinians are spread throughout the capital and their villas are well known locally. A large number of senior PLO leaders have become rich, either through siphoning off the cash that passes through their hands, or by using PLO muscle to do business on their own behalf.

The PLO always maintained a minimum of $1 million in cash in their Beirut account. The deposit is spread over a number of different current accounts in the names of the individuals on the PLO's finance committee, such as Abu Osama, Abu Ala and Fouad Shouabaki. While the opportunities for corruption are obvious, senior PLO members maintain that very few of their colleagues got rich by stealing from the organisation. However, Abu Musa, who, with Syria's backing, led the revolt in 1982 against the Arafat leadership in the Lebanon, maintains that more than twenty millionaires are close to Arafat, including his own cousin Moussa Arafat, who owns a large farm outside Damascus paid for with PLO funds.

As one of Arafat's critics puts it: 'The finance council of Fatah – numbering between nine and eleven – have almost to a man become millionaires. Fatah has used its funds to invest in banking, properties, a printing press, and the profits should be channelled back into the Fatah account. Instead, they go straight into personal bank accounts.'

Under the PLO charter, all profits are supposed to go back into the PLO or to the organisation originally responsible for the investment. However, there are no shareholders to raise such matters at an annual general meeting and no serious attempt at accountability.

The extent of the nepotism that surrounds Arafat is less easy to defend. His position of almost absolute power has led him to help his family in a way that has caused some resentment within the movement. For example, Arafat is leader of Al-Fatah's revolutionary council, which also numbers among its members his cousins, Haj Mutlaq and the aforementioned Moussa Arafat; his nephew, Nasser Kudwa; and his brother, Fathi.

Arafat is also known to be a particularly soft touch and hopeless about money matters. While this may cause problems for his financial advisers, it makes Arafat personally popular with his followers because he will always give small cash donations to his men if they are in trouble. His generosity can reach even further afield. In the late 1970s, the British embassy in Beirut was helping to organise a fund-raising drive for the St John's Hospital in Jerusalem, an institution renowned in the Middle East, and they decided to approach the richest group in Beirut, the PLO. Arafat said he would be happy to donate what was required, provided the British ambassador would meet him and accept the money personally. At that time, British diplomats were absolutely banned from meeting with the PLO, but despite this sanction, the ambassador agreed to the meeting, provided Arafat promised not to make it public. The two men met privately and the hospital got the money.

As the PLO has grown, it has become more important that it be led by men of some financial sophistication who can control its expansion in a logical and sensible way. However, this has not happened with the PLO. For example, Arafat remains very much in control of Al-Fatah. Given the size of the operation, it is incredible that he still signs all the Al-Fatah cheques – evidence partly of distrust and partly of the shambles surrounding their day-to-day money management.

In its infancy twenty years ago, the PLO had no money and no real structure on which to spend cash. The senior PLO men – from Yasser Arafat down – were forced to go on periodic tours around the Gulf, begging bowl in hand, to keep themselves going. Forward planning and a structured organisation were not really needed because the PLO existed strictly on a day-to-day basis. However, as the PLO has grown in complexity and its income has risen accordingly, the organisation has had to adapt to a changing role and an altered image of itself. While the world still viewed the PLO as a bunch of terrorist fanatics robbing banks and blowing up aircraft to boost their cause, the secret side of the organisation was being rapidly transformed.

Tragically, this transformation has taken place at the expense of the Lebanese people. Corruption was rife in that country before the PLO arrived, but the PLO systemised the corruption so that it permeated every aspect of the local society, upsetting traditions and a way of life that, in many cases, had been in place for centuries. Uprooted from what they considered to be their own homeland, the Palestinians had no feelings or consideration for their adopted country; Lebanon was simply a staging post to greater and better things, a platform from which to launch attacks on Israel and to conduct their business deals.

The lesson of what went on in the Lebanon has been well understood by other countries in the Middle East. When the PLO were expelled from the Lebanon in 1982, the organisation had some difficulty in finding countries that would play host to the exiles. In the end, Syria took 12,000, organised under Syrian control in the Palestine Liberation Army, plus another 3000 in refugee camps; Iraq took 400, Sudan 600, Algeria 500, North Yemen 800 and Tunisia 500. In addition, there are several thousand in Jordan, many of whom have been absorbed into the army.

Typical of a host country's experience is that of North Yemen. When they first arrived, the PLO men were housed in and around the country's capital, San'a. The fighters had been used to a dominant position in Lebanese society and to a wealthy lifestyle, but the North Yemenis did not take kindly to the arrogant behaviour of the young terrorists, particularly when there were a number of incidents of shopkeepers being robbed and young girls molested. In typical Yemeni fashion, the local people distributed their own brand of justice, executing and then beheading those who had attacked the women. The government now house the PLO fighters in two camps well outside the town, and they are not allowed to visit the city. It is a lonely and miserable existence.

In Tunisia, on the other hand, where Arafat has made his head-quarters, the signs of the wealth of the organisation are more visible. The PLO houses visitors in the expensive beachside Abu Nawas Hotel, where a third of the rooms are permanently reserved by the organisation. A fleet of PLO-owned Mercedes limousines ferries the organisation's leaders and local visitors around town. The payroll is paid in cash in Tunisian dinars or American dollars; at the bottom end of the scale, a fighter is paid $320 a month, an information officer $500. In addition, the same welfare system as existed in the Lebanon has survived the 8000-mile transfer to Tunis, so a PLO fighter who gets married may receive around $2000 to take care of out-of-pocket expenses.

While his followers may have suffered in the move from the Leba-non, Yasser Arafat clearly has not. He lives in a vast white palace with blue shutters in the fashionable Tunis suburb of Gammarth. The house, which is as large as anything owned by the President of Tunisia, has magnificent gardens that sweep down to the sea.

While the PLO has been removed from large areas of the Lebanon, the vast majority of the Palestinian refugees remain there with little prospect of being removed. However, the cycle that began with the civil war in 1975 is being repeated all over again. The money earned by PLO Inc. around the world is pouring back into the Lebanon, and already the infrastructure which formed the basis of the Palestinian business machine is being rebuilt. To protect their investments, a new generation of armed men, no doubt all PLO supporters, will emerge and the whole inter-communal strife will continue unabated.

The Israelis have always argued that the PLO have refused to improve the conditions of their followers in the refugee camps because their environment breeds successive generations of committed PLO followers and also generates widespread international sympathy. With the money available to the PLO, they undoubtedly could have built extremely comfortable quarters for their followers in the Lebanon, but Arafat and his colleagues have chosen a more anarchic route, and the Lebanese continue to pay the price for the PLO's arrogant and selfish approach. The result has been the destruction of one of the most beautiful countries in the Middle East. And the Palestinians as a nation are no nearer to achieving their goal of an independent state.

When Israel invaded Lebanon in 1982, they believed that if they could remove the PLO from the country, they would solve their security problem. The Israelis, like other governments faced with terrorism, had made a simple but fundamental mistake: they believed their own propaganda and genuinely thought that the PLO had remained a stagnant organisation, with a power base limited to the Lebanon's refugee camps. The Israeli counter-terrorist effort had been so occupied with trying to prevent the next bomb or rocket attack that they had apparently failed to notice how much the PLO had been evolving over the past fifteen years: it is no longer a rag-tag bunch of amateur killers. To understand the nature of that transformation, it is necessary to move east from the Lebanon to Syria.

5

Gilt-edged terror

JUST OFF Shah Bandar Square in downtown Damascus is a five-storey building of light brown cement. It looks more like the office of a low-level government department, unpainted since the colonials departed, than the headquarters of one of the wealthiest multinational corporations in the world.

Inside, the walls, which vary between dull grey and light green, are covered with several layers of filth, probably from the fumes emanating from the old-fashioned pipe stoves used to provide heat in winter. They constantly ooze a thick smoky cloud which makes the working environment particularly uncomfortable. On the ground floor, a man is sleeping on the main conference table which dominates the area. The walls of the main room are lined with books bearing both Arabic and English titles. The ones in English include *Arab Monetary Integration* and *Documents of the Non-aligned Countries*.

During the summer, the ground-floor rooms will be cooled by large, gently whirring fans that do little to counter the oppressive heat. Although the floors appear to have been swept, smudges and dirty fingerprints cover the light switches, and the general atmosphere is one of decay – all reminiscent of a scene from the film *Casablanca*.

The director's office is on the second floor. Outside the wooden door to his office is a telex machine with a list of international codes on a stand in front of it. The two secretaries who guard the entrance each have an IBM typewriter and a modern multi-button telephone sitting on their desks. Piles of economic digests and reports gather dust on the floor and against the wall.

The dark wood furnishings in the director's office are a cross between inferior mass-market 1930s art deco and 1940s utility. A large desk with two telephones, sofas and coffee tables covered in ageing coffee stains, full ashtrays, a few books and endless dust complete the decaying image. Only the colour portrait of Yasser Arafat and the handmade black and white poster, showing three versions of the same little girl's face, with the caption in English, 'THERE WILL BE A TOMORROW', hint at the real purpose behind this extraordinary building.

The man overseeing this squalor is Mohammed Zuhdi Al-Nashashibi, a senior member of a prominent Palestinian family, whose official title is secretary of the PLO executive committee and head of the PLO administration department. Because he is considered a highly pragmatic man, unallied to any faction, Western diplomats, particularly the Europeans and Australians, often seek his views on developments within the movement. As a member of the PLO executive committee, he is one of the fifteen most powerful men in the PLO, but as chief administrator, he is even more important. In addition, Nashashibi is the keeper of the keys to the rooms on the floor above his rather tatty office, and what those keys guard make him, apart from Yasser Arafat, the man most truly to be reckoned with in the PLO.

Nashashibi's keys open a locked heavy steel door leading from the fourth floor to the top storey. Behind this barrier lies a different world: a world of high-tech 1980s state-of-the-art computers; a world light-years away from the seedy old-fashioned appearance of the floors below, and even further removed from the popular image of the PLO terrorist.

In air-conditioned splendour, this whole floor, divided into two rooms, houses banks of Honeywell reel-to-reel computers. The main room, which is approximately twenty-five feet by fifteen feet, contains the computers and has a view of a delightful garden at the back of the house; leading off this is a smaller office about eighteen feet square, where the reels of computer tape are stored. The machines are carefully tended by young white-coated Palestinians, most of whom have been trained in the United States, some at MIT and Harvard. As one visitor to the closely guarded centre said: 'It was a completely different world, all high-tech and super-efficiency, not at all what one would normally associate with the PLO.'

The PLO is not generally recognised as having changed dramatically from the fumbling, impoverished organisation that added aircraft hijacking to the world's nightmares and popularised the kidnap-and-ransom business. Years of receiving enormous stipends from Arab countries, combined with an acute business sense and a constant plea of poverty, have given the organisation one of the healthiest financial profiles in international business.

Some unofficial sources have estimated that the PLO has assets in excess of $15 billion, but this is an exaggeration. However, it is generally agreed that, through the Palestine National Fund (PNF), the PLO has control of some $2 billion in assets, and taking into account the assets of all the different groups that make up the PLO, as much as $5 billion may be salted away. In 1983, approximately $600 million in current-account income was generated for the PNF, and of this, less than $100 million came in the form of donations from wealthy Palestinians or Arab nations: the balance was made up by investments all over the world. The total annual income of the various PLO factions runs to well in excess of $1.25 billion. This sum, which is greater than the total budget of some Third World countries, makes the PLO the richest and most powerful terrorist group in the world. As the complexity of managing their funds grew, the PLO adapted its organisation to take account of the huge inflow of funds. At the head of the financial pyramid is the Palestine National Fund.

Although the main computers are just off Shah Bandar Square, the headquarters of the Palestine National Fund is a few blocks away on Baghdad Street. This four-storey building is just as run-down and its offices appear much more cramped. The visitor to the PNF headquarters is greeted by the office manager, Darwish Abyad, a middle-aged man of at least 220 pounds, with a little rim of white hair encircling a bald pate. In his fading pin-striped suit, he looks more like a failed and miserable bank clerk than the man who controls much of the Palestinians' multi-million-dollar budget.

The three desks in the main room are piled high with large envelopes marked with the return address: 'Palestine Liberation Organisation Executive Committee' (in English). These envelopes must be destined for other Arab countries or the Third World since mail so marked would not get far in the West without being intercepted by different intelligence agencies.

When the PLO was originally formed, it had three main financial institutions: the Palestine National Council, the Executive Committee and the Palestine National Fund. To simplify the structure and to separate the financial management of the organisation from the politicking that bedevilled every area of the PLO, the PNF was given ultimate control.

The first head of the PNF was Abdul-Majeed Shoman (the head of a wealthy family known as the Rothschilds of the Palestinian people), now chairman of the Arab Bank. Traditionally, the role is combined with outside interests, although as the influence and wealth of the PNF has grown, so has the requirement for full-time senior staff.

In order that the PNF be as free as possible from factional fighting, it was determined that it should be as independent as possible. To this end, it was decided that the chairman of the PNF would be the only official elected directly by the Palestine National Council; others would be either salaried staff or co-opted into the PNF by existing members of staff. 'That made the PNF chairman the strongest person in the PLO,' according to one former director of the PNF. In 1981, the PNC began electing the fund's director as well as its chairman, but the strength of the most senior figure in the PNF, the chairman, remains undiminished.

Shoman's successor as head of the PNF was Dr Youssef Sayegh, and he was succeeded in 1974 by Dr Walid Khimawai. Trained as a gynaecologist, he left Israel in 1973 and worked out of Damascus, Beirut and Amman. Khimawai was the first PNF chairman to make the job full-time, and the Fund's influence and wealth grew most during the period of his leadership.

According to Khimawai, the PNF's role is 'controlling and receiving all contributions and taxation, every income that comes to the PLO organisations'. This policy should theoretically embrace the different organisations under the PLO umbrella, but in practice, this has been impossible to enforce: the Arab leaders who support the different PLO factions would be unhappy to see their attempts to buy loyalty and influence thwarted by the organisation pouring all the donations into a common pot. And the individual group leaders want to make the most of what little independence they have, and to parlay their own money for soldiers and for power. Therefore, while all the groups pay lip service to the PNF and to the PLO, they all maintain their own budgets.

During the Khimawai era, the brief of the PNF was simply to put some controls on spending, but according to Khimawai, this was expanded to embrace other duties: 'We added to these financial activities all the economic relationships of the PLO, such as joining economic institutions, Arab or international, attending economic conferences and such things.'

However, when Khimawai retired to Amman in 1981, the activities of the PNF were split into three main departments to accommodate the expansion of the PLO. The PNF itself remained responsible for financial management, but a department of economic affairs and a bureau for statistics were established in 1981.

Khimawai was succeeded as head of the PNF by Dr Hana Nasser, who, while not as public a figure as Yasser Arafat, is certainly as power-ful, if not more so. His role could be likened to that of the company secretary or chief accountant for General Motors or ITT – a major in-fluence on events and financial policy though not in front of the cameras.

Perhaps surprisingly, Hana Nasser is a Christian born in Jaffa in 1935, although his family later emigrated to the Ramallah district on the West Bank. He graduated from Bir Zeit High School in 1951, and in 1955 he received a BSc in physics from the American University of Beirut. In 1955, he taught at Bir Zeit University, which, although state-run, the Israeli government has always maintained is a hot-bed of subversion and PLO propaganda. In 1967, Nasser received an MSc from Purdue University, Indiana, and in 1972, he became president of Bir Zeit and retained that title until 1981, despite the fact that he had been expelled by the Israelis on 24 November 1974 for what they termed 'hostile activities'.

At the 1983 Palestine National Council summit in Algiers, Nasser was elected chairman of the PNF. Alongside him, Dr Salah Dabbagh became head of the economic department of the executive committee, with Darwish Al Ariad as managing director of the PNF. These three men were, until recently, responsible for the collection, investment and ultimate distribution of much of the PLO's wealth.

Nasser appears to have done a poor job as chief accountant of the PLO. In recent years, the organisation's budget has been heavily overspent and they have had a problem generating sufficient cash to pay for all the ambitious projects that Nasser authorised. Originally, Nasser was due to retire after the 17th conference of the Palestine National Council, which took place in Amman in November 1984. However, his critics were expected to use the conference to attack his management of the PNF and he resigned in advance. He was immediately replaced by Jawid el Gussan, a close friend of Yasser Arafat, who has been given a remit to introduce some strict financial controls to balance the PLO books.

Gussan is from a rich and well-known Palestinian family who originally came from Ramallah, which was occupied by Israel after the 1967 war. His father was a prominent local councillor and his sister is married to Anwar Nosaiba, the former Jordanian defence minister and current chairman of the East Jerusalem electricity board. Gussan is a successful businessman in his own right, with a wide range of companies operating mostly in Kuwait and the United Arab Emirates. He is seen as an Arafat loyalist and a moderate.

All the senior men on the financial side of the PLO are far removed from the street hoodlums who appear regularly on the nightly television news, and the contrast could hardly be greater. All are well-educated, English-speaking, urbane and articulate, giving an air of plausible and confident commitment to a cause in which they undoubtedly believe. Little of the fanatic is in their talk; on the contrary, they appear sober and well-adjusted, and while their loyalty to the Palestinian cause is unquestionable, their decisions are generally hard business decisions and have little to do with emotion or wild and temporary enthusiasms. In that respect, they differ little from their counterparts in the boardrooms of large corporations anywhere in the world.

PLO members often refer to the PNF as their 'finance ministry' and that is very much the role it plays – quite separate from the PLO's constant terrorist attacks against Israel, and periodically against each other; the subversion of the Lebanon which has resulted in that country's disintegration; and the assassination of enemies abroad. That having been said, the PLO itself would argue, with some accuracy, that these violent acts are now only a minor part of the PLO's worldwide operations. As its wealth has grown, the terrorism and reliance on military force has declined. Simple decisions about whether to launch a terror attack in Jerusalem have become infinitely more complex, with economic and international political repercussions taking precedence over purely military objectives.

This new pragmatism has caused considerable resentment within the movement, with the hardliners, such as George Habbash's PFLP, arguing that military force is the only means by which the Israelis or the world will understand the PLO cause. But cooler heads have prevailed, and the more moderate PLO leaders can now justifiably say that their wealth is more effective than any terrorist attacks. Through its economic muscle, the PLO has become part of the worldwide business establishment, which has given it a great deal of political credibility. This has infuriated the Israelis who, as they bear the brunt of the terrorist attacks, understandably still characterise the PLO, both for internal consumption and for international propaganda purposes, as a purely terrorist operation, while realising that such a simple image is at least ten years out of date.

To understand how the PLO see themselves, it is necessary to listen to the men who run the PNF. These men, who are totally committed to the Palestinian cause and who, in almost every case, have either known about or supported terrorist activity at some time, have evolved politically

112

into more sophisticated animals. For example, Dr Salah Dabbagh, the head of the PNF's economic department, says that the PLO is an organisation 'involved in social, welfare, economic, cultural and educational activities'. This simple view conveniently ignores the terrorism committed by the organisation. However, the fact that Dabbagh, a man previously committed wholeheartedly to violence as a solution to the Palestinian problem, should talk in such a way illustrates the kind of change that has taken place in the thinking of the PLO leadership. Dabbagh explains how the PLO has evolved:

> The basic issue which the PLO was first faced with was that the Palestinians do not have a homeland, do not have an identity and they do not have a sense of belonging. That was why the PLO was first engaged in military activity, for the liberation of the homeland, because no matter how you improve the living conditions of the Palestinians, if he does not have an identity or a homeland, he is still missing a great deal. That is why part of the activities of the PLO are directed towards the military regime. But that does not mean we lose sight within the PLO of the objective of the PLO, which is improving the lot of the Palestinians, and that is why we are trying as much as we can to give our population an identity, a sense of belonging, a dignity if you like.
>
> On the social level we have the Palestine Welfare Society which caters to the families of prisoners of war, of the martyrs and of the injured.
>
> On the educational level, we have kindergartens, we have high schools, but unfortunately we do not have a university that is run by the PLO. We have thought of creating an open university, which is an ambitious programme and which is being supported by Unesco. We have done a feasibility study which was assisted by Unesco and the Arab Fund for Economic and Social Development, which is situated in Kuwait and which has already given $10 million for the project. The project is still in the planning stage but we hope within two or three years it will get the go-ahead.
>
> We would like to expand in the areas that aim to improve the living standards of the Palestinians. Recently we have drawn a great deal of assistance from various national and international organisations such as the Islamic Bank and the United Nations.

There is, in fact, general agreement that fully seventy to seventy-five per cent of the PNF's annual budget is devoted to administrative and welfare issues. Of this, by far the biggest drain is the cash disbursed to what the PLO describes as 'martyrs' families', and internal PNF estimates put the number of families covered by the PNF as high as 20,000. There is also money disbursed to an additional 40,000 injured and maimed, who have either suffered during the various Lebanese wars or during Israeli attacks.

Each faction fully realises that their support among the Palestinians as a whole is very much dependent on a humane follow-through of their terrorist activities and the acceptance of responsibility for the consequences of their own actions. At the same time, they recognise that it makes good sense to have the cash handouts administered from one central authority so that there is both continuity and consistency. So all the factions contribute directly to the Fund and update their own martyrs' lists, which are then put on to the PNF's central computer.

The sums paid, which vary enormously depending entirely on personal circumstances, are small by Western standards, but quite adequate in the Middle East. Through a complex weighting system, the PNF is able to make allowances for inflation, changes in the exchange rate or altered personal circumstances. Thus, as each year goes by, so the allowances are adjusted upwards. In many respects, the system is little different from that applying to pensioners in the West.

For the PLO, such a sensible and fair system ensures continued loyalty even from those who are victims of some of the more extreme policies of the various factions. It also ensures some measure of dependency from thousands of families, most of whom are within range of Israel and can be expected to support and succour terrorists operating in their midst. Such strong control is extremely difficult for the Israelis (or any other government) to counter as, in many cases, the PLO is the sole source of income for a family.

Once the PLO was granted observer status at the United Nations in 1974, its credibility among many Arab countries and in the Third World was greatly enhanced. For the first time, instead of being a political pawn in Middle East politics, the organisation began to be taken seriously. The PLO is now either officially recognised by or has offices in 77 countries around the world and this number gets larger every year. With political stature has come a huge increase in income. Sources within the PNF indicate that, between 1974 and 1981, assets increased sixteen or seventeen times. This can be attributed to generous donations from Arab countries and to better financial management, which has, in turn, brought a bigger investment income.

As the PLO's political base has developed, its priorities have also changed. When the PLO was first formed, nearly all of its income came from donations, and almost all of that was earmarked for military training or for arms. Now, donations are responsible for less than twenty per cent of income, and more than seventy per cent of the annual budget is spent on development projects, education and welfare.

The PLO has become a reliable client for formal business loans from such organisations as the Islamic Bank, the Abu Dhabi Fund for Economic and Social Development and the Arab Bank. During 1981, for example, this type of business deal increased 100 per cent, and despite its eviction from the Lebanon, the PLO continues to benefit from a credible business reputation.

The PNF resembles the finance ministry of any legitimate (as opposed to terrorist) government – constantly looking for the best investment that will give the maximum return on capital, while at the same time attempting to ensure that some money is spent on the welfare of the people they claim to represent. (The question of representation is a thorny issue since no real elections to any part of the PLO are ever held, and therefore, in a democratic sense, the PLO cannot claim to represent the Palestinian people. However, the longer the PLO is allowed to build its financial base – with all the social infrastructure that implies – the less likely it is that any credible rival, Israeli-sponsored or otherwise, will emerge.)

The PNF and the PLO generally pride themselves on their sound financial management. As Salah Dabbagh pointed out: 'President Reagan doesn't believe in deficit financing. Neither do we.' The major difference between the two is that the PLO has succeeded in putting its policy into practice and (barring the odd financial hiccup) keeps a very healthy balance sheet.

In 1978, as the PNF had become more than a simple accounting system, the fund invested in computers to keep track of the cash. Purchased by a roundabout route from the United States, the computer system works in English and is operated by technicians educated in the West, primarily the United States.

The Israeli invasion of Lebanon in 1982 dented Arafat's image and weakened his position as leader of the PLO, with the result that some of his followers staged a rebellion. At the time of writing, control of the PLO's financial centre in Damascus is in dispute. It is still unclear who has control over the buildings around Shah Bandar Square, although it seems likely that Arafat remains in charge. However, even if Arafat has lost access to the Damascus computers, the PLO had already taken the precaution of spreading their administrative organisation around the Middle East. As one senior PNF official defiantly said: 'They can bomb us. We have five other branches. The computers are spread out for security and safety. The lessons of Beirut in certain cases were very severe. We are now well equipped to handle emergencies.'

The other computer systems are believed to be located in Kuwait, Amman and Tunis, as well as two in Algiers. Despite their increasing involvement with Western financial centres, the PLO has not based any of its operations outside the Middle East. According to PNF official: 'They wouldn't be very safe outside the Arab world.'

In 1978, the PNF employed around forty-five people full-time to operate the computers based in Damascus. As the Fund has expanded and the computer centres have become spread around the Middle East, more than 100 highly trained Palestinians now keep the records.

In the early days, the computers were simply used to handle the money and ensure that the accounts were up to date, but today, the computers also keep track of all the PLO's military hardware. This makes available an up-to-date inventory of ordnance, ammunition stocks and the personnel available to fight at any one time. For a modern army to use computers is not unusual. For instance, the French Foreign Legion, who were part of the multinational peacekeeping force in Lebanon in 1983, brought their own computers to do exactly the same job.

Seeing the benefit of the computer revolution, all the other major PLO factions, including the PFLP, the DFLP, the PFLP-GC and Saiqa, have invested in their own systems to monitor their own investments and income from around the world.

The twenty-five member central council of the PNF meets once every three months, formerly in Beirut or Damascus, but now in Amman. To prevent the PNF becoming too politicised, most of the members are independent of any particular faction; although some of the factions do have representatives, they will never form a majority on the council. At its meetings, the council deals with all aspects of the fund, from balancing the budget to short-term investments and long-term financial planning.

Unlike more legitimate operations, the PNF does not produce an annual report, even for internal consumption. Only one full pamphlet on funds, which dealt with the 1978 financial year, was ever issued, in 1979, but the reports from the various departments tend to spell out the complexities of the share of PNF money that the individual factions receive. Some element of ambiguity is helpful to avoid recriminations, and also, of course, an annual report would give the Israelis useful intelligence, which the PLO considered to be an unnecessary bonus for their primary enemy. In fact, the PLO has successfully concealed its wealth and sources of income from the Israelis who, despite their much vaunted intelligence service, do not have nearly as detailed a dossier as they would like on the PNF.

In 1983, for the first time in many years, the PLO ran a budget deficit. Arafat publicly blamed this on the decrease in contributions from the Arab states (although poor financial management also played a major part) and has repeatedly asked for a higher level of contributions from them. This does not appear likely since the Arabs are suffering their own cash-flow problems because of a fall in the price of oil. They also seem disenchanted with the PLO as a favoured child likely to bring kudos to their countries, and other worries, such as the spread of Shi'ite fundamentalism, are of far greater concern than the future of the PLO. In 1984, for example, the PLO received less than $100 million, with Kuwait and Saudi Arabia contributing the bulk of this. (The other Gulf States favour funding the PFLP rather than the PLO, which has had the effect of creating a balance within the PLO between Arafat's Al-Fatah and Habbash's PFLP.) The PLO is again discovering that the Arabs are fair-weather friends and that they must rely on their own resources if they are to achieve their stated aims.

Although terrorist groups can rapidly accrue capital and a sound financial base by operating outside the law and paying no taxes, they have a poor fallback position. Operating with a deficit therefore decreases the PLO's ability to borrow funds from a bank (even one as obliging as the Arab Bank). The PLO has had to tighten its belt and embark on a moderate austerity programme which has basically involved liquidating some of their assets, particularly those on Wall Street. However, given the enormous assets now available to the PLO, the organisation will never fall apart because of cash shortages. Like any other business or organisation, they will, from time to time, have cash-flow trouble, but if anything can be learned from the history of the PLO during the last twenty years, it is that the Palestinians are survivors.

The four main sources of income for the PNF are taxation, donations, state sponsorship and investments.

Every Palestinian is obliged to donate five per cent of his or her income as taxes to the PLO, and in two places, Libya and Algeria, this amount is deducted at source before the workers receive their salaries. In the case of Libya, Colonel Gadaffi has had a habit of keeping the money for his own use, depending on his attitude towards the PLO at that particular time. The five per cent from each Palestinian's income goes into the coffers of the PNF.

However, the independent factions also tax their members at rates which, in a number of cases, are similar to those used by some Western countries. The Marxist DFLP, for example, has a peculiarly capitalist approach to such matters and has instituted personal income taxes at the following rates (in Lebanese pounds)

500	5%
1000	10%
1500	20%
2000	30%
2500	40%
3000	50%
4000	70%
5000	90%

Because these extra taxes are collected from people under the group's control, who are not necessarily the same as those who are their supporters, such tax collections are not always popular, but they do represent a sizeable chunk of each faction's income. Al-Fatah, for example, gets some $60 million a year from taxing its supporters – around ten per cent of its total annual budget.

The PNF, as well as each faction, has a list of supporters who can be relied upon to donate large sums of money – generally upwards of $100,000 – in time of need. As the PNF has become increasingly self-sufficient, it has relied less on the individual donation, although the factions still depend on such income to some extent. The factions make the rounds each year, as do the Jewish fund-raisers in the United States. And, like the Jewish groups, in time of crisis, such as a war, the factions do not simply rely on unsolicited donations but actively seek cash support from their friendly and rich supporters. Some wealthy Palestinians and Arab sympathisers in the Gulf actually give frequently to a number of different groups, hedging their bets so that, if a Palestinian state is ever established, they will be seen always to have been on the side of the faction that comes out on top.

Sponsorship by Arab states has declined enormously in recent years, because the governments in the Middle East have become increasingly disillusioned about the prospects for a Palestinian state, and also because, as the PLO and its factions have acquired their own wealth, state sponsors are less able to exercise control.

For a country such as Syria, the primary reason for supporting the

PLO and a faction like Saiqa is the influence such support brings with it. Syria helped launch As-Saiqa ('Thunderbolt') in October 1968 as the military wing of the Vanguards of the Popular War for the Liberation of Palestine – which had been formed prior to the 1967 Arab–Israeli war by members of the Palestinian branch of the pro-Syrian Ba'ath party. Saiqa has always considered itself a rival to Al-Fatah, which was undoubtedly the reason it was established and continues to be supported by Syria. Syrian involvement with the PLO has kept President Assad at the centre of Middle East politics. Without the PLO, Assad's stature in the Middle East would be considerably diminished, and he would be seen for what he is – the brutal and repressive leader of a bankrupt country that owes its financial existence to Saudi Arabia and its military ability to the Soviet Union.

The PLO has benefited from the insecurity of Gulf leaders and from the Arabs' love of intrigue, but despite this, the PLO and all its different factions have intensely disliked the Arab leaders for the loyalty they have expected because of their donations, and all Palestinians now talk with some satisfaction of their new independence. In 1983, the PLO received less than $100 million in state-sponsored donations, one-sixth of the total budget, and in 1984, the figure was even less, with only the Kuwaitis and the Saudi Arabians continuing to give cash. Ten years ago, the PLO was almost entirely dependent on state donations for its existence. Should all state funding be withdrawn today, it would undoubtedly be noticed, but the PLO would survive.

The investments made by the PLO are difficult to distinguish from those made by the different factions because of the intense secrecy surrounding each group's financial activities and the nature of those investments. The PNF has invested in Wall Street and the London stock market but, according to one senior PNF member, only when it is 'financially sound'. The investments are made through shell companies in Europe – Luxembourg is a favoured base – or simply with a bank acting as a front. In late 1982, the PNF converted its whole portfolio of stocks into money market certificates: 'The interest was higher and it is much easier to get our hands on the cash in times of crisis,' explained a PNF financial expert.

The PNF also has blue-chip investments in West Germany, France, Japan and Belgium, as well as real estate in Paris and London's Mayfair. According to one member of the PNF, the PLO's large amounts of ready cash and its solid reputation as a payer of debts have assured that 'firms come to us; we don't have to go to them.'

For years, the PLO was the recipient of generous loans from the international banking community, but in 1981 it became confident enough to enter the lending business itself when it lent $12 million to the Nicaraguan government, and it plans to increase such activities in the future. Through such actions, the PLO is able to gain the loyalty of other countries through the umbilical cord of major loans. This technique of purchasing loyalty is familiar to the West, but is slightly more unusual for a group characterised as a terrorist organisation.

Nicaragua also appears to have played a key role in the PLO's ambitions to develop an international network of airlines that can help transfer people, arms and drugs around the world. At the end of 1979, the PLO gave a Boeing 727 airliner to Aeronica, the Nicaraguan state airline, and since then, the PLO has donated several others to the airline, leading some sources to suggest that the organisation now owns twenty-five per cent of Aeronica, although this has been impossible to confirm. What is known is that Carlos Zarouk, the Nicaraguan minister of transport, is of Palestinian origin and has links with the PLO, particularly through George Hallak who, some sources say, is the key figure in the PLO attempts over the past ten years to purchase and run aircraft all over the world.

George Dibbs Hallak (also known as Dibbs, Hallaq and George Andrews) was born in Akka in the Lebanon (formerly Acre, Palestine) in 1940, and has three Lebanese passports (numbers 074315, 210673 and 796462). Hallak, who now lives in Athens where he has two houses, first came to the attention of the authorities in the West in 1968 when he was involved in airline ticket frauds and erroneously claimed to be the marketing director of Air Mid East, which was supposedly registered in the United States but did not, in fact, exist. Two years later, he was arrested in Saudi Arabia on charges of fraud, and was tried, convicted and deported. The fingerprints and photographs taken by the Saudi police at that time remain on file with Interpol in Paris.

Hallak then formed the Beirut-based Caledonian airlines (not to be confused with the British Caledonian airline), which was used as a front for ticket frauds which hit Air Ceylon, Yemen Airlines and Air Guinea. All these seem like the actions of a small-time crook, but sometime in the late 1970s, Hallak appears to have come to the attention of senior officials in the PLO, and they have turned his knowledge of the airline business to good advantage. Using Hallak's expertise and its own money, the PLO is believed now to have bought substantial shares in Maldive

Airways, and it also has some involvement with Sierre Leone Airways, which has two Palestinians on its main board.

In 1984, Hallak went to both Australia and New Zealand to purchase two F28 Focke Fellowship aircraft. Both were flown to Sana'a, the capital of North Yemen, from where one flew on to the Maldives and the other disappeared. He also appeared in Dallas, Texas with the apparent intention of buying a local airline. However, FBI officials, who had been alerted to his presence, began following him, and obviously warned, he left for Athens without purchasing anything. That same year, on 1 August, Hallak placed an advertisement in the *Montreal Gazette*:

DC8 PILOTS
Captains, co-pilots, flight engineers and mechanics, for employment with Maldives Airways to relocate in Maldives. Immediate availability. Please respond to: Captain George Hallaq, telex Athens, Greece 222910.

Hallak is now the general manager (operations) of Aeronica, and there have been rumours that he may be appointed the Nicaraguan ambassador to Greece. Such a powerful position for a man who is known to have links with the PLO will not be welcomed by the aircraft industry or counter-terrorist forces.

In the area of general investment in such items as companies or property, the distinction between the PNF and other PLO groups again becomes blurred. At all levels, the PLO makes considerable efforts to disguise the source of money used for an investment. For example, when buying a building in Paris, the PLO purchased it in the name of a Palestinian who was a supporter of the PLO. (No intelligence agency keeps lists of such supporters. Likely terrorists or gunrunners are known, but financial advisers are not considered sufficiently important.) Or, in another case, the PLO might use one of several shell companies it has in Luxembourg or Lichtenstein, a common tactic that effectively disguises the origin of the money from the different intelligence agencies who take an interest in such matters.

This secrecy is taken to extraordinary lengths between the PNF and the factions and between the factions themselves, whenever investments are concerned. Because of a lack of trust among the groups, the investments tend to be compartmentalised so that no one can ever be tempted to appropriate income from one group for another. Each faction has its own fund manager who is given considerable responsibility and a high degree of independence. As one PFLP leader said: 'Sometimes even we do not know where the money is and it is often best that way.' Fuad Shobaki, the Tunis-based fund manager for Al-Fatah, apparently 'knows all Arafat's secrets', though he is rarely seen in public. His job is that of the anonymous and unassuming company accountant, a role he plays perfectly.

A recurring pattern in the PNF's investment programme is that large and liquid funds are invested on the international markets, whether in money market certificates or in gold on Wall Street, in Zurich or in Hong Kong, and the longer-term investments are made using the worldwide Palestinian mafia. Like the Jews, Palestinians have risen to positions of power in financial centres everywhere and are, therefore, able quietly to lend their support when asked.

In the Middle East, Palestinian companies often turn to the PLO or to one of the factions for help in financing expansion, by investing in the company's stocks. This shows loyalty on the PLO's part and helps the cause, and the funds are readily available from the PNF at reasonable rates of interest. The PNF has invested – rarely as a majority shareholder – in hundreds of companies, and because the PNF tends to invest in companies with Palestinian connections and because Palestinians tend to deal with Palestinians, they have all been able to prosper.

The oil boom also helped the PLO by placing large numbers of Palestinians in key advisory positions to rulers in the Middle East or as heads of the finance ministries of various countries. Because of these placements, the PLO's supporters have awarded multi-million-dollar contracts all over the Gulf, and as a result, a number of large Palestinian companies have prospered.

The autonomy given to the different factions has led to a wide portfolio of investments that belong nominally to the PLO, but more accurately, provide a means of income for the different groups. One PFLP leader says that his organisation 'has investments everywhere, long term and short term for liquidity. We do have our investments, all of them, in the Western world. When you have capital, you naturally look for profits.'

However, the PFLP, as well as being involved in sensible and commonsense business operations, runs a worldwide forging network, providing false documents to anyone with the ready cash. This operation has helped the PFLP through some lean times, although it is not as profitable today, now that the heady revolutionary days of the 1960s and early '70s have led to the 1980s when terrorist revolution is not as fashionable.

The DFLP favours investment in light industries, particularly plastics and textiles, run by locals, or else the DFLP buys a stake in the company after it is up and running. The DFLP even produces an annual calendar, which is given free to favoured clients and sold to supporters.

Al-Fatah, which has the largest resources, naturally has the biggest investments and the most ambitious schemes. Other factions often speak with some envy and resentment of its resources: Arafat has his hands firmly on the pursestrings of the PLO and is largely able to dictate just how much cash each faction receives, despite the apparent independence of the PNF. Understandably, over the years Arafat has ensured that he and Al-Fatah receive the lion's share.

Al-Fatah has invested in property in Mayfair and Paris, and owns a Belgian charter airline, hotels in Paris and Damascus, and a Cyprus-based shipping line. Also, Saudi Arabia, one of Al-Fatah's main, direct supporters, has supplied oil to the organisation at a discount, which it has then resold on the international market. Some sources suggest that American oil companies have purchased such oil, but this has been impossible to substantiate.

The PNF keeps a financial hold over the different factions within the PLO by controlling the amount of money each gets from central funds. Since 1969, a percentage formula has been determined which dictates how much cash each group gets, and under the present arrangements, Al-Fatah receives sixty-seven per cent, the DFLP and the PFLP each receive seven per cent, Saiqa gets twelve per cent, and the Arab Liberation Front and the PFLP-GC divide the remainder between them. Al-Fatah is responsible for paying the Popular Struggle Front and the Palestine Liberation Front.

In 1983, a large number of PLO members, led by Aby Musa, rebelled against the leadership of Yasser Arafat. Backed by Syrian money and forces based in Lebanon, Musa beseiged Arafat in Tripoli and eventually forced him to flee the country. President Assad of Syria had hoped that Arafat's defeat would destroy his credibility as a leader but, true to form, Arafat the survivor managed to hold on to the control of Al-Fatah and the PLO, not least because he continued to control the money supply through his influence on the PNF. The subsequent negotiations between Arafat and the rebels over a reconciliation have been, in large part, over money. All the groups advocate a redistribution of PNF income, and inevitably, the different groups disagree over just how the distribution of money should be reorganised. As one senior PFLP man said: 'These figures don't coincide with the strength of the various movements.'

Most groups agree, for example, that the twelve per cent allotted to Saiqa is far more money than its membership or activities warrant. Indeed, the only reason Saiqa was allotted such a relatively high percentage in 1969 was in acknowledgement of Syria's influence, as Saiqa's backer, on the future of the PLO and their position as host to many PLO operations based in Damascus.

Finding a resolution to this will require all of Arafat's considerable diplomatic skills. Any solution will almost inevitably involve al-Fatah, Arafat's own organisation, taking a smaller percentage, and he will be reluctant to accept this because a reduction in Al-Fatah's income will commensurately reduce his available cash and thus his influence. The alternative is a fragmented PLO, which would also seriously undermine Arafat's influence, thereby making it likely that some deal will be struck.

The PNF also administers the various offices located abroad. Whether accorded diplomatic status or not, the offices operate like embassies with rotating, salaried staff and prestigious accommodation that is generally centrally located. Funds for the offices are transferred, whenever possible, from Damascus or another of the PNF centres, to the local branch of the Arab Bank. Accounts are rarely held in the name of the PLO but instead in the names of the senior PLO representatives in the countries concerned.

As in the career structure of any other foreign service, those who are more able are promoted from the less important offices in such countries as Finland to the more important ones such as Britain or the Soviet Union. Again like any other service, the calibre of the diplomats also varies widely, and in the last few years, the central organisation has had some difficulty finding people of sufficient quality to represent them abroad. Previously, Palestinians were promoted out of the field – often successful terrorists or planners of terrorism – and pushed out, untrained, to the diplomatic circuit. However, as any foreign service officer knows, the skills are different, and the low level of sophistication displayed by their representatives concerned the PLO leadership. Also, the heads of offices abroad appropriated large sums of money that were never accounted for. Matters have improved somewhat following a determined effort, led by Yasser Arafat, to raise the quality of entrants into the PLO foreign service.

Rumours have circulated of PLO officials' salaries being as high as

$20,000 a month. Officials at every level firmly deny this and agree that even the most senior officials are paid a fixed rate of $600 a month. However, some do receive fringe benefits, including free housing and generous expense accounts. While the level of pay may not be high, there are still many opportunities for corruption, and undoubtedly, because of the loose financial controls on the operators in the field, huge sums of money have disappeared. It is difficult to find a poor Palestinian leader: most have large cars, all have their own homes and some have expensive holiday homes. This is perfectly understandable in view of the fact that they control vast wealth and are usually rewarded less well than their counterparts with similar responsibilities in more legitimate industries or businesses in Western countries. But the PLO was established as a revolutionary movement fighting on behalf of an oppressed nation, and some of its members have difficulty in reconciling such high principles with the apparently high lifestyle of many of the revolution's leaders.

Some critics inside the PLO, who consider themselves more ideologically pure than the majority, argue that the financial success of the PLO has undermined the possibility of a political success. They argue that many of the PLO leaders have become so satisfied with their evidently comfortable lifestyles that they have little reason to want to alter the status quo. The establishment of a Palestinian government would mean the end of much of the freeloading and the beginning of accountability, a word that is anathema to many.

Despite the machinery for an apparently efficient financial operation, the PLO is almost always short of ready cash. After the 1982 Israeli invasion of the Lebanon, according to its own estimates the PLO lost around $350–400 million in income from destroyed businesses, as well as the loss of vast amounts of military equipment. However, although the Israelis hoped that the expulsion of the PLO would be a mortal blow, this appears to have been a serious miscalculation.

The rebellion against Yasser Arafat later that same year – largely orchestrated by President Assad of Syria – was intended to capitalise on Arafat's weakened power base and replace him with a more pliable leader in the shape of Abu Musa. This also failed and Arafat, largely because he has skilfully retained the loyalty of the men who control PLO finances, has maintained a commanding position in the movement.

Paying no tax and completely unrestricted by borders or government restrictions, the PLO has been able to invest in a wide portfolio in all the major Western financial centres. These investments have been handled well enough to give the PLO a return that would be the envy of many major multinational corporations.

Any discussion of the future of the PLO should concentrate on the organisation's evolution from a gang of hoodlums who hijacked planes in the 1960s, into a sophisticated multinational corporation that uses terrorism and sound investment planning in equal measure to achieve its aims. In the same way as Israel will not disappear from any map of the Middle East, the PLO has grown to such a size and is so financially secure that it would be virtually impossible to remove.

Much of the rhetoric that comes from both Israeli and PLO leaders is simple posturing, and both now appreciate the other's strengths. To their considerable disgust, the Israelis now realise that, by concentrating on the military aspects of the PLO, they have allowed the organisation to blossom. No incisive military action can affect the Swiss bank accounts or the Wall Street investments, and as long as the PLO maintains its financial strengths, it will be listened to, because money still talks, particularly if the assets place it alongside the Fortune 500 companies.

For a group still widely considered to be a terrorist organisation, the PLO's record of money management is extraordinary. While the world has been concentrating on the bombings and the murders that inevitably capture the headlines, and while the policy-makers have been arguing endlessly about the nature of a Middle East peace, the PLO has been quietly getting rich. At the same time, it has been forced to change dramatically from the basic terrorist organisation the world knows – it has been an extraordinary transformation.

While the PLO may not have achieved its aim of establishing a Palestinian state, its longevity and financial success have made it a role-model for the rest of the terrorist world. At the same time, of course, the rise and rise of the PLO should be looked on as a case study for the failures of traditional counter-terrorism.

The Israelis, who are supposed to have the finest secret service – the Mossad – and the most effective counter-terrorist forces in the world, have signally failed to destroy the PLO. They have followed policies aimed at capturing the terrorists or getting sufficient intelligence to prevent them carrying out their next act, and in their limited way, these have no doubt done something to curb the terrorist activities of the PLO. But while the Israelis have been looking only in one direction, the PLO have moved down two different roads – the one taken by the gunman and the bomber, and the other taken by the accountant and the investment analyst – and Israel's blinkered vision has enabled the PLO to grow to its present size and strength. In particular, its immense financial wealth has given it unprecedented political power, something that the hijacking terrorists of the 1960s failed to achieve.

All those terrorist groups that survived the Sixties, when world revolution seemed just around the corner, have modified their political stand with a healthy dose of sound capitalism. None has been as successful with this as the PLO, bu all are rapidly following the PLO's lead.

The PLO have become the principal terrorist players on the international investment scene. No other group has shown the PLO's vision and industry; they instead tend to limit their activities and successfully turn to their own advantage the conventional approach of government forces to countering terrorism.

Very different from the PLO but in many respects more dangerous and ruthless, the IRA have successfully changed their role from political terrorists to that of underground gangsters in their fight against the British in Northern Ireland.

Part Three

THE IRA

6

Noraid

IN 1984, the Irish Republican Army were responsible for 414 terrorist acts – murders, attempted murders and explosions – which resulted in the deaths of sixty-four people, nine of them British soldiers. In addition, the police and army recovered 187 weapons and 3.8 tonnes of explosives. Alarming as these statistics are, they actually represent the lowest level of terrorism seen in Northern Ireland since 1970.

Although 528 people were charged with terrorist offences during 1984, the British government estimate that the total strength of the IRA comprises no more than around 300 men and women. This small number, who are prepared to detonate a bomb or kill a policeman in the cause of a united Ireland, are backed up by several thousand sympathisers. Between them, they cost the British government £4 million ($6 million) a day in their attempts to control terrorism. For their part, while the British may have become increasingly successful in countering the IRA, the organisation has branched out from simple terrorism into organised crime to provide the estimated £4.5 million ($7 million) a year they need to pay the gunmen and support a growing political base in Northern Ireland.

The IRA has become such an integral part of Catholic life that it will never be eliminated – there is no senior army officer, policeman or politician who believes that terrorism can be defeated. However, the IRA will never achieve its goal of a united Ireland with both north and south pledged to oppose the Marxist Provisional IRA, which they fear equally. It seems an impossible situation: the violence will continue with both sides fighting a war neither expects to win. To understand how the British government and the IRA came to oppose each other with such tenacity, it is necessary to look at the history of the Anglo-Irish relationship.

England – and, more recently, Britain – has been associated with

131

Ireland for more than 450 years. The relationship has been marked by bloody brutality on both sides, and the Irish have a distinctive record of terrorist activities against the British that is almost unequalled in modern international relations.

After 1534 – the year in which the Earl of Kildare's son assassinated Henry VIII's chancellor of Ireland – England began to extend its control to include the whole of the island. Even then, Protestant England had an uneasy relationship with Catholic Ireland. The two leading aristocrats, the Earls of Tyrone and Tyrconnell, who, with Spanish aid, had led a rebellion from 1595 to 1603, fled into self-exile in 1607. With their lands in the north confiscated by the Crown, Scottish and English settlers began to arrive and take over management of huge tracts of vacant land in the nine counties of Ulster, which in some places is only twelve and a half miles from the Scottish shore. This colonisation forced many Catholics to move to the poorer southern areas of the country where the land was less hospitable and where the population was forced to eke out a meagre living from ever smaller plots of land as land ownership was denied them and their numbers increased.

The English civil war in 1664, which pitted Catholics against Protestants throughout the British Isles, caused a further polarisation in the Irish community. The Catholics strongly identified with Charles I against the rebellious Oliver Cromwell, who was supported by the Protestants. During the war, there were widespread massacres of Protestants in Ireland, and when Cromwell won, he put down the Irish Catholics with utter ruthlessness. The arrival of the Catholic James II on the throne in 1685 gave the indigenous Irish a brief respite before the Protestant William of Orange defeated James at the Battle of the Boyne in 1690 and the cycle of persecution began again. The Battle of the Boyne is still celebrated by the Protestants in Northern Ireland, who have continued to describe themselves as Orangemen.

Even Protestant loyalty to Britain was not guaranteed, however. In 1798, inspired by the French Revolution, the Protestants revolted against the British and attempted to establish an independent state. The British response was typically ruthless, and an Act of Union followed which formally attached Ireland to the United Kingdom.

The more secure economic base that existed in Ulster, which was heavily settled by wealthy British landowners, plus its close proximity to the British mainland, ensured for its inhabitants the lion's share of the industrial development that took place in Ireland in the early nineteenth century, and this also helped to widen the gap between north and south,

Protestant and Catholic, rich and poor. In addition, the largely Protestant landowners in the north were able to increase production faster than the individual farmer, while in the south, the small farmer still lived a marginal existence, feeding his family and producing only a small surplus for sale.

When things went well, the small farmer's existence was possible, but the potato famines from 1845 to 1849 resulted in the death from starvation or disease of more than one million people and caused many thousands of others to turn elsewhere for survival. Over 780,000 of them emigrated to the United States, which at that time was just beginning to show promise as the land of opportunity. (Today, Irish-Americans are the second largest single element in the American population, with about forty million US citizens tracing their ancestry back to Ireland.) This exodus was to play a significant part in the nurturing and development of modern terrorism in Northern Ireland.

Two immediate by-products resulted from the famine in Ireland. The southern Irish came to hate the British, whom they blamed, with some justification, for the exploitation which resulted in the starvation of the poor farmers. In addition, the poor Catholics, desperate for work, began to move to the richer north. This antagonised the Protestants, who saw the Catholics as a threat to their jobs and way of life. In an attempt to limit the influence of the Catholics in the north, the Protestants laid the ground rules which discriminated against Catholics in housing and employment. They created Catholic ghettos and kept Catholics from voting and from getting their share of available jobs.

As the nineteenth century turned into the twentieth, the Catholics began to voice their ambitions for independence from Britain. Various bills were introduced to Parliament but all failed, and finally, following the outbreak of World War I, the Irish nationalists rose in revolt. Seeing this as an act of betrayal, the British put down the Easter Rising of 1916 and executed some of the Irish leaders. This pushed the Catholics into the arms of the nationalists' political party, Sinn Fein (Gaelic for 'Ourselves Alone'), which, in the election of 1918, won an overwhelming majority of the Irish seats in the Parliament at Westminster. Instead of taking their seats, however, the Sinn Fein MPs declared their independence and proclaimed a government to be based in Dublin.

This revolt, too, was put down with the aid of a locally raised militia, the Black and Tans. The Irish Republican Army emerged during this period and, led by Michael Collins, carried out a successfull guerrilla campaign against the British.

The present conflict between Sinn Fein and the British government stems from the official partition of Ireland into north and south. Under the Government of Ireland Act of 1920, two parliaments, one in Dublin and the other in Belfast, were established, both subordinate to the British government in London. Negotiations took place over the exact border between north and south, and in the compromise that resulted (with 'Northern Ireland' comprising six of the nine counties of Ulster), a large body of Catholics, particularly in the border area, unfortunately remained in the north. It is this group which has consistently been the most fertile recruiting ground for the IRA.

The Government of Ireland Act was followed, in January 1922, by the Dublin parliament, the Dail, accepting a treaty that gave the south independence from London, although with dominion status. Since then, persistent rumblings have occurred between some elements of the Catholic population in the north, who wish to be reunited with the south, and from the Protestants in the north, who fear that in a united Ireland they will become a persecuted minority.

The IRA grew in the late 1960s due to widespread discrimination against the Catholics by the Protestants. Not only were the police almost entirely Protestant, but Catholics received the worst housing and had an unemployment rate three times that of the Protestants. As civil rights activists were matched by the rise of Protestant extremism, the Catholics found that the Protestant police were unwilling or unable to protect them. In such a fertile environment, it is hardly surprising that paramilitary groups sprang up, and the more militant of these turned to terrorism in an attempt to achieve change.

The IRA divided into two distinct strands in 1969, with the 'Provisionals' moving away from the 'Officials' who, they argued, were too prepared to compromise. The Officials (OIRA), who were Marxist –Leninist, believed that they could use the electoral process to gain power, but the Provisionals (PIRA) violently disagreed with this and felt that they could achieve their aim of a united Ireland only through armed revolution. Ironically, the Provos, who are now Marxist, presently have a policy of standing at local and general elections while at the same time continuing to employ terrorism.

From the onset of modern terrorism in Northern Ireland in 1969, the United States has played a key role in its support. The enormous Irish –American population has always felt a strong sentimental attachment to 'the old country' and this has been translated into a steady stream of cash and guns to the IRA, which has, in part, enabled them to survive.

The key figure today in Irish—American politics is Michael Flannery. Born in 1902 in Knockshegowna between Nenagh and Roscrea in what is now the heart of the Republic of Ireland, he joined the No. 7 Batallion of the Tipperary No. 1 Brigade of the IRA at the age of fifteen. By the time the guerrilla war against the British and the Black and Tans began in 1919, he was a seasoned campaigner and, as he tells it, helped form the famous Flying Columns – to harry the British in an early and sometimes successful version of highly mobile guerrilla warfare.

In early 1922, the southern Irish parliament accepted a British offer to become a dominion. To many hardliners, including Flannery, this smacked of appeasement, and civil war broke out between the Irish, a war that in many respects was more bloody than the one against the British. It was this civil war that nurtured the convictions of many of those Irishmen who were to make their homes in America and form the core of support for the IRA. They believed that violence was the only way to combat the British and that no negotiations should be tolerated. It was an unsophisticated approach to what was (and is) a highly political campaign.

His refusal to support the treaty with the British forced Flannery to go on the run. Although he has never killed a man, he claims he came closest to it when he was arrested by Irish Republic troops at a farm near Nenagh. He had swapped his own Webley pistol for a US Bulldog revolver, and when he pointed this at the soldier climbing through the farmhouse window, the weapon jammed solid.

After two years in the Curragh, Portlaoise and Mountjoy prisons, he left for the United States along with a number of other Irish activists, landing in New York in 1927, and began to work for the Metropolitan Life Insurance Company. In the 1930s he became head of the Clan na Gael, the American branch of the Irish Republican Brotherhood, an early forerunner of the IRA. He currently lives in the affluent New York suburb of Jackson Heights. A practising Catholic, his apartment has its quota of votive candles and religious portraits.

Flannery really came to prominence in IRA affairs after the launch of the latest round of violence in 1969, when he was approached by the IRA as a potential source of funds. His first contribution was a cheque for $5000 which he sent direct to an IRA man in Belfast. The bank in Belfast returned the cheque uncashed and, realising that he would require a slightly more subtle approach, Flannery established the Irish Northern Aid – Noraid – organisation based at 273 East 194th Street, in the Bronx, New York City.

As the violence in the north grew, Irish-Americans helped Noraid to flourish. (It now has ninety-two chapters in the United States, from Boston to San Francisco, with a paid-up membership of 5000.) At the same time as the organisation expanded, a myth grew that Noraid was the main source of income for the IRA. Indeed, most people in Britain and many Americans firmly believe that the United States is primarily responsible for funding the IRA. However, this is little more than propaganda that has been carefully nurtured by both the British government and the IRA for their own particular purposes.

The British have always considered the United States a crucial area in the 'hearts and minds' campaign in Northern Ireland. Even though the Irish lobby has a powerful voice in American politics, the British have consistently attempted to counter this by playing on American guilt for the atrocities in Northern Ireland that they have supposedly helped to finance and arm. Such propaganda has been successful, and Washington has never voiced any real criticism of British policy.

For the IRA, the image of a huge body of support in the United States has helped foster the idea of a strong and legitimate organisation backed by the most liberal country in the world. Legitimacy is, after all, the Holy Grail of terrorism, and perceived American support has done much to underwrite the IRA's campaigns of terrorism.

However, the public impression of the American role in IRA affairs is different from the reality. In the early 1970s, Noraid managed to supply more than fifty per cent of the cash needed by the IRA, but of its current budget of more than £4 million ($7 million), the Provos receive less than £135,000 ($200,000) from the United States. Other groups such as the Irish National Liberation Army (INLA) and the Officials receive far less, and the support they receive is not significant enough to make any impact on their operations.

When Noraid was first founded, its leadership had high hopes that the organisation would not only serve as a channel for contributions but would also act as a political pressure group to rally US support for a united Ireland. While considerable progress has been made, Noraid has never managed to bridge the gap between being a minority pressure group and being considered a serious political lobby which Washington would have to treat with respect.

Noraid has benefited from an already existing structure of organisations that bind together many of the Irish–American working class, including the Ancient Order of Hibernians (which claims 100,000 members in the United States) and various union branches, particularly those for the police and dock workers (called 'Longshoremen' in the US), which have a high proportion of members of Irish descent. While these groups have contributed money, other sums have also come from collections at Irish bars and clubs in Boston, New York, Philadelphia and elsewhere.

Noraid's major publicity and fund-raising event is an annual New York dinner – mirrored by others in cities around the United States – held at the Astorian Manor. Each dinner is expected to raise between $20,000 and $30,000 and to act as a focus for Irish–Americans all over the country. At the 1975 dinner, sitting at the top table were Teddy Gleason, president of the powerful International Longshoremen's Association and vice-president of the Irish National Caucus, another pro-IRA lobbying group; and Paul O'Dwyer, a New York politician and lawyer, whose hatred of the British made him a gunrunner for the Zionists in the fight for the State of Israel in Palestine.

In 1979, 1800 people attended the dinner and $26,000 was raised for Noraid. On that occasion, the list of dignitaries reflected growing support for the organisation from a wide political spectrum. Among the guests were Congressman Peter Rodino, chairman of the House Judiciary Committee, and one of the investigators into the Watergate affair; John Henning, the former US ambassador to New Zealand, Under-Secretary of State during the Kennedy and Johnson administrations and, in 1979, secretary and treasurer of the California branch of the AFL-CIO; Robert Abrams, Attorney General of the State of New York; Denis Dillon, Attorney General of Long Island; Congressmen Lester Wolf, Hamilton Fish, Benjamin Gilman and Mario Biaggi; Thomas McNabb, national president of the Ancient Order of Hibernians; Teddy Gleason; John Lawe, president of the Transport Workers Union; (the Teamsters); Philip Brennan, president of the Labourers Union; and James Comerford, chairman for thirty-five years of the annual New York St Patrick's Day parade.

The parade has become the symbol of the Irish–Americans' attachment to their forebears' homeland, and recently, it has been used by the IRA to display the degree of support they can claim among the 100,000 Irish–Americans who attend and march each year. However, in 1983 the Irish government, the New York Roman Catholic archdiocese and many of the Irish–American political establishment boycotted the parade because Michael Flannery, the aforementioned head of Noraid and a known gunrunner to the IRA, had been elected grand marshal.

The 1983 boycott and the unwelcome publicity it attracted lessened the political content of the parade as a vehicle to maintain the façade of Irish–American unity. In 1984, Teddy Gleason, the Longshoremen's president, was elected grand marshal as a compromise between the hardliners and the moderates. However, Michael O'Rourke, a convicted IRA bomb-maker who at that time was in a New York jail fighting an extradition case brought by the British government, was also elected to the lesser post of honorary grand marshal. Encouraged by his fellow IRA supporters, O'Rourke, in an interview from his jail cell, boasted about his past exploits: 'I made between 700 and 1000 mortars and rockets for use against British troops in Northern Ireland. I'd only know when they were used when I read the papers.'

Despite his Italian ancestry, Democratic Congressman Mario Biaggi, who represents the Bronx and heads the *ad hoc* committee on Northern Ireland which claims the support of 133 US Congressmen in Washington, has been the prime mover behind support for the IRA. The American political process is particularly vulnerable to pressure from minority groups, and the Irish–American vote is significant in many areas. Therefore, many of the guests who attend the Noraid dinners around the country acquire some political advantage from being openly associated with such a prominent Irish–American group.

In the 1970s, support for the Provisionals and for Noraid was gradually becoming politically acceptable. Noraid propaganda had partially succeeded in portraying the British as an occupying force in Northern Ireland, or at least it had sufficiently blurred the distinction between political activism and terrorism.

However, in 1977, the British did achieve a propaganda coup when four prominent Irish–American politicians – Senator Edward Kennedy; the Speaker of the House of Representatives, Thomas 'Tip' O'Neill; Senator Daniel Patrick Moynihan of New York; and the then Governor of New York State, Hugh Carey – issued a statement condemning support for the IRA. The *New York Times* dubbed the quartet the 'Four Horsemen', and President Carter endorsed their stand in a statement later that year. But even this high-level opposition did not have a serious impact on the inexorable rise of Noraid support.

The British have believed for many years that Noraid is directly connected with terrorism, but the spur that finally prodded American law enforcement to action against Noraid was the assassination of Lord Mountbatten on 27 August 1979.

That Monday morning dawned clear and bright. It was one of those late summer mornings for which Donegal on Ireland's western coast is justly famous, when the mist curls in off the sea and gently gives way to bright sunshine on the lush green banks that mark the descent of the Dartry Mountains into Donegal Bay.

For thirty years, Mountbatten had come to this part of Ireland to find brief moments of peace in a land he loved and with a people he held in great affection. His years as a naval officer, chief of the British Defence Staff, Viceroy of India, Admiral of the Fleet, Allied Commander-in-Chief in Southeast Asia and First Sea Lord had put considerable pressure on him. To escape, Mountbatten brought his family to Classiebawn Castle on the outskirts of the tiny village of Mullaghmore in County Sligo.

In all the time that Mountbatten and his family had been coming to the village, there had never been any indication that he was under threat from the IRA, who were in control of large areas just over the border in the north. On the contrary, as a second cousin and confidant of the Queen and first cousin of Prince Philip, he was thought to be immune from harm. British intelligence felt that an attack on Mountbatten by the IRA would be counter-productive and damage their political image around the world. Thus, that Monday morning, only two police officers had been deputed to keep a fatherly eye on the Earl and the members of his houseparty.

Shortly after lunch, Mountbatten set off on a fishing trip with his daughter, Patricia; her husband, film producer Lord Brabourne; her mother-in-law, eighty-two-year-old Lady Brabourne; and the Brabournes' fourteen-year-old twin sons, Nicholas and Timothy. In the village, they were joined by a fifteen-year-old local boy, Paul Maxwell, who, aside from being a friend of Nicholas, acted as guide.

The twenty-nine foot green-and-white open-decked motorboat, the *Shadow V*, was anchored just off the pier in the village. The Mountbattens had used the vessel for years, its simple clinker-built construction and panting two-stroke engine perfectly suiting the surroundings and the rather limited mackerel fishing expeditions the family favoured.

Shortly after the boat pulled out into the bay, a fifty pound bomb, stowed among the fishing equipment, exploded, scattering pieces of the boat and its occupants across the bay. Seventy-nine-year-old Mountbatten was killed instantly, along with his grandson, Nicholas, and the local boy, Paul Maxwell. The elderly Lady Brabourne died in hospital the next day, and the remainder of the party suffered serious injuries.

Both the INLA and the Provisionals claimed responsibility, the latter announcing that the bombing was part of a 'noble struggle to drive the British intruders out of our native land'. However, they did express regret at the death of Paul Maxwell: 'Latest intelligence before the attack said that there would be additional members of the Royal family, and not civilians, on the boat. It should have been a more mature man [serving as pilot], an older man who would have been able to weigh up the political company he was keeping and the repercussions of it.'

Three hours later, at Warrenpoint just over the border in Northern Ireland, an army truck was blown to pieces when it passed another truck carrying 1200 lbs of explosives hidden beneath a load of hay. IRA gunmen opened fire on the British troops, several of whom had been killed or injured in the blast, and prevented ambulances arriving by road.

In a previous reconnaissance, the Provos had realised that, if the British were unable to provide support for the troops, a helicopter would have to fly in reinforcements and would be forced to land near the only piece of cover close at hand, a ruined stone house. When the helicopter arrived, the same member of the IRA active service unit responsible for the truck bomb detonated an additional 1000 lbs of explosives hidden in the house.

Eighteen British soldiers were killed at Warrenpoint – the highest number of casualties inflicted by the IRA in one incident since 1921.

In normal circumstances, the carnage at Warrenpoint would have received wide publicity, but it paled beside the murder of Mountbatten and his family at Mullaghmore. In Britain there was outrage at the attacks, and Mountbatten's funeral produced an outpouring of sentiment and the sort of scene of pomp and majesty that the British manage so brilliantly. However, although the loss of a man who was undoubtedly much loved was genuinely felt in Britain, the 'Monday Massacres' had an invaluable (to the British government) impact in the United States.

The Mountbatten murders marked a watershed in Irish–American politics. Not only did the IRA lose a great deal of sympathy from previously supportive Irish–Americans, and some of the traditional leaders in the United States begin to question the younger, Marxist-orientated Provisional leadership, but for the first time, the FBI and other law enforcement agencies bowed to pressure from the British government to move against IRA supporters in America, and particularly Noraid.

* * *

It is an interesting hallmark of Michael Flannery and the old guard surrounding him that, whatever the political complexion of the IRA or the divisions that occurred among Irish–Americans in the United States, their support was unwavering. Originally, Flannery backed the IRA because his own experience in the civil war of the early decades of the century had shown him the value of cash support, particularly to the families of those killed or jailed. 'It is my experience from being in jail and on the column in Tipperary,' he said, 'that morale could be seriously affected by men worrying about their wives and children. If we help these people, it will help the IRA to have contented men. My intention is to help the IRA. People have a moral duty to support the IRA and I'm one hundred per cent behind it.' This view is perfectly logical but, of course, it does not take into account the IRA's changing policies since 1969.

As the more traditional and strictly republican Official wing of the IRA declined and was overtaken by the Provisionals, the organisation became more radical. In fact, it is now dedicated to the establishment of a Marxist state in a united Ireland, presumably under the leadership of Sinn Fein's president Gerry Adams. (Adams, British intelligence monitoring of his telephone reveals, insists on callers referring to him as 'Comrade'.)

On the other hand, the majority of Noraid's support comes from the conservative and staunchly anti-Communist trade union movement in the United States. Consequently, as the Provos have become more radical, the trade unions have moved away from their unqualified support of the group and have become more questioning in their loyalty. At the same time, attacks such as the Mountbatten assassination and the bombing of Harrods in 1983, in which a young American tourist was killed, have also alienated the politicians who were beginning to support Noraid and a united Ireland.

Even the attitudes of the IRA's oldest and most loyal backers are changing. While Flannery and his friends have comfortably supported the violence as a 'just war', which they can compare with the romantic days of their youth, they have little in common with the young men in Northern Ireland who preach a brand of politics unheard of two generations before. In particular, the decision by the Provisionals to combine the bullet and the ballot box has baffled the old guard; they are unable to relate to an election campaign in which the Provos (in the guise of Sinn Fein) run for seats in the Parliament at Westminster or to the European Parliament in Strasbourg. After all, one of the main reasons for Flannery leaving Ireland in the first place was his disgust at De Valera's agreement to work within the political process and abandon armed violence. These are simple men who have a relatively straightforward view of the war and its logical outcome. The subtleties of the Gerry Adams style of fighting are not for them, and in the past five years they have come to feel increasingly alienated. The differences between the old guard and the newer Irish leaders have contributed to the reduction in Noraid's ability to raise funds, and a sharp decline in political support in the United States.

In 1981 there was something of an upswing in Noraid's fortunes. A number of prisoners, convicted of terrorist offences, went on hunger strike in the Maze prison in a protest against conditions. Initially, the IRA leadership did not support the strike, but when they appreciated its propaganda value and the resolution of the men at the heart of the strike, they decided to give the action their full backing. Ten IRA men eventually died of starvation, and while the hunger strikes did not restore the political dimension, there was a brief resurgence in the fund-raising.

In the first six months of that year, Noraid raised more than $250,000, the highest contribution to the IRA coffers since $172,000 had been raised in 1972. However, the structure of Noraid, like those of many terrorist support systems that have been around for a long time, had become very cumbersome so, of that $250,000, only $93,000 reached Northern Ireland. The balance was retained to pay for salaries and propaganda in the continental United States.

Unfortunately for the IRA, the hunger strike was only a passing rallying cause that briefly united Irish–Americans behind the IRA. Since the middle of 1981, the fortunes of Noraid have continued to decline rapidly. For example, at the annual dinner at the Astorian Manor in November 1981, senior politicians were noticeably absent. British intelligence now believes that the cash passed to the Provisionals from Noraid is less then $200,000 per annum and declining each month.

Under current legislation, Noraid as a 'foreign agent' is required to file papers with the US Department of Justice listing annual income and its disbursement. In this way, the US and British governments are able to keep some track of the finances of the organisation, although the FBI and British intelligence agree that Noraid declares only one-quarter to one-fifth of the cash it collects. The balance is either retained in the United States for the purchase of arms, or covertly sent to Dublin and Belfast.

Money collected in the United States is shipped from Noraid's New York offices to two organisations: An Cumann Cabhrach at 44 Parnell

Street, Dublin (where the IRA news-sheet *An Phoblacht* is published) and to the Green Cross in Belfast, another support organisation for the IRA. Messengers, many of whom are believed to be vacationing New York police officers of Irish descent, carry cash at least twice a month to Ireland.

In the early days, Noraid officials attempted to distance themselves from the IRA, claiming that Noraid was simply a charity designed to provide financial assistance to the families of IRA members suffering hardship as a result of sectarian strife, but no intelligence or law enforcement agency has ever made any real distinction between the two. Therefore, Noraid has dropped much of the pretence, which partly accounts for the decline in income: Irish–Americans happily donated money to what they saw as an essentially humanitarian cause but are more reluctant to see their dollars going directly to underwrite terrorism.

Noraid has been persistently accused of supplying arms to the IRA, and it is true that the IRA, as well as a number of other terrorist organisations, have undoubtedly benefited from the relaxed laws applied to arms purchases in the United States. However, the arms conduit from the United States to the Provos has been neither as successful nor as continuous as is popularly believed. Intelligence believe that from 1968 – just prior to the latest round of violence – until February 1983, 2817 weapons were captured which had been smuggled from the United States to Northern Ireland. However, during that same period, more than 8000 weapons were captured by the RUC and the British Army.

The Provisionals and the other groups have consistently complained about a shortage of modern arms. In 1969, the IRA were ill-prepared for action. They had few modern armaments, depending largely on Lee-Enfield .303 rifles of World War II vintage, American Springfield rifles, the odd Thompson sub-machine-gun with the circular magazine so beloved of Chicago gangsters in the 1930s, and even one German Schmeisser machine-gun saved from World War II. However, by 1972, the IRA had begun to modernise and had acquired several Armalite AR-16 5.56 mm rifles from the United States (and subsequently the AR-18 from Japan). With a twenty-round magazine and the ability, through its bullets' tumbling action, to create devastating wounds, the Armalite quickly became the favoured weapon of the IRA and remains so to this day. The AR-16 in its Colt Commander version has a folding stock and so is readily concealed – an additional attribute – and it is accurate at up to 500 yards, a range at which it can penetrate some body and some vehicle armour. Like anything of any permanence in the Ulster conflict, the Armalite has swiftly become part of folklore, as is evident from a thirty-yard-long inscription on the walls of Derry above the Bogside (a Catholic ghetto): 'God made the Catholics, but the Armalite made them equal.'

The use of sophisticated modern weapons boosts morale within the IRA and also gives the organisation credibility as a fighting force. Because of this, on several occasions in the 1970s, journalists were given demonstrations of the Provos' M-60 heavy machine-gun. This particular weapon, which was smuggled from the United States, was too valuable to use in battle and was kept safely out of danger in the Irish Republic where it was used entirely for propaganda. (They now have seven or eight M-60s, and these are used regularly in the north.)

The Provisionals also possess two .5 Browning machine-guns which they recovered from a World War II bomber that crashed and sank in Loch Neagh. Provo members dived and recovered the guns, but they have been unable to make them work properly.

With such a shortage of arms, one gun often tends to be used for a multitude of missions. An Armalite of American origin, which was found in February 1984 in Dunloy, Northern Ireland, after two IRA terrorists had been shot, was identified from eight previous missions: the attempted murder of policemen in Ballymena in January 1979 and in Cullybackey that December; the attempted murder of Ulster Defence Regiment (UDR) soldiers on Galgorm Road, Ballymena, in February 1980, at Bridge Road, Dunloy, in February 1982 and in Toomebridge that May; the attempted murder of an RUC reservist in Cloughmills in September 1983; the attack on Randalstown police station in November; and the murder of RUC man, John McFadden, at Rasharkin, also in November 1983.

In normal criminal circles, the weapon would have been ditched as soon as it had been used in a killing or attack of any kind. Forensic scientists can easily match a bullet with a particular rifle, and using the same weapon again and again merely stacks up a body of evidence for the future.

The IRA's shortage of adequate munitions is due in part to a British intelligence effort to interrupt the arms flow from around the world. They have been helped by the apparent incompetence and lack of sophistication in the ranks of the IRA. In 1982, for example, a three-man Provisional team with £1 million in cash travelled around Europe trying to buy arms on the black market. They visited France, Belgium, West Germany and Italy, and at each stop, they were taken in by crooked arms dealers who, after demanding substantial sums as deposits promptly vanished. The trio returned to Belfast empty-handed and minus their £1 million. The British intelligence agents who had been keeping an eye on them from the start of their trip were astonished that no action was taken against the three.

Until 1979, the United States had not co-operated with British intelligence for the control of illegal arms flowing from the US to Ireland. Following the Mountbatten assassination, the FBI changed their neutralist policy and agreed to act on any information they received from British intelligence. They set up a six-man squad, whose sole job was to monitor known Irish–American activists and to interrupt the flow of arms and illegal cash from the United States. The result has been a series of court cases in the last five years which have severely damaged the infrastructure of the support groups in the US and cut their financial base to such an extent that the US no longer makes a significant contribution to the IRA's war chest.

The key to the first major FBI case against Noraid officials was George DeMeo, a bearded and bespectacled Corsican with close-cropped dark hair, who owned a Yonkers gun shop and was a sometime resident of North Carolina.

Two big gun and ammunition thefts in 1976 – the robbery of the National Guard Armory in Danvers, Massachusetts, near Boston, and one at the US Marine camp at Camp Lejeune, North Carolina – marked the beginning of the law enforcement campaign against the IRA gunrunners. The National Guard Armory robbery was carried out by a Boston Polish–Irish gang known as the 'Roxbury Rats', who stole some 100 M-16 rifles and at least eight M-60 heavy machine-guns. These guns were passed to a Boston fence called Charlie Gallant, who in turn passed them to a Noraid official, Bernard McKeon, who shipped them to Dublin in crates labelled 'Standard Tools'. At Camp Lejeune, over one million rounds of ammunition and several guns were stolen. The shipment of arms stolen from the armoury in Massachusetts was intercepted in Dublin in 1979 after the local police received information from British intelligence. However, at least 600,000 rounds of the ammunition stolen from Camp Lejeune reached Northern Ireland.

The common link in both robberies was George DeMeo, who was arrested and put on trial in North Carolina in 1980. Both British and US intelligence officials testified against him and he was sentenced to ten years in jail.

DeMeo, in the hope of diminishing his time in a high-security prison, approached the Justice Department and offered to use his contacts with Noraid to set up a 'sting' operation which would cut through the IRA's arms pipeline. The FBI codenamed the sting 'Operation Bushmill'.

The first step was to get DeMeo out of jail. He was encouraged to appeal against his sentence, and although the Justice Department officially opposed his application through papers filed at the North Carolina court, they privately approached the judge to ensure that DeMeo was released. DeMeo then immediately got in touch with George Harrison, a sixty-six-year-old Brink's armoured car guard.

Harrison had been born in Ireland and, like many other senior Noraid officials, emigrated to the United States while he was still a young man. He rose through the ranks of Noraid and was now treasurer of its Brooklyn branch. He is an idealist who believes that every cause fought by oppressed peoples around the world, whether they are Palestinian, Basque or whatever, is a just fight. However, the cause closest to his heart is that of a united Ireland, and for twenty-five years, as he admitted on British Independent television's *World in Action* programme after Operation Bushmill, he had been shipping guns from New York to the IRA, often with ordnance supplied by DeMeo.

HARRISON: If it was within my power to – er – send – er – erm – er – a shipload of weapons to – er – the Irish Republican Army tomorrow morning, I would do it.
Q: Are you proud of that?
HARRISON: I am very proud of it.
Q: How many weapons do you think you have shipped over there?
HARRISON: Well I – er – prefer to let my attorney . . . it's in the court records. I – I – I don't want to go into specifics and that, but however, I didn't send enough, I wish I should have, I should have sent a lot more.
Q: But we're talking about thousands of weapons over the years here, aren't we?
HARRISON: Well, I would suppose, yes.

In February 1981, DeMeo, with bugging equipment concealed on his body, met Harrison and discussed the possibility of DeMeo supplying armour-piercing shells to fit a 20 mm cannon. On 17 May, Harrison was driven by his close friend Thomas Falvey, a fifty-five-year-old construction worker, to DeMeo's house in Pelham outside New York, to meet John White, the man who, DeMeo had told Harrison, would be able to supply all the guns that he wanted. 'White' was actually

FBI special agent John Winslow, who was also fully rigged with bugging equipment. In the room where they were scheduled to meet, a video recorder had been concealed to obtain photographic evidence of the meeting.

Winslow told Harrison that he had access to 350 stolen MAC-10 .45 machine-guns, which he would sell for $250 each. Harrison responded that he was expecting $50,000 in a month's time and would take any guns or ammunition that Winslow had to offer.

One month later, on 17 June, Winslow – again in his 'John White' persona – met Harrison and agreed to supply forty-seven machine-guns for $15,000, including twelve AK-47 Kalashnikov rifles. Harrison accepted, but the next day Winslow telephoned to say that the price had gone up to $16,800. FBI agents, who had placed a wiretap on Harrison's phone, heard him immediately call Michael Flannery with the news.

That same evening, the FBI followed Harrison to Flannery's Jackson Heights apartment. When he went through the door, he was carrying a blue plastic shopping bag, and when he came out, a large white envelope was sticking out of the top of the bag. Harrison drove to Falvey's house where he was to meet Winslow. When the latter arrived, the AK-47s were unloaded into Falvey's garage and Winslow was paid in $100 bills taken from the white envelope in the plastic bag.

Shortly afterwards, the FBI agents saw Harrison and Falvey leave the house with what they thought was one of the rifles concealed in the all-purpose blue shopping bag. They moved in, and although the bag contained only beer, both Harrison's and Falvey's homes were found to hold a treasure trove of arms and information relating to the arms smuggling business. The FBI uncovered a large store of arms at Falvey's house and a carefully itemised list at Harrison's, which detailed his twenty years of arms smuggling for the IRA, involving more than 1000 weapons and 900,000 rounds of ammunition worth more than $1 million. (The IRA have traditionally kept meticulous records, which in the early 1970s led to a number of major successes by British intelligence operating in Northern Ireland. In an attempt to counter this, the IRA's Army Council banned account books that could incriminate individuals outside the cell structure. These instructions obviously had not reached across the Atlantic.)

Documents found in Harrison's house led the FBI to Patrick Mullin. Born in Galway, Mullin became involved in the movement after he witnessed the 1972 Bloody Sunday massacre when British paratroopers fired on civil rights marchers in Derry and thirteen people were killed. Small, slight and balding, he was employed as a foreman with a telephone company and seemed to be out of his depth with the hard-nosed company of the other Noraid members. However, police found thirteen rifles, twenty-five machine-guns, ammunition and a flamethrower piled up underneath the pool table in the basement of his house.

David Gormley, a Vietnam veteran and a staunch Irish republican, was also arrested on evidence found at Harrison's house and charged as a regular bagman for the arms buyers. Although at the time of the bust he was on holiday from his job as an engineer, the FBI found enough evidence to implicate him in the arms deals.

Three months later, as he was coming home from Mass, Michael Flannery was arrested and indicted with the others. The police had delayed arresting Flannery because he was the most senior of the group and his arrest was potentially the most politically sensitive. Tall and white-haired with a single streak of ginger running through it, his craggy features and rasping Brooklyn accent are familiar to many Irish–Americans around the country, and over the last quarter century, Flannery has become the closest thing to a symbol that the Irish republican movement in the United States possesses. Caution was therefore required, but the FBI were convinced that they had enough evidence to convict Flannery.

Inevitably, Paul O'Dwyer was asked to defend the accused Noraid members. O'Dwyer, no stranger to Noraid trials, and a prominent member of the organising committee of Noraid's annual fund-raising dinners, provided the services of his law firm free. He embarked on a bold defence that shattered the prosecution's case despite the fact that all the defendants admitted to smuggling the arms to Northern Ireland.

O'Dwyer's defence dramatically suggested that DeMeo was, in fact, a CIA agent, and that all the accused had believed they were working for the United States government at the time of their arrest. Evidence was produced that purported to show that DeMeo had indeed worked for the CIA in the past. This included a memorandum sent to the CIA by the late FBI director J. Edgar Hoover in 1967, in which Hoover said he thought DeMeo was working for the CIA in a plot to assassinate Fidel Castro.

The facts were that, in 1969, DeMeo had been arrested along with Earl Redick, a former US army intelligence officer, with five tons of weapons bound for the African state of Chad. DeMeo assured Redick that the case would not come to trial because his friends in the CIA would have the charges dropped. Indeed, just days before the trial was to begin, all charges were dismissed.

The CIA denied that DeMeo had ever worked for them or had any connection with the Agency. However, as the defence correctly pointed out, the CIA was obliged to make such a denial if DeMeo was an agent since the Agency never acknowledges its covert agents. The prosecution were put in the position of proving that DeMeo was not a CIA agent, an impossible task, and the jury acquitted all the defendants, much to the FBI's disgust.

In fact, the CIA probably were using DeMeo as an informant in an attempt to keep track of arms supplies to Ulster, and it is probable that he had been supplying them with hard intelligence for many years. This would account in some measure for British intelligence's high success rate in capturing arms that had been smuggled from the United States. However, it is a quantum leap to say that the CIA had actually been running the arms pipeline and that the Noraid members had been acting on behalf of the US government.

While this case had ended in disaster, the FBI's squad monitoring IRA supporters were already preparing for their next sting. While tapping Harrison's phone, they had overheard a conversation with a man named Gabriel Megahey who had not previously appeared in their files. Inquiries to British intelligence in Belfast and London revealed that Megahey, who had worked on the docks in Southampton, and was now a barman in New York.

During the early 1970s, Southampton was the main conduit for arms into Britain, and the munitions for the 1974 campaign of terror, when soldiers and civilians were killed by bombs planted in London and other major cities all over Britain, had been imported via Megahey. He had easily smuggled the munitions because of his contacts within the docks, but police had found a bomb factory hidden in a Southampton garage in 1974 and Megahey had been implicated. He was served with an exclusion order banning him from entering Britain, and because that phase of their terror campaign in Britain was at an end, the Provo command moved him to New York.

The brash and youthful Megahey (he is now 47) was not immediately popular with the established old guard in the Noraid hierarchy. The left-wing politics and casual attitude shown towards the killing of innocent civilians by Megahey and his associates were anathema to long-standing members such as Flannery and Harrison. Instead of co-operating, the two groups went their separate ways and Megahey set up his own arms-smuggling operation.

The FBI put Megahey under full-time surveillance, which included a twenty-four hour tail, phone taps and photographic records of meetings. He became known to the FBI squad as 'Panicky' because he was so careful about shaking tails. According to one FBI agent: 'He was so surveillance-conscious and professional in the way he handled himself. We conducted many, many surveillances of him, both electronic and physical. There were times when we surveilled him throughout the streets going to various meetings when he would walk backwards, go in and out of subway cars, the *French Connection*-type individual.'

Megahey was so skilful at covering his tracks that the FBI had given up hope of ever getting enough evidence to bring to a court of law. And then, in June 1981, Michael Hanratty, a thirty-five-year-old electronics engineer and surveillance expert, walked into the FBI office in New York.

Hanratty claimed that an American, Andrew Duggan, had approached him to arrange the supply of arms to the IRA. Hanratty later claimed that Duggan had told him that the IRA 'wanted to make larger strikes, rather than just shooting down one man with one gun. They wanted to shoot down a whole planeload.'

In the past, IRA arms purchases had centred around rifles, pistols, explosives, detonators and ammunition. No evidence exists that the IRA has received anything approaching the sophisticated weaponry possessed by other terror groups such as the PLO; on the contrary, the IRA had preferred small and strictly limited operations. (However, compared with groups such as the PLO, the IRA use what weapons they have with great skill. Their bomb-making techniques, use of modern detonators and timers as well as their tactics show good training and a high capability. No other terrorist group in the world can match their skill on the ground.)

At this time, the British army's successful deployment of helicopters in the areas bordering on the Republic of Ireland had created some frustration within the organisation. Helicopters are particularly suited to counter-terrorist operations in rural areas because of their spotting and rapid reinforcement capabilities. The IRA had therefore decided to attempt to buy – among other things – surface-to-air missiles (SAMs) which would be capable of shooting down helicopters.

The receipt of Hanratty's information, immediately set in motion an elaborate FBI operation, codenamed 'Operation Hit and Win', aimed at trapping another IRA arms smuggling gang. Initially, Hanratty, accompanied by FBI agent Enrique Ghimenti posing as an arms dealer, met Duggan at a hotel in Manhattan. Duggan told the two men he was merely an intermediary, and after some preliminary discussion, which included the possible purchase of SAMs, they agreed to concentrate on the details at a future meeting.

That meeting occurred in New Orleans in a specially converted room above a bar, fitted with both microphones and video cameras. Two IRA men turned up to meet the three FBI agents, all of whom were posing as arms dealers. The IRA men agreed to buy five Redeye missiles at $10,000 each, and then the discussion moved on to other items on the IRA shopping list, including grenade launchers, ammunition, detonators – even the purchase of a submarine. The IRA men were particularly impressed by the Heckler & Koch 9 mm MP5SD which the FBI had brought with them. Ironically, the Heckler & Koch silenced machine-gun is a particular favourite of the British Special Air Service (SAS).

At one point, the IRA men considered test-firing the machine-gun into a pile of telephone books that the FBI agents had kindly stacked on the floor. However, it was decided that the bullets would probably go straight through the floor and hit the customers drinking beer in the bar downstairs, thereby attracting a certain amount of unwanted attention.

A third and final meeting took place a month later, and on this occasion the elusive Megahey walked in and gave his firm order for the Redeye missiles, which the FBI recorded on video. The FBI could hardly believe their luck. As one of the agents recalled, 'For him to walk in, talk to an undercover FBI agent on camera with microphones rolling, stating that he was the number one in the United States – the feeling in the next room was one of ecstasy to the point that we were almost leaping from the pipes.'

Megahey, ever cautious, told the FBI men that, to avoid any last minute hitches, he proposed an exchange of hostages who would be held by both sides until the weapons were safely out of the country. 'If any of my men get nicked, you are dead,' Megahey said. 'If I am going to jail, someone is going down in a hole.' On that cheerful note the meeting broke up.

Megahey was arrested a few days later, along with Duggan and two brothers, Eamon and Colm Meehan. On this occasion, no CIA involvement could be produced by the defence, and all four men were convicted and sent to prison.

In the course of 'Operation Hit and Win', the FBI came across a number of other IRA sympathisers who were not sufficiently involved in the case to justify their arrest. Among them was Liam Ryan, a natural-ised American citizen who had been born in Northern Ireland. He works as a meter reader for New York's electricity supply company and lives with his Irish girlfriend, Helen O'Sullivan, in a Bronx apartment.

The FBI believed that Ryan was involved in obtaining false docu-ments for the 'Hit and Win' team both to buy the guns and to smuggle them out of the country. Although there was insufficient evidence on this occasion, the FBI finally brought Ryan to court in April 1985. His arrest marked the conclusion of another coup against the IRA which had involved co-operation between the CIA, FBI, British intelligence and the Irish government.

At the beginning of September 1984, an eighty-foot trawler, regis-tered in Ipswich, Massachusetts, set sail from Boston for Ireland. On board were rockets, Korean-manufactured grenades, 100 West German automatic rifles, fifty-one pistols and revolvers, shotguns and a 0.5 calibre heavy machine-gun which could pierce armour at a distance of one and a half miles. The total value of the cargo was over $500,000.

The trawler was tracked by a CIA surveillance satellite, and its rendezvous with an Irish trawler, the fifty-six-foot *Marita Ann*, was reported to the Irish government, which seized the vessel and confis-cated the cargo.

The Irish justice minister, Michael Noonan, said that the money for the arms had been raised by Noraid and that they had organised the shipment of the arms from Boston to Ireland. Although this was denied by Noraid, when Liam Ryan was arrested the following April and charged with offences relating to the illegal purchase of arms, the Brooklyn courthouse was packed with Noraid supporters. The best-known figure in the public gallery was the New York lawyer, Martin Galvin, Noraid's publicity director. When the judge set bail at $750,000, the sum was immediately met by Noraid members including Galvin, who gave a personal guarantee of $500,000. Ryan is pleading not guilty to the charges.

The FBI drive to stem the flow of arms from the US to Ireland resulted in several other cases, and the impact was so great that, by the middle of 1983, Noraid was forced to establish a fund for the various defendants who were coming before the courts. The Irish–American Defense Fund set as its goal the raising of $200,000, all earmarked for defence costs. The thirty-six members of the committee that headed the Fund included Tommy Gleason, president of the International Longshoremen's Asso-ciation, Barney Walshe, president of the Boston Trades Council, and senior officials from the Teamsters, the police and the firemen's unions around the country.

A glossy brochure, which was distributed widely, required donors to fill in a card pledging contributions of between $20 and $50 a month. The brochure pointed out:

> The defendants are not wealthy people. Prominent lawyers have volunteered their services *pro bono*. Nevertheless, high expenses are being incurred to ensure a fair trial. For example, travel and hotel expenses of defense witnesses must be paid; court transcripts must be purchased; the families of some of the defendants need financial assistance.
>
> The finance committee of the Irish–American Defense Fund estimates we need $200,000 this year to meet minimum expenses. The fund urgently needs your help to assure that these individuals have the best possible defense.

Until the FBI began its investigations, the IRA successfully portrayed the attacks on Noraid as pure propaganda by the British. For many Irish–Americans, this was a convenient fiction that effectively salved any problems their consciences may have had about giving money for terrorism. However, the spate of trials taking place on America's East Coast have changed all that. These provide clear evidence of Noraid's involvement in the arms business, and this has caused a considerable decline in the group's income. Appeals on behalf of those who have been arrested for smuggling arms are not likely to be successful without the funds to back the defence. With some justification, the Noraid defence fund promotors say that part of their aim is to make Americans aware of 'the current campaign, at Britain's behest, to intimidate all individuals and Irish–American organisations actively aiding the struggle against British colonial rule in Ireland.'

This campaign took on new urgency in July 1985, when President Reagan put forward a supplementary clause to the current extradition treaty between the United States and Britain. This clause recognises for the first time that terrorists should not be immune from extradition simply because they claim to be attempting to achieve a political objective. In the past, this argument has been successfully used by a number of IRA terrorists who have fled to the United States, to avoid being extradited for trial in Northern Ireland. The supplementary clause was put forward by President Reagan as a direct result of personal pressure by Britain's Prime Minister, Margaret Thatcher. However, the measure is not expected to pass through Congress despite considerable pressure from the administration. The Irish–American lobby has been very active on Capitol Hill, and as one Congressman put it: 'There are no votes in passing this and we have an election coming up.'

Nevertheless, the British are pleased with the events of the last two years. With income falling and prosecutions of activists rising, Noraid will probably never again recover to be an effective support group for the IRA. Five years ago, Noraid appeared to be on the verge of having a major impact on the American political process. The British have always dreaded the possible growth of a significant body of opinion in the United States that would support the view that Britain is a colonial power occupying Northern Ireland; this was certainly what all the senior IRA men operating in Belfast and Dublin hoped for. With the United States backing their cause, victory would be in sight.

In 1984, however, Gerry Adams' response to the question of how important American aid is to the Irish republican movement showed a change of attitude:

> We are grateful to the various American organisations that support us, but the fact is that, if all American funds were cut off tomorrow, it would not affect us at all. American support will be much more important in the future when we will want international recognition for a new government of a new Irish state.

If present trends continue, not only will Adams not have his funds, but Noraid will be silenced as an effective lobbying voice.

Noraid's financial status and Irish–American support for the IRA have been influenced by the different propaganda forces at work. In the early 1970s, Noraid effectively argued that all money donated to their organisation was spent on humanitarian causes in Northern Ireland. This was never true: from the outset, Noraid provided cash and arms directly to the IRA and, to a large degree, helped in the growth of the terrorist movement.

During this period, the British government was reluctant to take the initiative and combat the organisation, thereby allowing Noraid to gather a growing body of support. Only when the threat from Noraid changed from the financial to the political arena did the British take the organisation seriously. As more politicians appeared at the fund-raising dinners, the British government began to consider a propaganda campaign of its own.

154

To some extent, the IRA played into the hands of the British. Its increasingly militant stand, which evolved into the Marxist philosophy of the current leadership, provided a useful tool in the propaganda war. The prospect of a pro-Moscow government in either Dublin or Belfast filled most of the staunchly conservative Irish–Americans with dismay. At the same time, the increasing horror of IRA terrorism, symbolised by the Mountbatten murder, gave the British another propaganda weapon which helped prick the consciences of Noraid supporters.

Most important of all, however, was the ability of the British to convince a traditionally neutral American government to take positive action through the courts, and this has proved to be the turning point in Noraid's affairs. Through purely constitutional methods within the existing structure, the American legal process has brought Noraid to its knees, and it no longer poses a serious political or financial threat to the British fight against terrorism in Northern Ireland. The campaign against Noraid is the first and best illustration of co-ordinated international moves that concentrate on the financing of terrorism. It shows that the elimination of an organisation's monetary sources can have a more direct impact than many years of counter-terrorism, which traditionally concentrates on the gunmen and the bombers rather than on their paymasters.

Britain, the one country besides Israel with a long and bloody record of combating modern terrorism, has, however, learned little as the IRA developed from a bunch of hoodlums into a wealthy and relatively sophisticated terrorist organisation. To understand this failure, it is necessary to examine in detail the development of the IRA mafia in Northern Ireland.

7

The IRA mafia

THE BORDER area between Northern Ireland and the south is known locally as 'bandit country' and is a favourite haunt for local IRA gunmen. For decades the wild border has been a haven for smugglers and bandits of all descriptions. It has hundreds of tiny tracks known only to the locals and is virtually impossible to patrol; the rolling hills, broken by steep crags and narrow defiles, provide perfect concealment. As an old Irish couplet aptly puts it:

> *Ye'll never find an honest man*
> *'Twixt Carrickmore and Crossmaglen.*

With such a perfect area of operations, the IRA have made every effort to claim the border and to deny access to the British army and the local police – the Royal Ulster Constabulary (RUC). They have been partially successful, thereby forcing the British to operate from heavily defended patrol points dotted along the border. The British regularly come under mortar and rifle attack, and their efforts to counter IRA terrorist operations have been hampered by the latter's extensive knowledge of the local terrain and their ability to slip across the border to the south, often only minutes away.

The centre of this isolated area is the tiny village of Crossmaglen, which has the appearance of an armed camp. Access to the border post is by helicopter only, and the buildings are all either sandbagged or have netting strung over them as protection against mortar attack. The IRA regularly open fire on the army in what has become a test of wills between the opposing sides.

A few minutes by helicopter along the rugged border area from the army post at Crossmaglen lies the farm that has become one of the symbols of the British army's impotence, as well as being the IRA's most lucrative source of regular income. The £165,000 ($250,000) farm, its white buildings nestling in the middle of green fields, belongs to Thomas Murphy, known as 'Slab' to his friends from his fondness for dropping concrete blocks on the legs of people he doesn't like. Slab, a burly forty-two-year-old six-footer with a substantial paunch which invariably hangs over baggy trousers, held up by a broad leather belt, lives at Larkins Road, Ballybinaby in County Louth in the Republic, five miles from the only border post in the area that has not been blown up in recent years. Habitually wearing a tweed cap and anorak, he is good-looking with a prominent chin and thin face framed by long, dark sideboards and topped with curly, short, black hair, and with his three brothers, he lives and works at the farm.

For many years, Slab has been the head of one of the IRA's most vicious active service units (ASU) in the border area, which has made dozens of attacks on the security forces. He also is on the northern command of the IRA, which makes him one of the most powerful godfathers in the organisation. However, what vastly increases his value to the IRA is the fact that the main barn on his farm exactly straddles the border between Northern Ireland and the south.

This large corrugated-steel barn, constructed in 1970, has made Slab something of a legend to the police and army and has made him a hero to his colleagues in the IRA. Because of the barn, he is able, through skilful manipulation of currency and Customs regulations, to contribute every year a minimum of £165,000 ($250,000) and, in some years, as much as £2 million ($3 million) to the IRA. In 1985, British intelligence believed that he was contributing £8,000 ($12,000) a week.

For many years, Slab has operated a fairly sophisticated smuggling operation that takes advantage of subsidies offered by the European Economic Community. For example, the Common Market at one time paid farmers in southern Ireland a subsidy of £8 ($12) per animal exported to the United Kingdom, of which Northern Ireland is a part. To operate the swindle, Slab ferried pigs into Ulster from the south and filed subsidy claims at a British Customs post at Newry, County Down, in the north. The pigs were then smuggled back to avoid tax penalties that were levied on livestock taken from the north to the south, and the business was repeated again and again.

Slab's barn serves as a particularly useful tool for the movement of farm stock and other produce subject to different subsidies between north and south. In order to prosecute for this, Customs must prove that

157

the same load is going back and forth, but because the barn actually straddles the border, Slab can always argue in court that the load had been changed in the barn. To date, this argument has prevented the British from taking any action, and they are further hampered by the inaction of the police in the south who, the British believe, are themselves heavily 'subsidised' by the proceeds from Slab's smuggling operations.

When the pig subsidy was abolished, Slab simply converted his operation to grain, currently earning an £12-a-ton ($18) subsidy from the Common Market, payable to the owner when the grain crosses into the south. The produce is smuggled north, and then exported legally into the south, collecting the subsidy along the way. He has also dealt in cattle. In October 1985, the Court of Auditors of the European Common Market produced a report that detailed massive frauds totalling more than £450 million ($700 million) a year. One of the cases that the inspectors studied was that of Slab and his farm. As a result of their investigation, they privately admitted that the cattle in the area were being sent back and forth across the border so regularly that 'they knew the way by themselves'.

Slab's operation is almost constantly observed by British intelligence, often in the form of an undercover team. To prevent any action the British might take against him, Slab has cleared the area around his farm of all hedges and trees that might conceal members of the SAS or other security force undercover teams who are responsible for much of the covert work in the province. In addition, he has built earth ramparts around the farm buildings and erected floodlights to illuminate the area during the hours of darkness. Each evening, Slab or his employees patrol the farm with Alsatian dogs to flush out anyone who might be concealed. As a result, the SAS must operate from a concealed hide on a hillside some distance away.

Despite the level of Slab's contribution to the IRA, he has not been widely exposed as a prominent member of the organisation. The only photograph of him in existence was taken by British intelligence using a 1000 mm lens from an observation post, and his name has never before appeared in print.

Even without publicity, Slab's constant nagging presence has caused some frustration in the security services. For example, in one morning alone, an SAS team watched a load of grain rotating through Slab's barn so fast that they reckoned they had seen him make £17,000 ($50,000) for the IRA coffers. On a second occasion, when another load of grain was making a series of two-way trips, the SAS team determined that there was just a thin load of grain with sand underneath. To prevent this load from passing through again, a two-man army team hid up in a tree and, as the lorry passed underneath, sprayed the load with blue paint.

At a more serious level, various plans have been devised to remove Slab. In 1979, the army proposed sending an SAS snatch squad to take him physically from his barn to the north for trial. However, government lawyers believed that they would be unable to make a case against Slab which would stand up in court, and he was left alone. Later, in 1981, a senior army officer put up a plan to the British high command that involved manufacturing a bomb from materials normally used by the IRA and planting it in the ditch that runs along the track between Slab's house and the barn; as Slab carried out his usual surveillance one morning, the bomb would be detonated. 'The intention was that it would look like an IRA own goal,' recalled one senior army officer involved in the scheme. However, the plan was rejected at army headquarters on the grounds that such extra-legal killings set a dangerous precedent which could result in anarchy in Northern Ireland. At the moment, Slab believes that, if he sets foot in the north, he will be arrested, and as for the British, they prefer to keep him penned up in the south rather than having him roam freely in the north.

British intelligence believe that Slab was previously in charge of the most successful active service unit in the South Armagh area, and personally credit him with ordering the deaths of 104 members of the security forces. The rest of the unit is composed of Patrick Murphy, Slab's brother; Alex Murphy (no relation); Paddy Monaghan; Brendan Mulvenna and another sixteen hard-line terrorists. However, as Slab rose in the IRA ranks, he was forced to hand over the leadership of the ASU and, for some years, concentrated on planning and developing new ways of raising money. As it turned out, the ASU was far less effective without Slab's guiding hand, and in 1985, he was once again asked to take charge of terrorist operations in the area. He did so, and within weeks, security forces noticed an increase in activity.

Partly because of Slab's results, the army have established a secret project known as 'Operation Condor', which is designed to take the initiative from the terrorist by establishing a chain of visible and secret observation posts along commonly used lines of communication between the north and the Republic of Ireland. 'We know everybody and everything that moves in the area, and this has a serious psychological impact on the terrorists,' commented one army officer.

In his more senior capacity, Slab also monitors the activities of those IRA men who have fled from the north to the south. For example, the town of Dundalk, just over the border in the south, as well as being the centre of much of the planning and recruiting for particular murders or robberies in the north, also currently plays host to 300 known IRA members. As all of these men are a drain on the IRA coffers, it is Slab's job to weed out the scroungers from the genuine terrorists.

The various senior army officers who have encountered Slab have a sneaking admiration for him and his operations. All agree that he is a masterly villain who knows his craft, and all concur that he is the most wanted of all the IRA men operating in the border area.

Slab's example has proved an inspiration to others, so that smuggling is now a thriving industry that costs the Dublin government an estimated £100 million ($150 million) a year in lost revenue. In 1983, Irish customs officers made 8,200 seizures or detections of crimes committed – three times as many as four years before – but this was only ten per cent of the total amount estimated to be involved.

Besides the differences in Common Market subsidies, the different tax rates between north and south have helped the criminals. The sales tax (VAT) on luxury goods such as television sets and alcohol is thirty-five per cent in the south compared with fifteen per cent in the north. Local officials believe that, in 1983 alone, 24,000 colour television sets were smuggled illegally into the south.

Customs officials wearily point to the 240 unauthorised crossing points along the 270-mile border, nearly all of them in relatively inaccessible areas. To patrol such vast areas, the Customs have just nineteen mobile teams. Not surprisingly, the Customs prosecuted only forty-seven smugglers in 1983, and these were given such small fines that they would have little deterrent effect on others involved in the trade.

The British army has made various efforts to block the unauthorised crossing points, but all have proved unsuccessful. If the army dynamites the tracks, the IRA either fill in the holes or drive around them. Recently, the army have blocked the roads with huge concrete-filled steel tanks. To counter this, the IRA have simply borrowed earth-moving equipment from the nearest building site, dug huge holes, pushed in the tanks and then resurfaced the tracks.

The situation in the border area resembles an elaborate but deadly game of chess, with the IRA always retaining the initiative. This has led to some frustration among the security forces. In a memorandum dated

September 1981 that has become a legend among the army in Northern Ireland, the officer responsible for border security set out what he saw as the problems of countering the IRA in the area. All of what he says is relevant today as the situation has only changed for the worse. His views provide a fascinating insight into the workings of the military in Northern Ireland and provide a remarkably frank assessment of the threat and capabilities of the IRA. It is worth drawing on the memorandum in some detail as the lessons spelled out in it could equally be applied to almost any country facing a serious terrorist threat: ignore the sources of income to the terrorist and the problem grows in direct relation to the terrorist's ability to exploit society to his financial benefit. The memorandum begins by pointing out that the godfathers, the terrorists, and their active supporters in South Armagh, seem to enjoy a secure and comfortable life, living and operating along and across the border. The officer feels that there is inadequate targeting of the terrorist community and doubts that any master plan or list of priorities exists to unite the efforts of the various security forces operating in the area. He notes that this lack of co-ordination is exacerbated by a lack of will on the part of the government's civil agencies to enforce the law in their own field. Major abuses of laws and regulations are allowed to continue unimpeded, and the terrorists are the first to take advantage of this situation.

Whilst recognising the difficulties facing government officials operating in South Armagh, the officer goes on to say that he feels they are seriously demoralised and indifferent to their duties. He concludes that when the general public can see that the terrorist community grows and prospers illegally and the law enforcement agencies fail to prevent them, they are inevitably led to consider the terrorists as the more powerful influence in their lives. The officer's assessment of the problem is that, while the security forces are handicapped by lack of useful information in advance and hard evidence, in the event, the civil services, who could provide the evidence of many infringements, do nothing about it. 'Were both agents of the state to get together under the aegis of a determined co-ordinator, great progress in the fight against terrorism would be made', he says.

The officer expresses the opinion that the fight against terrorism should involve everyone and that soldiers would be better employed on a specific anti-smuggling operation with a good chance of success, than on a conventional operation dependent on good luck. Such co-operation would achieve three things: the terrorist community would come under pressure and eventually make a mistake; the general public, whether republican in sympathy or not, would be pleased to see 'the leeches on society being targeted and harassed'; and the government would show its will to enforce the rule of the law, thus restoring confidence and normality.

The memorandum concludes with a recommendation for the appointment of a regional co-ordinator who would oversee a common strategy of counter terrorism. 'Short of this, there seems little prospect of increasing significantly the present unimpressive attrition rate against the terrorists in South Armagh.'

The memorandum was endorsed enthusiastically until it reached the then Commander (Land Forces). His response was quite firm: 'I would not like to see it offered to Northern Ireland Office [the civilian arm of the British government in the province] or the RUC. We may not be winning in S. Armagh but it will not help to allow ourselves to once again fall into the error of tearing ourselves apart.'

Throughout the campaign against the IRA, the army has been reluctant to become too closely involved in the political battle. The British army has always stayed clear of political controversy, seeing its role as the impartial executor of government policy, irrespective of which party is in power. This hands-off attitude has considerable benefits in a democracy, because it allows the politicians to run the country without any interference or threat from the armed forces. However, in an environment such as Northern Ireland, the army should play a vital political as well as military role. Their unwillingness to grasp this particular nettle must be partially responsible for the inexorable rise in the power and wealth of the IRA.

The official response to the terrorist threat has been formulated wrongly because of a reliance on the conventional image of the terrorist as an armed hoodlum who (being a simple soul) kills opponents, often with great brutality, and robs banks, usually for small sums of money to live on from day to day. While this view might have been realistic twenty years ago, it is no longer true today.

Inevitably, the terrorists will call the shots in their bid for political power. They make the moves which force the existing establishment to react or, they hope, to over-react. However, unless the counter-terrorist forces can adapt to the changing threat, the terrorists will be in such control that they will become impossible to stop.

When the latest crisis in Northern Ireland began in 1968, the IRA were still in the traditional role of the terrorist: they were primarily bumbling amateurs struggling from day to day, with no money, few clear objectives, a loose command structure and obsolete arms, many of which dated back to the previous 'Troubles' in 1919. However, the old high command quickly gave way and a new generation of terrorists emerged, who were better educated and intelligent enough to realise that, for the IRA to succeed, they would need modern arms, clear aims, a cell structure to avoid penetration by British intelligence and, above all, money, and lots of it.

The IRA's current policy was spelled out in 1977 by Gerry Adams, a senior member of the IRA high command. In a speech on the future of the movement, he argued that, for the IRA to achieve long-term success, the organisation would have to expand and develop its political base, while at the same time continuing its campaign of bombing and assassination. This has now been formally adopted as IRA policy, and is known as 'the ballot paper and the Armalite' strategy or, more collo- quially, 'the ballot and the bullet'.

Adams, almost single-handedly, has moved the IRA on from the ineffectual, faction-ridden terrorist organisation it once was into a militarily effective group with a firm power base in the community in the north. Under his careful guidance, the IRA is, as far as the British government is concerned, more of a political threat now than at any time in its history – despite the fact that terrorism is being contained, and as a military force, the IRA has lost much of its potency. The British security forces have considerable respect for Adams and consider him to be the key to understanding the military strategy of the Provisional IRA and of the IRA's political wing, Sinn Fein. Adams claims that Sinn Fein is entirely independent of the IRA, but the British believe that the two (like the IRA and Noraid) are indistinguishable.

Adams was brought up in Belfast's Ballymurphy housing estate, a bastion of conventional Catholicism, and in the 1960s, while still in his teens, he had an early exposure to sectarianism when Catholics demon- strated *en masse* against the discriminatory housing policies of the Protestant government. According to army sources, he was made Belfast commander of the Provisional IRA while in his early twenties, and in 1971, he was interned by the British government.

The following year, William Whitelaw, then Northern Ireland Secretary, convened a secret meeting between the British government and the IRA. Gerry Adams, then still interned, was flown from jail by helicopter to England. Although nothing significant occurred at the meeting, it was a formative experience for Adams, who realised that the British government could be forced to negotiate.

Over the next few years, Adams moved increasingly towards a hard-left political position, and the policies of Sinn Fein moved with him. Sinn Fein has always been dedicated to a united Ireland, but what the character of that new nation would be has changed from that of a simple republic to that of a state which would owe more to Karl Marx than any other political philosopher.

The following points are central to Sinn Fein's manifesto:

★ All foreign ownership of land would be banned, and any such owners as currently exist would have their land taken from them.

★ All farming land would be run by co-operatives.

★ There would be widespread nationalisation of the main industries and financial institutions; personal ownership of industrial companies would be outlawed.

★ The new country would withdraw from the Common Market and would become allied with the non-aligned states.

★ Outside interference in Ireland's political and religious affairs would be banned, and the import of all foreign material, whether literary or technical, would be strictly controlled.

★ The system of government would become decentralised, with 'people's committees' and 'people's courts' dispensing administration and justice.

The establishment of such a state, which resembles in almost every way the ideals of the Soviet Communist model, causes alarm in Dublin as well as Belfast. Neither north nor south, whatever their other differences, wish to see a united Ireland of the Gerry Adams kind. However, the 'bullet and ballot' strategy has proved so effective that neither country seems to be able to counter it effectively. Adams seems to be a genius at exploiting the weakness of the British government and turning it to his own advantage.

For example, during the hunger strike of March 1981, Danny Morrison, then director of the Sinn Fein publicity machine, suggested that one of the hunger strikers, Bobby Sands, run for a seat in Parliament at Westminster. Adams agreed, and although Sands was in jail at the time, he was elected a British Member of Parliament. The London government reacted by immediately passing a law prohibiting convicted prisoners from putting themselves forward for election to Parliament. When Sands died, Owen Carron, another Sinn Fein nominee, took his place.

Adams himself was elected to Westminster in 1983, although he has not yet taken up his seat. In 1984, he said:

The IRA mafia

> The gun existed before the ballot box campaign because the IRA military campaign was being carried on before Sinn Fein became involved in electoral politics. But the armed struggle meant that a few people carried on the battle and the rest had to be spectators. The political campaign is important not so much because it gets people like me elected, but because it shows the size of Sinn Fein's and the IRA's support. Before that, the IRA was dismissed as 'a tiny group of criminals'. Since we got 103,000 votes at the last election, we've now become a 'Marxist' organisation. What's happened is that we have got the spectators involved.

In fact, for a comparatively fledgling political party, Adams has been remarkably successful at the ballot box. In the 1982 election to the Northern Ireland Assembly, Sinn Fein won 10.1 per cent of the votes; in the 1983 General Election, they won 13.4 per cent; in the 1984 elections to the European Parliament, they won 13.3 per cent; and in the local government elections in 1985, they won 11.8 per cent of the vote. Of the fifty-nine Sinn Fein councillors elected in the 1985 elections, ten had convictions for serious terrorist offences and had, between them, served more than 100 years in jail. All of the offences were committed on behalf of the IRA.

The British government estimate that Adams needs three times as much money to support Sinn Fein's political campaign as he does to operate the IRA as a simple terrorist organisation. For example, the security services estimate that the 1983 General Election campaign in which Adams was elected cost Sinn Fein £1.30 ($2) a vote, or £137,000 ($206,000). This is far higher than is officially allowed under British electoral law, but one of the advantages for terrorist groups turning to the established electoral system is that they already have an underground network in place for moving money illegally between individuals and groups. It is easy to divert that money to fund political campaigns, particularly when you do not feel confined by any moral obligation to obey the law. The amount of underground money they can pour into their political campaigns without official sanction is only limited by the depths of their wallets.

However, despite this, political campaigns can prove to be very costly, and for the IRA, whose political powerbase has been developed only recently, the elections of the last four years have proved a strain on their resources. This has been compounded by joint action of the Irish and US governments.

In February 1985, the Dublin government passed special legislation to seize over £2 million ($3 million) held in a Bank of Ireland account in

165

the Republic. The money had been paid by Associated British Foods after the IRA threatened to carry out a series of kidnaps and bombings in the Irish Republic unless the cash was handed over. It had been transferred from a bank account in Switzerland to the US in May 1984, when an account was opened at the Manhattan office of the Bank of Ireland on Fifth Avenue by a man using a false passport. The same man, who police have been unable to trace, then drew the money out of the account and personally carried it to the Irish Republic, where it was deposited in yet another account, at the Navan branch of the Bank of Ireland.

The Irish government asked the US Customs to help trace the money, and their New York office notified the Irish that a New York bar owner named Alan Clancy appeared to be involved. Clancy, a well-known figure in Noraid circles whose bars are used to collect funds for the organisation, is a staunch Irish Republican who moved from his native Ireland in the 1970s. Joseph Patrick Doherty, a man wanted on terrorist charges in Britain, was arrested in one of Clancy's New York bars in 1983. Irish and US officials learned that Clancy had used his own name to try and get access to the account at the Bank of Ireland in the Republic, and he was still trying to get hold of the money when the government froze the account. He is now under investigation by a grand jury.

Also under investigation is William Burke, senior vice-president of the New York office of the Bank of Ireland and another figure prominent in Irish republican circles. In 1984, he was nominated to the post of grand marshal of the St Patrick's Day parade in New York and came third.

The money was earmarked for the council election campaign of May 1985. The loss of the money led to a bitter internal struggle in the high command of the IRA, with Gerry Adams insisting that money which would otherwise be spent on financing terrorist acts, be diverted for the election fund. The hardliners argued that elections contribute nothing to forcing the British to leave Northern Ireland. The result of the row was that four key hardliners – Ivor Malachy Bell, Anto Murray, Eddie Carmichael and Anne Boyle – were all expelled from the Army Council, the IRA's ruling body.

Despite all the evidence to the contrary, Adams continues to dismiss suggestions that he has been underwriting the election campaigns with money generated through terrorism. When asked where Sinn Fein got their funds, he replied, 'We run cake fairs and things.'

'You have to bear in mind that election campaign money comes entirely from ready cash and it is all new money,' said a senior official in the Northern Ireland Office. The result is that they have been very short of cash and this is likely to get worse.'

To pay for their new and expensive policy of combining violence with participation in elections, the IRA have been forced to revise their tactics away from simple bombing and killing into projects that bring in large sums of money, while at the same time giving them a firm grip on the system they are attempting to undermine and eventually overthrow.

For example, in the early 1970s the Official IRA began conducting a series of frauds on building sites involving tax-exemption certificates, which enabled them to collect the thirty per cent income tax rather than handing it over to the government. A major contractor who obtains a contract from a large organisation normally sub-contracts work to smaller companies such as plasterers and electricians. If a sub-contract is worth, say, £800,000 ($1.2 million) a year, the major contractor would pay the sub-contractor in twelve monthly payments of £66,000 ($100,000). The sub-contractor should then put aside around thirty per cent (the standard rate of income tax in Britain) of his total wages bill, to account for income tax due from his employees.

However, because of the irregular nature of the business, sub-contractors have been given a special concession by the tax authorities – the Inland Revenue – which allows them to pay the tax in one sum at the end of the year, rather than every time they pay their employees, and those sub-contractors who qualify for the concession are supplied with a tax-exemption certificate. Normally, a sub-contractor would supply the major contractor with one of these certificates to establish his legitimacy, thus enabling him to settle his tax account at the end of the financial year.

Unfortunately, forged tax-exemption certificates, originally imported from England and selling for between £3000 ($5000) and £13,000 ($20,000), became and have remained widely available. This has enabled sub-contractors to claim that they, in turn, have passed work to other sub-contractors and can show tax-exemption certificates to prove it. However, when the Inland Revenue attempt to trace the last building company in the chain, they find it does not exist and is often registered in the name of a dead man. The company with the certificate can claim that they acted in good faith and the Inland Revenue have no way of getting their tax money. Because the tax-exemption certificate is generally valid for three years, and the Inland Revenue are not particularly efficient about chasing late payers, one certificate can be used many times for a whole series of frauds.

Although the Official IRA was the first to take advantage of this fraud, the other paramilitary groups quickly followed. To avoid expensive and potentially damaging competition between the different terrorist groups, Belfast has now been divided into sections, with the Official IRA controlling construction in much of the Markets and Shorts area of the city, the Provisionals in the Ardoyne and the INLA in the Poleglass area.

As the scheme has become more popular, so additional refinements have been made by the terrorists. Most building-site workers claim unemployment benefit – 'doing the double' – which enables the paramilitary groups to lower their levels of pay. In fact, most terrorists now insist that any workers employed on the building sites under their control must claim unemployment benefit. This not only blackmails the workers, who effectively become locked into the terrorist employment structure, but it also vastly inflates the profits that each of the underground organisations can make from a particular contract. Additionally, the overall economy is affected because all the people working for the terrorists are officially unemployed. Therefore, several thousand people who actively contribute to a healthy underground economy become part of the depressing official economic statistics.

The Protestant paramilitary organisation, the Ulster Defence Association (UDA), dabbled briefly in the building frauds business at the end of the 1970s, but backed out after they discovered that the vast majority of the building work was taking place in the depressed Catholic areas. Instead of continuing to develop their particular end of the fraud in competition with the IRA, they did what any sensible businessman would do: they made a deal. Regular meetings are held now between the Provisionals and the UDA, resulting in Catholic workers under the control of the Provos working at building sites in UDA-run sections of Belfast, with the Provisionals passing on an agreed percentage of the profits from the fraud to the UDA.

When the authorities, and particularly the police, began to notice the fraud in the mid-1970s, they decided the whole matter was the responsibility of the Inland Revenue, who have their own fraud investigation department. The Revenue later decided that the fraud, judged purely in financial terms, was too small to bother about (at that time, it generated less than £165,000 ($250,000) a year), and no investigation was carried out. Ten years later, the fraud has grown, according to police estimates, into a £40 million ($60 million) a year business, of which the various paramilitary groups, both Protestant and Catholic, take a net annual profit of around £10 million ($15 million).

'Much of the blame for the scale of the frauds lies with the Inland Revenue,' one senior police officer in Belfast has pointed out. 'They accept forged documents late and do nothing to enforce the law. They have consistently taken the view that it is not cost-effective to clamp down in this area. The result has been a mushrooming of the business to the multi-million pound scheme it is now. Their performance is just criminal.'

However, the Inland Revenue is not completely at fault. In the context of tax frauds nationwide, the building-site frauds in isolation may not be that significant, but within the context of the problem of terrorism in Northern Ireland, they take on a whole new dimension. The problem has always been that, in Northern Ireland, civil servants, who are responsible to their political masters in London, have consistently taken a more relaxed view of financial corruption and the financing of terrorism than have their army or police colleagues.

Civil servants, perhaps understandably, are invariably more concerned about the short-term consequences of any particular act or decision and its potential impact on their political masters in London, and thus, they would pay more attention to a rise in overt terrorism such as bombing, assassination or knee-capping. Although combating these problems may be of limited benefit, rather like sticking a finger in the collapsing dyke, there is little long-term impact on terrorism. As a result, on the one hand terrorist acts have been contained, while on the other the influence of terrorist groups has grown enormously over the last ten years. This difference between the perception of civil servants and that of other agencies fighting terrorism has led to a mistrust that, in turn, has led to a lack of co-ordination and differing aims.

The civil servants argue that the police often have a tenuous grasp on reality and wildly exaggerate the nature of the problem. One senior official in the Northern Ireland Office said:

> We have always found it extremely difficult to deal with the police. One week the most important thing might be gaming, but the next week they have moved on to something totally different. It is extremely difficult to get an accurate figure on any particular aspect from them, and indeed we have given up trying to produce figures. Rather, we try and estimate the relevant importance of different rackets.
>
> For example, there was one particular instance where we had an

estimate from the RUC of a racket turning over £10 million ($15 million) a year. Using exactly the same figures as a starting point, intelligence came up with an estimate of £130,000 ($200,000) and we put the figure even lower than that. So we find their figures are often in cloud cuckoo land.

Whatever the nature of the disagreements, the police remain convinced that to combat the terrorist groups an understanding of their financial resources is fundamental. The Northern Ireland Office, on the other hand, have abandoned attempts to evaluate the scale of the terrorist financial underground and no longer keep records on the subject. As the political process produces policy that differs increasingly from the reality as perceived by the police and the army, so the chances of the successful implementation of such policies grow ever more remote.

Of course, the terrorist organisations have taken full advantage of this apparent lack of co-operation and co-ordination. While the civil servants have concentrated on countering the perceived conventional terrorist threat, the IRA's paramilitary groups have been quietly building an enormous and highly effective underground structure which now permeates almost every level of business and industry in Northern Ireland.

The policies of the paramilitary groups, both Protestant and Catholic, have evolved beyond simple terrorism and are designed to exploit existing sectarian divisions while at the same time making the different groups richer and thus broadening their power bases. They have also been able to exploit the paranoia that has resulted from their own activities.

In the early 1970s, the IRA's recruits would normally raise money by selling 'protection' to local shop owners, publicans or industrialists. Typically, this would involve small sums, which had the advantage for the terrorists of being low risk and a regular source of income. As the terrorist business has expanded, however, the type of protection it offers and the cost have expanded as well. Today, while the corner pub might still be contributing around £50 ($75) a week to a particular terrorist group, in the meantime every major business in the province has been sucked into the protection racket. As one senior civil servant said: 'Belfast has got to the stage now where contracts automatically have ten per cent built in on the cost of everything from a pint of beer to window glass for houses, to pay off the paramilitaries.'

Ten years ago, protection would be demanded in a quite

straightforward manner. The gang – typically three or four strong – would march into the premises, brandish a weapon and demand money; if the owner did not pay up, they might break a few windows or beat him up. Today, the whole operation has become much more sophisticated and gentlemanly. Any contractor or business new to an area controlled by one of the paramilitary organisations is approached by representatives of the group concerned, but now the approach is generally made by an apparently legitimate security company that has been established by a terrorist group to provide a legitimate veneer for what remains a simple racket.

For example, the UDA have set up a number of companies – such as Task Point Security based in Donegal Road and Leader Enterprises in East Belfast – that have boards of directors, pay their taxes and in every way act inside the law. Those two companies alone have an annual turnover in excess of £200,000 ($300,000). 'Prospective clients approached by these companies generally accept the offer of services,' said one senior police officer. 'There is no need any more for the terrorists to produce guns or anything, although the prospective client knows full well what sort of trouble may be just around the corner if he doesn't pay up. Without overt threats, it is very difficult for us to prove anything.'

The security companies owned by the UDA run radio-controlled vans and patrol dogs and their 'guards' have uniforms, just like any other security outfit. In fact, they do a good job. In any event, the security control exercised by the terrorists is so strict that little occurs in a particular area without the sanction of the terrorist leaders.

This new and apparently legitimate source of funds has been increasingly popular among the terrorists. The Belfast Yellow Pages, in 1970, list only seven security firms for the city, but today there are more than sixty. Of course, the legitimate security firms have had extraordinary difficulties competing with terrorist-supported ones. Although they may be able to match the price, they do not benefit from the concealed threat of a beating or shooting if a company does not accept their competitor's proffered bid.

That threat is a real one, which the IRA periodically underlines with a salutary killing. At the beginning of August 1985, the Provisional IRA approached Seamus McEvoy, a forty-six-year-old father of six and prominent contractor, who worked in both the south and the north. They demanded an immediate payment of £8000 ($12,000) as protection. He refused. Three weeks later, gunmen came to his home in

Donybrook near Dublin and, when he answered the door, shot him twice in the back of the neck. With the brilliant blurring of politics and economics that is their hallmark, the IRA let it be known that McEvoy had been killed not because he had refused to pay them protection but because he had done some construction work for the Royal Ulster Constabulary.

Terrorism appears to acknowledge its own expertise and to produce its own pecking order. Just as the Protestants have ceded expertise in building-site frauds to the Catholic terrorists, the Catholics have allowed the UDA to dominate the security market. The Provisionals have not yet graduated to operating security companies as fronts, instead allowing the UDA companies to control the security on Catholic sites in exchange for a cut of the profits – a happy arrangement for both parties. It makes the best use of each terrorist group's particular talent while at the same time ensuring that the lines of control in different areas remain clear and that no unseemly battles erupt over the control of territory.

Of course, periodic freelance operations are carried out by the different groups, particularly the INLA, which tends to go its own way instead of co-operating willingly with other groups. For example, just before Christmas 1983, when the INLA was short of money, they approached three different restaurants and nightclubs with a demand for £2000 ($3000) from each to fill the coffers. All their demands were met. However, such incidents have become increasingly rare as the protection business has acquired a semi-legitimate air.

One of the reasons the security firms have been successful is the climate of terror established by the terrorist groups. Apart from simple shootings and bombings, they have attacked property and people, as well as carrying out robberies to produce the cash needed to finance their activities. In 1984, the police noticed a disturbing new level of co-operation between Protestant and Catholics. Regular meetings are now held in a pub on the Shankhill Road in Belfast (where Catholics would normally be shot), with the purpose of assigning areas of Belfast to various Protestant and Catholic paramilitary groups. The two sides generally co-operate on robberies involving £50,000 ($75,000) or more. A typical plan might include the INLA robbing a business in a UDA area and the UDA agreeing to dispose of the stolen goods, or the UDA might rob a warehouse in Provisional territory and the Provos will help fence the proceeds. Such a division of labour makes the police's job virtually impossible because their normal sources of inside information generally do not cross the religious divide. The organisations also exchange intelligence information such as the registration numbers of unmarked police cars or the locations of police or army surveillance units.

However, as the protection business has blossomed in the north, there has been a general tendency for the terrorists to move south over the border to rob shops and banks. In part, this is a result of the lower security and a less efficient police force in the south, but the terrorists understandably have become reluctant to jeopardise their own regular, highly lucrative income from the protection business. After all, they can hardly demand money for providing protection and then rob the premises they are supposed to be guarding. Even amidst the chaos in Northern Ireland, this would be a little difficult to accept.

As the terrorist organisations – and particularly the Provisionals, the most politically sophisticated of them – find new ways of making money and thereby increase their income, they are forced to find new outlets for their cash. As Al Capone and the Mafia discovered, one of the problems with earning large amounts of ready cash is the need to get the notes back into circulation, a task that is not as easy as it might seem. The Mafia established seemingly legitimate cash businesses such as laundries (hence the term 'laundering') and rubbish disposal. The IRA have chosen taxis and clubs to launder their cash.

Once the IRA made the decision to move into the taxi business in 1972, the high command proceeded to eliminate the competition. A sustained campaign was launched against the city-run bus system, and buses were systematically stoned and firebombed. The media portrayed this as the repressed Catholics of Belfast expressing their frustrations through aggressive actions. In fact, it was the IRA clearing the way for their own transport operation. Citybus, which operates the transport system in Belfast, had to retire more than 300 buses at a cost of nearly £10 million ($15 million) so that the IRA could sustain their monopoly on transport in the Catholic areas. Without the buses, the city loses £2 million ($3 million) a year in revenue.

In June 1972, the IRA's first consignment of five second-hand black cabs arrived from London. Within three months, 600 cabs were operating and the buses had been driven off the road. The IRA's taxi network consists of two cab companies operating as fronts for the organisation. They employ eighteen full-time workers, own two garages and an interest in a tyre company; all told, the companies claim assets in excess of £1 million ($1.5 million).

The IRA's taxi companies, Falls Taxis and People's Taxis, together have around 350 cabs and employ 800 drivers. Each driver pays £35 ($50) a week to be a member of the Taxi Drivers Association and contributes £500 ($750) a year for group insurance which is organised centrally by the Association. When the cabs first began to operate, no attempt was made to licence them or to comply with the law requiring insurance. However, the government introduced legislation that has forced the cabs to become more legitimate. They are now insured through their own company and have become reinsured through the legitimate market at Lloyd's in London.

The IRA control all aspects of the taxi business. The cab drivers generally rent their cabs from Provisional companies, have them repaired at a Provo garage and buy their fuel from Provo diesel stations. Such control over the city's transport is also useful to the Provisionals for the movement of guns and assassins around the city.

No one doubts that the cabs provide a useful social service and are popular with local residents. 'Should the government try to introduce legislation to outlaw black cabs,' one government official commented, 'there would be a massive hostile response from the people as they give a better service than the buses. You can make them comply to legal requirements but apart from that, there is damn all you can do.'

However, with the improving security situation and the abolition of the 'no-go' areas established by the terrorists, which barred police and security forces from entering some Catholic enclaves, some buses do now operate in Catholic areas. This competition has eliminated much of the profit that the Provisionals were making from the cabs. 'They are not prepared to put their prices up to match the buses as they have taken a decision that what they are providing is a service to the community and, as such, they should continue to subsidise it if possible,' a police officer explained.

With their eye on the main chance, the Protestants swiftly followed the Provo's example, and now, under the auspices of the North Belfast Mutual Association, the Ulster Volunteer Force (UVF) operates around ninety cabs in the Shankhill Road and Shore Road areas of Belfast. Officially, the cab drivers pay the Association £1.50 ($3) a week to cover administration costs, and if they buy their diesel from the Association, they save an additional £150 ($225) a year in insurance premiums. However, at a March 1983 trial in Belfast, it was alleged that, when a person applied to operate a black cab, he had to pay an 'unofficial' initial fee of £90 ($135) and a weekly sum of £30 ($45). The taxis were also suspected of acting as a collection agency for people paying protection money to the UVF. Each driver was charged with bringing in between £3500 ($5000) and £4000 ($6000) each week for the UVF coffers.

While the cabs may not be enormously profitable for either the Protestants or the Catholics, they have made the different terrorist groups acceptable parts of the society that they have set out to destabilise.

In the autumn of 1972, two senior members of the IRA, Seamus Loughran and Gerry Maguire – at that time interned by the British government in Cage 4 of the Maze prison – developed the idea of establishing a co-operative which could act as a conduit for IRA funds earned by other means, and could also serve as a potential profit centre for apparently legitimate business activities. To raise the necessary £4000 ($6000) to start the venture they apparently sold wooden harps, Celtic mementoes and imitation guns that they made in the prison and sold outside. This romantic ideal of prisoner rehabilitation created an attractive picture, but IRA-generated funds from protection and robbery also helped produce early seed money.

With the help of lawyers, in order to comply with existing legislation, the IRA established the Andersonstown Co-operative Industrial and Provident Society in 1972, and its first purchase was the Glen Ten butcher's shop in Andersonstown. The co-op's executive committee was composed entirely of men who had been interned by the British government as suspected members of the IRA, with Maguire as chairman and Loughran as secretary, both of whom were on the Brigade staff of the Provisional IRA in Belfast.

The co-op expanded with the establishment of a construction business, and they then bought a supermarket in Andersonstown for which they paid over £750,000 ($1 million). Next the co-op bought a house at No. 5 Andersonstown Road (for a headquarters), and purchased the Suffolk Inn in the same area for £130,000 ($200,000). Like any other business, they applied for a bank loan. The Ulster Bank, their normal bankers, turned them down, but the Allied Irish Bank advanced them a loan of £100,000 ($150,000).

Over the next two years, they bought land on the corner of Suffolk and Glen Roads, and applied for planning permission to build five shops and a playground. This project never got off the ground, but they did buy a nearby engineering factory after the owner had been shot during an attempted robbery.

At its sales outlets, such as the pub and the butcher's shop, the co-op kept the prices of its goods much lower than the market rate because the organisers of the scheme viewed the co-op as a social service. Others believed that the IRA wanted to gather support in the Catholic areas of Belfast, and to change their image of simple gunmen, uninterested in the future of the people they claimed to represent, into one of caring and concerned community leaders.

The co-op helped the local people by passing on some of the benefits of their cost-effective operation. This was financed in part through lucrative contracts won from the housing executive, a local government organisation responsible for the construction and maintenance of housing in the area, and which decided which tenants would be allocated which property. Incredibly, a British government-sponsored body was responsible for giving work to the Andersonstown Co-op in a misguided attempt to give maintenance work to local firms. For reasons that have never been made clear, the housing executive failed to appreciate what the police and the army knew: the co-op was simply an IRA front. The housing executive were therefore instrumental in contributing thousands of pounds to the IRA at a crucial period in their development. In 1975, for example, the co-op was awarded a contract to repair some flats in the Moyard area of West Belfast. Within three months, the average price for repairs had soared from £1350 ($2000) per unit to between £8000 ($12,000) and £10,000 ($15,000).

Wherever possible, the IRA have tried to turn their money-making schemes to political advantage, and the co-op was no exception. Their involvement with the housing executive ensured an effective intelligence network within that organisation. In the late 1970s and early 1980s, the executive was responsible for providing subsidised council housing for working-class people in Belfast. Housing is permanently at a premium there, with some tenants waiting years to be moved from slums to more modern housing. Using their sources inside the executive, the IRA would learn which houses were ready for occupation and which family had been offered the property. If the family were not Catholic IRA supporters, the night before they were due to move in the Provisionals would bring in a family of their own supporters who could then claim squatters' rights. The IRA won a number of friends among the Catholics as they gained a formidable reputation as an independent and effective housing agency, able to get things done despite the bureaucracy of the executive.

The army became alarmed by the IRA's successes which encouraged a Protestant backlash. The army set up a special squad which staked out all houses that were about to be occupied by housing executive tenants;

when the IRA showed up with their chosen family, they were arrested. The scheme soon became too expensive for the IRA and they abandoned it.

The co-op caused the security forces and the British government some concern, each viewing it as a more serious long-term threat to the province's stability than that posed by the gunmen. The co-op was the subject of several highly critical newspaper articles, and one that appeared in *The Sunday Times* in 1975 resulted in Maguire and Loughran suing the newspaper for libel and the co-op suing for defamation. After sixteen days of evidence, the jury retired to consider their verdict on the morning of 24 October 1979. An Ulster policeman, strategically positioned underneath an open window of the juryroom, heard them make up their minds within half an hour; however, for form's sake and to avoid being accused of bias, they waited six more hours before announcing their decision.

The jury dismissed the libel case, concluding that the two men 'were guilty of illegal activities, including robbery, fraud, and intimidation, that they associated with terrorists and were responsible for keeping irregular accounts, and that they sought to enrich themselves and their relatives by means of the criminal activities referred to in the article.' However, the jury did find that the Andersonstown Co-op had been defamed when the article alleged that it had been a front for the Provisional IRA, and the co-op was awarded £200 ($300) damages, a paltry sum given the gravity of the allegations.

The publicity generated by the libel case damaged the co-op considerably. Its reputation as a legitimate business, which had always been questionable, was ruined, and any lucrative government contracts it had dried up. It was eventually wound up in 1982 with debts of £60,000 ($90,000).

The co-op didn't actually make any money for its members, and given the mismanagement of other business activities in which the IRA have been involved, the co-op was most likely a consistent drain on resources. Terrorists are extremely good at using their muscle to beg, to steal or to borrow but do not operate as well in a semi-legitimate way (with the exception of the protection companies). When they have to file accounts and turn in a regular profit, they are less effective.

This may change in the future as a younger and better-educated recruit is drawn into the Provisional's ranks, attracted by the Marxist dreams of leader Gerry Adams. Unlike most terrorist organisations, the Provos are unusual in that they have attracted few middle-class recruits.

The group's working-class origins have resulted in a distinctive bias towards working-class business activities.

The most successful of the terrorists' business ventures, which perfectly combined the need to make money with social influence, was the development of the drinking clubs. As lawlessness began in Belfast at the beginning of the 1970s, a large number of illegal drinking clubs – or *shebeens* as they are known locally – sprang up all over the city. This was due partly to local demand for cheap liquor and partly to the terrorists' need to recirculate hot money while, at the same time, providing a social service. Most of the breweries paid the IRA for protection and were willing to supply drink at cut-rate prices in return for protection for the pubs they controlled and for their distribution warehouses. The shebeens in Belfast and elsewhere in the province were, almost without exception, run by members of different terrorist organisations, either Protestant or Catholic. For example, on the Falls Road, the Provisionals controlled the Sweety Bottle, Dr Hook's and the Zebra Crossing, while the Official IRA ran the Cracked Cup and the Long Bar.

Belfast rapidly took on the air of Chicago during Prohibition, except that there was little attempt to conceal the existence of these new speakeasies from the authorities. Eventually, under pressure from the British government, the police moved in and in a series of raids during 1977, shut down large numbers of shebeens (one was even found operating in an abandoned bus).

The breweries were beginning to pay heavy penalties for their earlier co-operative attitude. The terrorists were hopeless businessmen, and some breweries were owed as much as £750,000 ($1 million) by individual clubs. A united front of brewery owners forced the club managers to adopt a more business-like approach, beginning with the club managers paying their bills on time.

The paramilitary groups began to work inside the law, and some even applied for licences to operate publicly. The government found this perfectly acceptable because legitimate front men were apparently used. In 1983 nearly 600 members-only clubs were registered, with 254,270 members who bought over £27 million ($40 million) worth of drinks.

The police regularly inspect the clubs' books and each must file annual returns, but these give no indication either of a club's affiliation or of the amount of money creamed off to help finance the paramilitary groups. The illegal drinking clubs have almost entirely disappeared – police estimate that the Provisionals currently operate only ten in

Belfast – and the legal clubs have taken over the social role previously performed by the pubs, which are much more casual, welcoming customers off the street, and have been hard-hit by the expansion of the clubs.

The terrorist groups have operated the clubs within the law, although they often have placed their own illegal slot machines alongside those that may legitimately line the walls of a club. Along with the coercion that gets the machines into the clubs in the first place comes an agreement from the club management that the Provos or the UVF will receive all the proceeds from the machines. Since the police estimate that one machine can net £27,000 ($40,000) a year, this means that the terrorists make far more from slot machines than they ever did from Noraid.

The headquarters of Sinn Fein social life in Belfast is the Pound Lovey bar, where £500,000 ($750,000) was spent on refurbishing the bar and building, which includes a twelve-table snooker hall. The Pound Lovey is only one of twenty-two such bars in West Belfast that owe their allegiance to the IRA.

The increasing involvement of terrorists in organised crime first alarmed the British government seriously following a secret Northern Ireland Office study prepared in February 1983 which listed, in order of priority, the sources of finance for the Provisional IRA:

Covert
1 Bank robberies in the north and south
2 Extortion
3 Tax exemption frauds
4 Gaming machines

Overt
1 Clubs, social functions, shops, direct collections and subscriptions
2 Overseas sympathetic contributions

Although the figures for robberies in north and south have not been collated, in 1984 in Northern Ireland there were 622 armed robberies where £830,258 ($1.2 million) was stolen, compared with 359 robberies the previous year when £413.891 ($6 million) was stolen. Other statistics are less clear as no official figures are collected and it is often difficult to distinguish between terrorist activity and simple crime.

Some protection rackets, for example, are run in the name of the

PIRA but the money never reaches the organisation's accountant either because it is siphoned off by corrupt terrorists or because the gang involved have no involvement with PIRA. But police sources suggest that tax exemption frauds account for £40 million ($60 million) of business a year and drinking clubs sold more than £30 million ($45 million) of drinks in 1984. By comparison, contributions from supporters overseas and money raised from social events played a relatively small part in the funding of terrorist groups.

When the February 1983 report reached the Secretary of State for Northern Ireland, Jim Prior, it was agreed that a rackets squad would be formed in the RUC; that the Department of Health and Social Security would be encouraged to report frauds; and that tougher gaming laws would be introduced.

The rackets squad, designated officially C19 but known locally as the 'Al Capone squad', forms the centre of a new campaign against terrorism, but C19 consists of only fifteen members and two supervisors. Although they have had limited success, it is difficult to see how they will combat effectively a terrorist network which now permeates every level of Northern Ireland business.

In a parliamentary written answer on 16 February 1984, Jim Prior revealed the latest statistics on the security situation in the province. In 1971, there had been 1756 shooting incidents and 1022 explosions; in 1983, there were 290 shooting incidents and 266 explosions. This appears to be a great improvement, and any reduction in the killing and maiming in the province is indeed welcomed. However, the robbery figures are not as encouraging: in 1971, there had been 437 armed robberies and £273,300 ($410,000) had been stolen; in 1983, there were 622 armed robberies and £830,258 ($1.2 million) was stolen. These figures greatly increase if robberies in the Republic are also included. While terrorist activity has decreased substantially if viewed in conventional counter-terrorist terms (e.g. killings, shootings and bombings), an overall and disturbing increase has occurred in other areas not normally seen as purely terrorist activity.

Sir John Hermon, the Chief Constable of the RUC, said in his annual report for 1983 'Republican and Loyalist paramilitary organisations have established a lucrative foothold in criminal racketeering which, if not eradicated, will become a pernicious feature of the social and economic life of our community.'

*   *   *

British intelligence estimates that around 200 IRA men are currently on the run, and that the organisation can muster about 70–100 men for active service units. At any one time, no more than 100 people are actively involved, and another 200 may be on call to provide transport or a safe-house. Other groups, such as the INLA or the UVF, are much smaller and would not pose a significant threat if the IRA were no longer around.

Pitted against the terrorists are the 8000 members of the RUC along with 2000 reservists, combined with the might of the British army, British intelligence and the covert activities of the SAS. The British government currently spends just under £4 million a day in subsidies and fighting terrorism. In addition, the governments in London and Dublin have tried repeatedly to find a political solution to the problem. As a senior official close to Jim Prior said in a 1984 interview, any political solution in Northern Ireland with the aim of eliminating terrorism is pointless. 'They [the terrorists] are just too rich, too powerful and too much a part of Northern Ireland society.' The blame for this state of affairs must rest in large measure with the politicians who are responsible for adjusting to changing circumstances and dictating new policy. In combating the IRA, little attempt has been made to recognise an evolutionary process in terrorism.

In the late 1960s, the IRA was largely a bunch of old and idealistic republicans, many of whom had grown up as young men during the Troubles of the 1920s. They were poorly equipped and had little ambition beyond a united Ireland. Between then and today, a new generation of leaders has emerged that bears little relation to the old guard. Led by Gerry Adams, they are mostly extremely bright and dedicated revolutionaries who would like to see a united and Marxist Ireland, a prospect as worrying to the democratically elected government in Dublin as it is to the British government in Westminster. These new leaders believe that revolution can be achieved through a combination of armed might and economic subversion, which would tie down large numbers of the enemy while at the same time funding the revolution and involving the mass of the people in it.

While the counter-terrorist forces of the RUC and the British government have been concentrating on killing or capturing IRA leaders, the IRA have quietly and most effectively built a revolutionary infrastructure based on economic subversion. In the process the division between terrorism and pure crime has become blurred, and some terrorism is actually simple criminal activity and vice versa.

181

However, the basic message remains the same: economic terrorism has made for wealthy terrorists. The money that the IRA now have at their disposal has enabled the organisation to begin funding a network of advice centres across the country and to fight in local and general elections. This in turn will extend their power base and produce a situation similar to that which occurred in the United States after Prohibition, when known gangsters gained public office. The difference is that the gangsters in Chicago wanted power and money; in Northern Ireland, the gangsters are interested in power and changing society.

Even though the IRA have developed their financial resources, they remain constantly short of money. This is explained in part by the breadth of their ambition, which always outstrips their income, but it is primarily due to the fact that the organisation lacks financial control. The income collected in the terrorist coffers is far more than what they actually spend. This apparent discrepancy puzzles both the security forces and the IRA leaders. According to one senior British army officer who regularly reads the daily transcriptions of all the telephone taps in Northern Ireland, 'The biggest question asked by IRA leaders of each other concerns the vanishing cash. They don't know the answer and neither do we, although we suspect much of it is simply spent on drink.' Or, as another officer put it, 'The money is pissed against the walls of West Belfast.'

If the security forces had devoted as much energy to monitoring the economic development of the IRA as was given to countering more conventional terrorism, much could have been done to prevent their inexorable rise. The tax-exemption frauds could have been stopped before they were out of control, gaming laws to require annual notification of ownership and tax returns would not have taken seventeen years to be passed into law, and the law regarding licensing of security companies would have been enforced.

Two outstanding problems remain, which until they are resolved will prevent any lasting solution to the problem of terrorism in Northern Ireland: the role of the Dublin government and the lack of co-operation between the different security forces in Northern Ireland.

An absolute rule of terrorism is that, to survive, a terrorist group must have the sanctuary of a friendly country bordering the country in which the struggle is taking place. The Irish Republic provides exactly that sanctuary for the IRA.

The Dublin government has consistently been unwilling to take firm action against known IRA terrorists or to police the border between the two countries effectively. Therefore, the IRA have a bolt-hole where they are safe. The 200 terrorists and 400 associates and family members living in Dundalk in the Republic illustrate the failure of Anglo-Irish co-operation in this respect. However, the Dublin government is beginning to recognise that a Marxist IRA, which seeks power through violence, may be as much of a threat to their democratic values as they are to Belfast. As a result, the sharing of intelligence between London and Dublin and cross-border co-operation have greatly increased. The Anglo-Irish treaty, which was signed in November 1985, places great emphasis on joint efforts to counteract terrorism. The two governments have pledged to improve security co-operation along the border and to share intelligence on a more regular basis.

For the British to leave the north before the IRA is defeated would be a serious mistake and would almost certainly lead to a civil war in the north which would inevitably engulf the south. Indeed, current political and security assessments suggest that, in the absence of the British army, the Protestants, who are better trained and better armed than any other group in Ireland, would be forced to march south on Dublin. They would take the city and establish a Protestant – not a Catholic – united Ireland. This may be unduly alarmist, but it is a prospect that does not fill the Dublin government with much joy.

To persuade the Dublin government to act, the British themselves will have to be more effective against the IRA. Efforts to combat terrorism in the province have been hampered by the lack of co-operation between politicians, army and police, each interpreting his or her role differently. In particular, a crucial difference on the ground exists between the police and the army: the army want to kill terrorists, and the police wish to maintain law and order. These are not necessarily the same aims, and to date, the two groups have been unable to co-ordinate their policies.

In response to the bombing of the Grand Hotel in Brighton by the IRA in October 1984, aimed at the Prime Minister Margaret Thatcher, the British government established a new committee to co-ordinate intelligence. Nicknamed 'TIGER' ('Terrorist Intelligence Gathering Evaluation and Review'), the committee's purpose is to provide some overview of the information gathered about the IRA. However, this is a further example of the government's short-term and short-sighted approach to tackling the problem.

The key to destroying the IRA is to attack their economic base and to expose the corruption that is a feature of all terrorist activity. More than ten years have gone by since the IRA recognised that money was the key to their future political success. The British government must react to these changes before it is too late.

Part Four

KIDNAP AND RANSOM

8

The snatch business

Signor Ciro Cirillo, a senior politician in Italy's Christian Democrat party and the man charged with masterminding the reconstruction of the Naples area following the devastating earthquake of November 1980, took seriously the threats made against his life by members of Italy's Red Brigade terrorist group. He varied his route to and from work, and apart from his chauffeur, he always travelled with an armed guard. However, the precautions he took were hopelessly inadequate against the superior will and firepower of the Naples cell of the Red Brigade.

Returning from work on the evening of twenty-seventh April 1981, he was about to open the front door of his house when a car pulled up outside, shot dead both his chauffeur and his bodyguard and bundled Cirillo into the back of the car. He was driven away to a secret location where he was held for eighty-eight days.

The Red Brigade intended that the kidnapping of Cirillo – as well as increasing their own assets – could be used as a political gesture to win support among the Naples underprivileged. In their preliminary communiqués, the group demanded that, in return for Cirillo's release, the government should increase payments to the earthquake victims, put more money into the rebuilding programme and pay unemployment benefit to those who had been put out of work by the disaster. They also demanded the payment of an undisclosed ransom.

When negotiations between the Red Brigade and the government appeared to stagnate, a fellow Christian Democrat decided to approach Raffaele Cutolo, boss of the leading faction of the Naples Camorra, the mainland equivalent of the Sicilian Mafia. Although in jail, Cutolo wielded enormous influence and still effectively ran the Camorra.

As evidence of his status, while in jail Cutolo is attended by a valet, who supplies him with champagne and choice delicacies from local delicatessens, and there is a private phone line into his cell. Cutolo's carefully coiffed, wavy dark hair and fashionable gold-rimmed spectacles are a familiar sight on Italian television, as 'The Professor' is sought out for his views on crime and criminals. With a stylish flourish of crimson wax, Cutolo always stamps his letters with the circular 'RC' on his gold signet ring. He has almost unlimited power in Naples and the surrounding areas and, according to the Italian police, commands the loyalty of some 5000 men in an organisation that, as a Naples police chief put it, has 'greater power and turnover than General Motors'.

In negotiations attended by members of the Italian secret service and senior members of the Christian Democrat party, Cutolo demanded a slackening of police activities against his band, a reduction of his own sentence and a new psychiatric test to show that he was not responsible for his actions. This last clause would have resulted in him being transferred to the hospital from which he had escaped in 1979, when dynamite was used to blast an exit route. A final demand suggested that the Camorra, always rather more business-orientated than the simple terrorist, should receive many of the building contracts relating to the earthquake reconstruction programme.

Using his considerable influence with the Red Brigade, Cutolo was able to negotiate the payment of a ransom that the Red Brigade happily announced was around $1 million, which was to be used for the financing of future actions. What the world was not told was that the ransom had in fact been nearer to $2 million and that it had mostly been paid by the Christian Democrats, who thus undermined their own avowed policy of not dealing with terrorists. Raffaele Cutolo and the Camorra pocketed the balance for acting as middlemen.

Interestingly, one part of this deal seems to have been an agreement by the Camorra that, for their $1 million commission, they would assassinate a number of people designated by the Red Brigade. This is the first known example of co-operation between what was essentially purely a criminal organisation and a terrorist group that is ostensibly dedicated to the overthrow of the established order.

Signor Cirillo was released on 24 July 1981. He was found soon after six a.m., in the doorway of an uninhabited block of flats in Poggioreale, outside Naples, opposite the rubble of a high-rise building that had collapsed in the earthquake. He was thin and shaken but otherwise unharmed.

The sums paid out in the Cirillo kidnapping were not that unusual, and the way the Red Brigade's share was later distributed fell into a pattern that is fairly standard among terrorist groups. The Red Brigaders are somewhat pedantic about book-keeping – an unusual trait for terrorists, who tend to have no concept of effective financial management – and through account books that have been seized and the confessions of captured terrorists, it is possible to build up a fairly detailed picture of how the cash was eventually spent.

According to Carlo Alemi, the investigating magistrate in charge of the case, almost all of the money was spent by the Red Brigade within a year. After the kidnap, the cash was immediately divided up by the leader of the Naples cell, Giovanni Senzane, who had been passed the Red Brigade's portion of the ransom in a suitcase on a Naples city bus by a member of the Camorra. The money appears to have been apportioned equally between the Naples, Milan and Rome sections of the Red Brigade, with each section head responsible for handing out smaller sums to members. 'Being on the run, as most of the Red Brigaders were at this time, is an extremely expensive operation,' explained Judge Alemi. 'We have accounted for all the money with the exception of around $118,000. The ransom disappeared into a thousand different rivulets.'

At the time the ransom was paid over, salaried members of the terrorist group were paid between $176 and $470 a month, depending on status. It is a fact that, in every terrorist group around the world, there are very few examples of highly paid staff. This is more a function of their financial incompetence than any political or philosophical reluctance to accept larger sums. The IRA, for example, pay their hired gunmen less than £100 ($150) a week, the sort of sum that no self-respecting American gangster would consider as a daily retainer.

The ransom money was divided into bundles of $100,000 to $200,000 and handed to trusted lieutenants of the group. There was no attempt to invest it in bank deposits. On the contrary, the cash was always hidden under beds, beneath false floorboards or carried in briefcases when a member was travelling from one safe-house to another.

While two fairly large sums of money were spent by the Naples cell to buy two safe-houses in the suburbs of the city, the remainder appears to have been frittered away. Vincenzo Stoccoro, then a twenty-nine-year-old member of the cell, spent between $3000 and $4000 having major dental work done. He had at least ten teeth implanted with metal screws, and was subsequently known by the Naples cell as 'Iron Jaws'. Natalia Ligas, then twenty-three years old, had a reputation as one of the most

189

ferocious members of the Red Brigade, and had been involved in a number of murders and kidnaps since dropping out of the Faculty of Sociology at Rome university. With her share of the Cirillo cash, she went off for a month's holiday to the island of Capri. Such extravagance was evidently not held against her since, after the arrest of Giovanni Senzane, she took over from him as leader in Naples. Another Red Brigade couple bought a modest flat for $18,000, and spent $3500 on furnishings. They were then married in church and, with the remainder of their share of the proceeds, were able to afford an elaborate wedding reception.

Although the Red Brigade emerged from the revolutionary catalyst of 1968 and have survived, they appear to have developed financial resources that have little in common with those of other groups and, unlike the latter, in many respects they have retained a degree of political purity. There is corruption and extravagance, but certainly nothing on the scale of the PLO or the IRA. Instead, rather like the government of Italy itself, the terrorists appear to live something of a hand-to-mouth existence.

The original founders of the Red Brigade came from an 'historic nucleus' of former Catholic students in the sociology department of the University of Trento. They were inspired and led by Renato Curcio and his wife Margherita Cagol, who had both, like their followers, had a traditional middle-class Catholic upbringing until they had chosen the revolutionary path during the student unrest of 1968. (Curcio was later sentenced to a thirty-one-year prison sentence for forming the Red Brigade; Cagol was killed in 1975 during a gun battle with police.) The objectives of the BR (*Brigate Rosse*, or Red Brigade) is to 'mobilise, to extend, and to deepen the armed initiative against the political, economic and military centres of the imperialist state of the multinationals'. To achieve this aim, the BR believed it was necessary to 'develop and unify the Offensive Proletarian Resistance Movement'.

The 'historic nucleus' gained its intellectual strength from Curcio, but it was a fellow student from the University of Trento, Giorgio Semeria, who provided the brilliant logistics and lean structure that was to prove so difficult for Italy's counter-terrorist forces to penetrate. The BR was organised on a cell structure, with each cell having five members and only one member of each cell knowing the contact in another cell. The cells formed into pyramid structures known as 'columns', which were established in all the major Italian cities, including Milan, Rome, Turin and Genoa.

In the mid-1970s the original 'historic nucleus' gave way to a second generation of activists who were both less intellectual and more violent than their predecessors. According to one expert on the Red Brigade, Vittorfranco S. Pisano, the activities of the BR can be divided into four phases.

From 1969 to 1972, while the 'historic nucleus' held sway, the operations of the BR were largely confined to the production of revolutionary propaganda. There were a few, very tentative attempts at violence, but these were generally limited to fairly feeble acts of sabotage in local factories and the fire bombing of cars belonging to senior figures in the police and judiciary.

As all terrorist groups have discovered, such limited action achieves very little; the group is a minor irritant and nothing more. Perhaps more importantly, it does not merit coverage in the press, which is the lifeblood of all terror groups. As a result of their failure to achieve even notoriety, from 1972 to 1974 BR's actions were stepped up and the first of the political kidnappings occurred.

Kidnapping had already proved to be an effective terrorist weapon in Latin America, and it is hardly surprising that Italy's terrorists should adopt this tactic for themselves. Sicily, the reputed headquarters of the Mafia, has for many years had a justified reputation as a kidnapping centre, although here there is no political motive and the kidnaps are undertaken simply to generate income. The Red Brigade quickly discovered that political kidnapping produced not only hard cash but also a great deal of very welcome publicity.

From 1974 to 1976, the second generation took over from the 'historic nucleus', and while they carried on with the kidnaps, they also embarked on a campaign of savage terrorism which included regular assassinations of public figures and the knee-capping of enemies.

The latest phase seems to have been instigated once the terrorists felt that they held the initiative in their war against the government. This has been very bloody, and at one time it looked as if law and order would collapse in Italy. However, there have been some striking successes against the BR, particularly with the capture and imprisonment of many of their leaders. Even so, the Italian government has been unable to find an effective and lasting method of eliminating the problem of left-wing terrorism.

Kidnapping for ransom remains the Red Brigade's favoured method of raising cash. They have consistently found it the most painless way of generating income, and their techniques are so refined that there is very little risk attached. This has not been lost on other terrorist groups or on the business community, both of whom have moved to take advantage of an obviously lucrative business.

Apart from the possibility of earning large sums, kidnap and ransom has an attendant political spin-off: a large number of the terrorists' targets have been Western businessmen, often representatives of foreign companies, who can be portrayed as symbols of international capitalism. Corporations are understandably very sensitive about the safety and security of their employees and invariably wish to be seen to be doing everything possible to secure their release. Less subject to the pressures of international opinion or the broader considerations of national policy, corporations tend to pay the ransom money, thus ensuring that they, or other similar targets, will be targeted again, and that next time the terrorist group will have enough money to do the job properly.

The publicity that goes with the kidnapping of a senior executive is, of course, an enormous bonus to a terrorist group, who become more widely known and, if they have chosen their target skilfully, may gain considerable kudos among the working class that they invariably claim to represent.

According to the US State Department's Office for the Combating of Terrorism, between the years 1968 and 1982 there were 409 kidnappings involving 951 hostages. Kidnappers escaped with their hostages in more than eighty per cent of the incidents, and collected ransoms in more than seventy per cent of the cases in which ransoms were demanded. Kidnapping attacks resulted in thirty-six deaths (including seven US citizens) and sixty-two woundings (including eleven US citizens).

Since 1968, kidnappers have operated in more than seventy-three countries, but Europe and Latin America are the most popular venues, with US businessmen – generally employees of multinational corporations – as the favourite targets. During this time, it is estimated that terrorists have been paid ransoms totalling $350 million, with US-based corporations paying in excess of $150 million.

In 1974, the Exxon Corporation went down in history for paying $14.2 million to Marxist guerrillas in Argentina for the release of Victor E. Samuelson, one of their executives – the largest single ransom so far paid by a US corporation. The $60 million paid for the release of brothers Juan and Jorge Born, who owned the grain-exporting firm of Bunge & Born and were held by the Monteneros in Argentina, remains the all-time record. In addition to the cash, which was paid by the brothers' firm in 1974, the terrorists insisted that the company distribute food and clothing worth $1 million, and install busts of the late President Peron and his wife Eva in all the firm's factories.

Almost every single terrorist organisation of any credibility has, at one time or another, kidnapped individuals, and all have done so with some success. It is extraordinarily difficult to isolate individuals from kidnap attempts. Generally, the kidnappers are quite prepared to use extreme violence, to gun down any guards or indeed anyone else who might get in the way. Also, a potential victim has no way of knowing when or by what method a kidnapper will strike. All it is possible to do is to limit the options available to the kidnapper and, at the same time, set up an effective negotiating process which will limit the damage – to get the victim out alive at the minimum cost.

Responding to an obvious market need and an inability of the legitimate law enforcement agencies to counter the kidnap threat effectively, business has stepped in with a series of packages which offer both insurance and training. Beneath its crusty exterior, Lloyd's of London, the biggest insurance market in the world, occasionally has the ability to spot a trend and ride it for all it is worth, and so it was with kidnap-and-ransom insurance. Although it has been involved in this since the Lindbergh kidnapping of 1932, it was at a very low level until the early 1960s, when Lloyd's began to offer specific deals on kidnap insurance. In the past ten years, that one market has been the single most important growth area in Lloyd's, and the underwriting syndicates directly involved have shown both the greatest growth and the largest profits. In 1984, for example, it was estimated that Lloyd's took premium income in excess of £120 million ($175 million) to insure vulnerable executives and politicians, primarily in the United States and Europe.

Premiums for such insurance generally start at 0.5 per cent of the sum covered, depending on the part of the world concerned and the detailed country risk analysis prepared by the insurer. Where Italy, Spain and South America are concerned, the more usual figure has been two per cent annually, or $20,000 for a $1 million pay-off. However, competition from abroad, particularly New York, has pushed rates down considerably in the last two years. For example, for ten years Lloyd's had insured a major international pharmaceutical company at a cost of $1.3 million for $10 million of cover, but recently the company was reinsured at less than half the cost for double the cover ($600,000 for $20 million). Detailed rates are increasingly difficult to estimate as kidnap-and-ransom insurance has become such an accepted part of day-to-day insurance. Now it is normally just added to a broad policy in the same way as a homeowner might take out a flooding clause as part of a more general insurance policy.

As the insurance market has grown, so has the sophistication of the companies involved in providing the insurance, and in ensuring that they have the minimum to pay out. In addition, of course, they hope to gain the release of any victim, unharmed, and to have negotiated the ransom down to the lowest acceptable level.

The boom in the kidnap business led Lloyd's, who are not usually known for their direct involvement in the more exotic end of the insurance market, to sponsor their own private counter-terrorist, anti-kidnap squad – Control Risks Ltd. The company was founded in 1973 under the sponsorship of Hogg Robinson, one of London's major insurance brokers, and with the enthusiastic endorsement of Cassidy's, a major Lloyd's underwriting syndicate which today accounts for more than seventy-five per cent of the world's kidnap-and-ransom insurance.

Control Risks' three founders were men whose backgrounds accurately reflect the current status of the organisation: Arish Turle, a former officer in the Royal Greenjackets regiment, who, after a spectacularly successful career in the SAS, resigned following a dispute with a senior officer while serving in Northern Ireland; David Walker, also a former officer in the SAS, who has subsequently left Control Risks to set up a company called KMS, which currenly earns around £2.7 million ($4 million) in commission from the Sultan of Oman to supply ex-British Army mercenaries for the local armed forces; and Mark Winthrop, who also has an SAS background and now runs a company called SCI specialising in personal security and microelectronics.

The development of Control Risks almost exactly mirrors the growth in international terrorism. In 1975, the company employed three people and had a modest turnover of £16,500 ($25,000). That figure jumped to £170,000 ($250,000) in 1976/77 and then to £333,000 ($500,000) in 1977/78 when the company employed a staff of twenty. In April 1982, the company broke away from the Hogg Robinson group to become an independent operation, based in London's Victoria. In its first full year as an independent, it employed around sixty-five full-time staff and grossed £2.43 million ($3.65 million). By 1984 there were 100 employees, and turnover was rising towards the £3 million ($5 million) level. Of that turnover, Lloyd's of London guarantee Control Risks Ltd fees of over £1 million ($1.5 million) a year. Control Risks charges, in addition to the Lloyd's retainer, a standard work fee of £600 ($1000) per day for each person involved in a case. Since 1976, Control Risks have spent 5083 days involved in an on-site advisory capacity in 126 extortion-related incidents in over fifty countries, of which seventy-nine were kidnap negotiations, and the remainder were extortion by product contamination, bombs and other forms of terrorist threat.

In January 1978, Joseph Smith of Bethesda, Maryland, a suburb of Washington DC, joined the board of Control Risks, and the American division of the company has played an important role ever since. It has a staff of eight based in Bethesda, and all the employees come from either the FBI, the Green Berets or the US State Department. It is currently headed by Dick Meadows, the man the American government had inside Iran waiting for the helicopters to land during the abortive rescue mission for the hostages at the US embassy in Tehran.

Control Risks has also appointed several well-known law enforcement and counter-terrorist experts as non-executive directors. These include: General Sir Frank King, the army commander in Northern Ireland from 1973 to 1975; Sir Robert Mark, head of the (London) Metropolitan Police from 1972 to 1977; and Major-General Richard Clutterbuck, a respected expert on terrorism.

As the operation has grown, so has the sophistication of the services the company provides. The essence of the whole operation is secrecy. As nearly all the employees are former intelligence officers or from (in Britain's case) the SAS, internal security is not a problem. In fact, Control Risks and the other rival companies that have sprung up in recent years have managed to operate with remarkable freedom in extremely delicate matters with the minimum of government interference, even though some of their methods may actually do considerable damage to the work of counter-terrorists around the world.

At the heart of all kidnap-and-ransom insurance policies is secrecy. The confidential document that Control Risks hands out to all its clients is headed 'Kidnap Procedure – Insurance', and stresses that the document can be used as the basis for instructions sent to selected executives but that the existence of the insurance must not be disclosed to them. It suggests that the instructions should be circulated to senior executives like any other top priority material.

There is invariably a prime clause in any such insurance agreement that the very fact that insurance has been taken out must remain confidential. If the insurer learns that this confidence has been breached, the insurance automatically becomes invalid.

It is this area of breached confidentiality that has caused considerable concern to law enforcement agencies and has resulted in kidnap-and-ransom insurance being outlawed in many South American countries, in Italy and, to a certain extent, in Spain. Law enforcement officers argue that, if the terrorists know that this type of insurance has been taken out or that there is even a chance that a potential victim is insured, it both makes a kidnapping more likely and ensures that the terrorists will get away with a larger sum of money than would otherwise be the case.

For example, the British government is seriously alarmed by the growth of such insurance because kidnapping for ransom is becoming increasingly popular in Northern Ireland and the Republic. Their worry is that the IRA may find out that someone is insured for this – either through their intelligence sources or from the insured person him/herself. The latter could then be kidnapped and, after the money has been paid over, claim it back on the insurance. A large sum of money is thus passed to a terrorist organisation in a way which guarantees no comeback. In the opinion of the security services in Northern Ireland, this has already happened in one case and more may be on the way. This concern is reflected in the Irish Republic. Dr Garret FitzGerald, the Prime Minister of the Republic, has asked the British government to stop Lloyd's issuing kidnap-and-ransom insurance. The request has been discussed by the British Cabinet but no decision on action has been taken.

Certainly, Italian judges argue that kidnap insurance is one of the main reasons for the successful and highly profitable industry that has grown up around the ransoming of prominent Italians. The insurance companies respond by saying that they have saved a number of lives by enabling victims to pay ransoms, and that they may have reduced the actual level of payment.

Moral issues aside, the business continues to grow. Control Risks currently has more than 480 clients – 227 in North and South America, 127 in Great Britain and 129 spread throughout other parts of the world. Over one-third of its clients worldwide are employed in the service sectors of banking, finance, insurance, the media, computers and high technology, and thirty-four of its clients are families or private individuals.

The client base of Control Risks includes eighty-three of the companies in the Fortune 500 – including four of the top ten companies listed and sixteen of the top fifty – and they also have clients from three of the top ten US industrial concerns.

This does not, however, give a true picture of the actual position of the whole body of this type of insurance. As one source close to Control Risks pointed out: 'Our list merely reflects the people we have direct contact with. Nearly every member of the Fortune 500 and any major international firm will have kidnap insurance of one kind or another. We simply haven't got involved because they have not requested a specific part of our service.'

For a fee that varies depending on the size of the company, Control Risks will enter a corporation and assess it for kidnap risk, building up an initial profile of the company that points out the weaknesses in its security system and where its executives might be particularly vulnerable. If a company then takes out insurance, a further, extremely detailed, company profile is developed, concentrating on areas of operation and likely targets.

In addition, senior executives covered by the insurance are examined and dossiers built up, which include personal habits, blood groups, fingerprints and handwriting samples (to identify the ransom appeals they hope will never be made). Both the insured and his or her family are briefed on what is likely to happen in the event of a kidnap. Film simulations are shown to familiarise the executive with the psychological trauma inherent in any kidnapping.

Depending on the level of insurance that has been taken out, the response to a kidnapping varies. At the highest level a team – generally two people – will fly to the nearest city and take over the negotiations with the kidnappers from the family. This periodically brings them into conflict with the local police, who tend to want to set traps to catch the terrorists, while the negotiators have a different priority: to get the hostage free at the minimum cash cost. At the lowest level, these negotiators will each be part linguist, part psychologist and part tough guy, although they never carry guns and do not endorse any violence in trying to free their clients.

Clients are all issued with a briefing list of what to do if they are kidnapped. The briefing document is confidential and suggests that before the company's adviser arrives, the kidnappers should be asked to provide proof that the victim is alive. Until a 'proof question', which only the victim can answer, has been answered, settlement should not be discussed. Discussion of settlement should be avoided in any case, although willingness to co-operate should be shown.

A codeword should be agreed to identify the real kidnappers from hoaxers. All calls should be recorded on tape, or failing that, details of the caller's sex, age, accent, tone of voice and mental state should be noted as well as whether the call is local or long distance, automatic, operator connected or from a call box and how long it lasts. A detailed record of events including date, time and type of all communications from the kidnappers, the date and time of all significant events and details of all meetings should be kept. No interviews are to be given to the press.

Such a thorough and painstaking procedure has paid off. For example, on 12 January 1977, shipowner Piero Costa was kidnapped by the Red Brigade who asked for over $2 million in ransom. Costa was insured with Lloyd's, and Control Risks flew a team out from London to take over the negotiations, which eventually lasted nearly three months. Finally a sum of $900,000 was agreed upon.

Costa's cousin, Giovanni Battista Costa, together with the victim's sister, Maria Costa, a nun, loaded the money into two suitcases and drove to an arranged point near Rome. Here they received written instructions which sent them to dozens of other locations around the city. At every point, they would find a new set of instructions and a new destination. Eventually, they found themselves in a dead-end street in an industrial estate, facing a blank wall. Standing next to the wall was a woman wearing a large poncho, obviously with a weapon concealed underneath, and a man who police are convinced was Mario Moretti, one of the founder members of the Red Brigade. These two took the suitcases, hurled them over the wall, jumped over themselves and disappeared.

Although this happened on 26 March, Costa was not released until 3 April. The reason for the delay was that each of the 100,000-lira notes had been covered with a powder which could identify anyone who handled the cash. (This is standard Control Risks procedure if a ransom is ever handed over.) The Red Brigade spent the eight days between receiving the ransom and releasing Costa in handwashing every single banknote, and it was not until they were sure that every trace of the powder had been removed that they set Costa free.

Another, more extensive type of laundering ransom money is a major problem facing kidnappers, and a small industry has become established to solve the problem. As a matter of course, in every single kidnap case the serial numbers of all notes handed over are recorded. It makes no difference if, in typical movie style, they are all small-denomination, used bills – they are still hot. As a result, the kidnappers have to allow a thirty per cent commission for clean money for every note exchanged. The ransom cash then surfaces over a period of years in different parts of the world. For example, after the kidnapping of Duke Maximiliano Grazioli from Rome, when Control Risks negotiated the ransom demand down from $2 million to $1 million, about a year later the money began surfacing in Costa Rica.

While the Costa kidnapping had been a textbook example of what could be done by effective negotiation, as far as Control Risks are concerned it had an unfortunate sequel: the ransom money was used to purchase guns, weapons and a safe-house for use in the kidnapping of Aldo Moro, the former Italian Prime Minister. He was eventually shot by the Red Brigade.

To the outsider, the whole business of kidnap and ransom is charged with high drama. However, the arrival of the insurance experts on the scene has, in fact, given the whole business a routine air where both sides know exactly the moves that are required in this intricate and potentially deadly chess game. After all, it is in the interests of all that there should be a peaceful and happy outcome. In Italy, for instance, there is now a scale of charges that both sides know are acceptable, with the typical rich person fetching a ransom of $0.5–1 million, the very rich $1–2 million and the super rich $2–4 million. The difficulty comes when deciding into which category a victim falls.

'The general victim is not a name you read about in the gossip columns. They have their armed guards and know they might be targets and so they really are too much trouble,' explained one kidnap negotiator. 'A much more likely target is the businessman whose company turns over a few million dollars a year, who thinks he is too small a fish for the kidnappers to fry.'

Just as potential victims have brought in the professionals on their side, so have the kidnappers. In nearly every kidnap-and-ransom operation, an abduction team is hired, along with a group of guards who will prepare a safe-house and look after the victim during the months of negotiation. But the most important recruit to the kidnappers' side is the negotiator who will match the Control Risks representative. This professional approach tends to remove the margin of error in discussions and to take the negotiations from the realm of high drama into the almost routine. Such professionalism undoubtedly helps to take the emotion out of an area where a hasty response could cause the death of the victim.

The Financing of Terror

In 1979, terrorists kidnapped the twenty-nine-year-old son of a wealthy Roman shopowner and dealer in coffee futures. He was grabbed outside an apartment in an affluent Roman suburb and, two months of negotiations later, the ransom demanded by the kidnappers had been reduced from $1 million to around $400,000. The 'final' increased offer from the family had been, on the other hand, the equivalent of the cost of a decent dining table, almost an insult and intended to indicate that funds were exhausted. The response of the terrorists was to send a bottle of blood to the family. A hurried council of war was called during which each member of the family was asked to suggest a response. The consensus was that double the family's offer should be made.

'My view was that this was the final squeeze of the sponge,' recalled the negotiator. 'The terrorists wanted to make sure that there really was no money left, so I recommended we up our offer by $1500, and the son was released two days later.'

While such poker games may appear amusing, the evolution of kidnap and ransom as a method of financing terrorism is very dangerous. Society appears to have accepted that the whole business should largely be taken out of the hands of law enforcement agencies and passed on to those whose only concern is to minimise the financial impact. In an unintentional conspiracy, the terrorist, the victim and the insurance companies have found a level at which they are all prepared to work. The kidnappers get their cash, the victims have insurance and the insurance companies get their premiums. Cosy as this status quo may be, its effect is felt far outside this simple triangular relationship.

For every penny that a terrorist group gathers in from kidnaps, a substantial proportion goes towards the funding of future operations and the maintenance of the terrorist organisation. The complacency that has been apparent so far in the development of counter-kidnap operations is extremely damaging to society, no matter how convenient it may be for the victim, the terrorist and the business community. However, despite the quite obvious disapproval of many police forces, there has been no real attempt to curb the growth of kidnap insurance and, indeed, many governments appear to be happy to abrogate all responsibility in the matter.

The evolution of the kidnap-and-ransom business has spawned a number of other areas that have enabled business to promote uniquely tailored services. Again, Control Risks has led the way in offering a computer-based information service – known as CRIS.

CRIS was established to take advantage of Control Risks' growing network of employees and sources around the world. The company relied to some extent on good on-the-ground intelligence so that their negotiators would be able to go out into the field properly briefed about the state of terrorism in the country where the kidnap had taken place, and also, if possible, with a breakdown of the personalities of the terrorists who might be on the opposite side of the (figurative) negotiating table. From a small collection of ordinary files, Control Risks have built up the most sophisticated data bank available on international terrorism. So detailed is it that MI6, Britain's counter-intelligence service, regularly consults the library.

For a fee starting at £1500 ($3000), businesses can tap into CRIS. Because the information they can access is edited in-house by Control Risks staff, what a company can actually obtain is a fairly detailed and monthly updated country risk analysis. Since the scheme began two years ago, CRIS has only generated twenty-five per cent of the business that was expected, partly because many companies have their own intelligence apparatus and partly because they prefer to believe that the threat is not that real. However, ever responsive to the needs of its favourite child, Lloyd's have agreed to make up the difference between subscription and cost.

Such detailed briefs are essential if protection companies are to do their jobs properly. In the early days of terrorism – in the 1960s and the early 1970s – kidnapping fell into a fairly uniform pattern. A person would be kidnapped as a way of raising cash to maintain day-to-day terrorist operations. There was little attempt at strategic planning by the terrorists, largely because their accounting systems were generally so inefficient. However, as terrorism has become more sophisticated and the demands of the infrastructure more complex, so terrorists have tended to evolve specific targets or a specific policy to pay for a planned broad-based terrorist programme.

The IRA are an excellent example of a group which has managed to survive considerable hardship while evolving politically. Of all the terrorist groups that currently exist, the IRA commands the most respect among counter-terrorist teams and among other terrorists. Even though they are thought to be, in some respects, slightly of the lunatic fringe – committing suicide through hunger strike is considered quite eccentric – there is tremendous respect for their political savvy.

The IRA have also led the way in learning how to use an established political system to achieve their revolutionary ends. Combining terrorism with political campaigning, they have tried neatly to straddle the divide between legitimacy and terrorism. However, this dual policy has proved expensive. As soon as a terrorist organisation begins to work within the existing structure, its operations become more visible, and if elections are involved, success is never simply a matter of coercion. Votes have to be won, and if the voters are to be convinced that terrorism is good for them, large sums of money will be necessary to support the rhetoric with social welfare schemes and other devices to transform the terrorist in the eye of the voter from a street-corner gunman into a social worker. To pay for this new policy, the IRA have attempted to exploit every money-earning scheme at their command, and this has included branching out into the kidnap-and-ransom business.

There is a large degree of autonomy between different IRA active service units operating in north and south Belfast. It is understood that the Northern Command of the Provisional IRA issued instructions in early 1981 to all ASUs to try and raise funds by every possible method to pay for the forthcoming elections, but no instructions were issued as to method, and the interpretation of the orders was left to individual local commanders. The result has been less than a triumph although, contrary to popular belief, the Provisional IRA and Sinn Fein did manage to raise one large sum for the fighting fund.

On Friday, 16 October 1981, Ben Dunne, junior boss of one of the Irish Republic's biggest chain stores and a prominent member of one of the country's richest families, was driving to Portadown, just over the border in the north, to open a new store. A car swerved into his path and his Mercedes was driven off the road. Four masked men jumped out of the vehicle, bundled him into their car and headed south for the Republic.

After about twenty minutes, the vehicle stopped and Dunne was taken to a nearby shed where he was hooded. Shortly afterwards, a man came into the shed and, warning that 'The British are close', moved them all out to a nearby ditch where Dunne was forced to lie with guns pointing at his head. He was then transferred to a house in the south, where he was kept, hooded, for the six days of his captivity.

The kidnapping of such a prominent man caused a considerable furore in all of Ireland. Such an action was a radical departure for the IRA who had traditionally confined themselves to bank robberies, simple extortion and petty crime. A massive manhunt was launched which concentrated on the border areas, a traditional stronghold for all the different terrorist groups fighting in Northern Ireland.

While the hunt was going on, the kidnappers had communicated with the Dunne family by telephone, asking for a ransom in exchange for his release. All public statements made both by the police and by the family have suggested that the sum demanded was £500,000 ($710,000). In fact, it was double that at nearly £1 million ($1.5 million). Father Dermod McCarthy, a Dunne family friend who had officiated at the wedding of Ben Dunne and his wife Mary nine years before, took on the role of intermediary.

The local police decided that no ransom money should be paid and did everything they could to prevent the cash being handed over. Police twice stopped representatives of the family from delivering a ransom which was then reported as £500,000 ($710,000). On a third occasion, Father McCarthy secretly met members of the gang in County Louth to negotiate, but had to fling himself into cover when a security patrol stumbled on the meeting and opened fire. The gang escaped and the priest was uninjured.

Dunne was eventually released unharmed after six days. The kidnappers left him at the roadside with three bullets – one from an Armalite rifle which they said would have been used to kill him, one from the revolver used to guard him in the hideout, and the third, also from an Armalite, for Father McCarthy to keep as a souvenir.

Three days into the kidnapping, the Provisionals began leaking to sympathetic journalists in Dublin and Belfast that the group who had carried out the kidnapping was a rogue unit acting without orders. The IRA had received some very critical coverage in the local papers, which argued that not only was the Dunne family highly popular and Ben Dunne responsible for a successful business that Ireland desperately needed, but also the family had not been unsympathetic to the cause of a united Ireland.

When Dunne was released, the Provos let it be known that this had been carried out on their instructions because the kidnapping had proved counter-productive in publicity terms and because the massive manhunt was hampering other, more important operations. In fact, the kidnappers had been acting with the full authority of the Northern Command of the IRA, who had issued the orders to raise money for the election campaigns.

In addition, contrary to what both police and IRA sources suggested at the time, a ransom *was* handed over: according to sources close to the Dunne family, just over £750,000 ($1 million) was passed to the active service unit that kidnapped Dunne. The British government view the payment of that ransom as an extremely dangerous precedent. Another cause for their concern is their belief that Dunne was actually insured against kidnap and the IRA may either have been given this information or have learned it through their own intelligence sources.

This was the first and, to date, most successful kidnapping designed to fuel the terrorists' campaign for a legitimate electoral mandate. Encouraged by this, the IRA decided to carry out a series of further kidnaps, which they hoped would bring in enough money to the Sinn Fein and IRA coffers to fund the forthcoming British elections and the elections to the European Parliament, due to be held in 1984.

Their target this time was not a businessman but Shergar, one of the most expensive horses on earth. Shergar had won both the Derby and the Irish Sweeps Derby and had been syndicated for nearly £10 million ($15 million) to a group of wealthy investors headed by the Aga Khan. When stud fees are taken into account, the real value of the horse was probably close to three times the syndicated sum.

The kidnappers had chosen their target well. The horse was at stud at Ballymany on the edge of the Curragh in County Kildare. It was a remote rural spot, and while the stables had been designed to provide the greatest comfort for the animals, there was little security. There were, it is true, closed circuit cameras monitoring Shergar's stable so that help could be swiftly on hand if such a valuable animal should suffer an accident. However, these devices were aimed at protecting the horse from itself and not from outsiders.

Such a relaxed attitude was perhaps understandable, as it had been extremely rare for terrorists – or, for that matter, anyone else – to take a horse for ransom. The only other occasion in recent times was in Italy in the late 1970s, when a Red Brigade group in Milan kidnapped a second-rate racehorse believing they had a priceless piece of horseflesh on their hands. The owner of the animal, keener to have the insurance than pay the ransom, refused to negotiate, so the Red Brigaders killed the horse and cooked and ate it. The terrorists, who were factory workers, were then greeted with a chorus of neighs every day when they turned up to work. Unfortunately, the Shergar saga was not to be so harmless.

At around 8.40 on the evening of 8 February 1983, at least six men in three cars drove up the long, winding driveway to the main stud buildings at Ballymany. They went unchallenged and the son of the head groom, James Fitzgerald, innocently answered the door to the late-night callers. The groom himself came downstairs to find his young son pinned to the floor by the gunmen. After securing his family in the kitchen, the terrorists forced Fitzgerald to take them to Shergar's stable and to assist them in loading the horse into a double horsebox that they had summoned up the drive by two-way radio. Police believe the gang must have been acting with considerable inside knowledge as the terrorists even knew that Shergar would not go up the ramp of the horsebox unless there was straw sprinkled inside.

Fitzgerald was taken along with the horse and, prior to being dropped outside a nearby village, was told to pass on a request for a £2 million ($3 million) ransom. Fitzgerald telephoned the bad news to the French stud manager, Ghislain Drion, who in turn got in touch with the Aga Khan in Switzerland.

Within hours, it was decided to bring in professional negotiators from Control Risks. Although the horse had not been insured specifically for kidnap, it had been insured against loss of stud fees, and Lloyd's would have to pay out in excess of £5 million ($7.5 million). Thus, they were particularly anxious that any negotiations should be handled with complete detachment and professionalism. The Aga Khan and other members of the syndicate shared this view.

A small team from Control Risks were immediately established at the stud farm and waited for negotiations to begin. Contact was made on the morning after the kidnap, the kidnappers asking for Drion, but the stud manager was not around at the time and the same thing happened that afternoon. However, contact was finally made with Drion shortly after. At this stage, the affair began to take on the elements of a French farce.

In his first conversation with the kidnappers, Drion, who himself has a marked French accent, found it impossible to understand the thick Irish accent over the telephone, and the kidnappers' spokesman found the discussion equally incomprehensible. He rang back later that day and spoke to one of Control Risks' negotiators. The kidnapper then switched the focus of the affair to France by demanding a contact number in Paris. This was provided. The switch to Paris had been made with the full knowledge of the Irish police who were, however, unwilling to let their French counterparts in on the act. The result of their chauvinistic view was that, later in the negotiations, the French police, once they discovered what had been happening on their territory, were most reluctant to help.

The following day, Thursday, the Paris number was telephoned and the ransom demand for £2 million ($3 million) was repeated. The negotiator then demanded proof that the horse was still alive. The following Friday night, the kidnappers told the negotiator in Paris that proof of the stallion's survival would be made available at the Crofton Airport Hotel in Dublin the following morning at nine o'clock. A negotiator turned up but no one appeared with any proof. A second rendezvous was agreed, and on this occasion, the kidnappers produced a colour Polaroid photograph of the horse with a copy of a newspaper – the 11 February issue of the *Irish News*, a Belfast paper – included in the picture.

The final conversation with the kidnappers took place late on the Saturday night after the photograph had been seen. It was a very brief conversation in which the caller asked if the money was ready. When told that the owners were not yet satisfied, the conversation ended with the words: 'If you are not satisfied, that's it.' Nothing has been heard from the kidnappers since.

With hindsight, both the negotiators and the syndicate believe that the negotiations failed because the kidnappers were operating out of their league. Part of the problem of the IRA running independent fund-raising operations is that there is inadequate control over the actions of the various active service units. In this instance, ambition exceeded ability.

What the kidnappers often perceived as impossible behaviour by the owners and the negotiators during the course of the discussions was often matched by equal exasperation on the other side. For example, at different times the kidnappers demanded a ransom to be paid in £100 notes, which do not exist; at 5.45 one evening, they demanded that Drion should personally deliver the £2 million ($3 million) ransom in Paris at noon the next day, an utterly impossible task in the time available; they ordered the negotiator in Paris to get authority from syndicate shareholders to pay the ransom within one hour but forbade him to telephone Ireland to speak to them; at 5 pm on Saturday, 12 February, long after the banks had shut, they demanded that the Paris representative get £2 million ($3 million) before the end of the night; and contrary to all conventional kidnap-and-ransom behaviour, the kidnappers refused to negotiate the original ransom demand.

The whole affair was something of a disaster for the IRA. There was considerable speculation in the early days of the kidnap about possible IRA involvement, but no convincing proof was found. It was only after the dust had settled and intelligence informers began to gossip that the truth became known. This was supposed to be the first in a succession of kidnaps and it was expected that Shergar would be the softest touch. The sums riding on the stallion were so enormous and the estimated insurance cover was such that the IRA believed that an amount close to what was being asked would be swiftly paid. It was a bad miscalculation, but it only spurred the organisation to try once again.

Just before 8 am on the morning of 7 August 1983, two men appeared on the hillside behind a house at Roundwood, County Wicklow in the Irish Republic. They beckoned to someone behind them, and a further four men appeared, all with their faces covered with black balaclava helmets and all carrying weapons. They moved purposefully towards the house nestled in the valley below.

Their target, Galen Weston, is head of a business empire that stretches from Dublin to London and Canada, and includes the Fine Fare supermarket chain as well as Fortnum & Mason in London's Piccadilly. Unfortunately for the IRA, the police had received a warning of the impending snatch and were waiting for the kidnappers as they stepped into the courtyard at the back of the house. There had been no indication of the ambush. Weston's estate car was parked outside the house, his invariable habit when he was staying there. (In fact, he was spending the day playing polo in England with Prince Charles.)

The police called on the gang to surrender, but a vicious gun battle ensued. Four of the kidnappers were wounded and all except one were arrested. In the courtyard of the house, police found two Belgian sub-machine-guns, a Gustav sub-machine-gun, a Browning automatic pistol and a Webley revolver.

At the subsequent trial of the five men who had been arrested, it was revealed that four of them came from Northern Ireland and the fifth was from Dublin. All were believed to be operatives for the Provisional IRA. All five were found guilty and sentenced to long jail terms. Gerry Adams, by then Sinn Fein MP for West Belfast, and Joe Cahill, former Belfast commander of the IRA, were in court to hear the judgement and waved encouragingly to the accused as they were led away.

Having failed with Galen Weston, the IRA struck again just under two months later, and this time one of Weston's senior executives, Don Tidey, was the victim. He had just left his home on the morning of 24 November 1983 to take his daughter to school when his car was stopped by another containing four men, all wearing local police uniforms. The bogus officers dragged Tidey from his car and bundled him into a yellow Ford Escort, leaving his terrified daughter behind.

Once the alarm had been raised, thousands of police and army personnel were mobilised for the search. The forty-nine-year-old widower was thought to have been taken north towards the border, but it was not until nine days later that the kidnappers made contact. In a telephone call to Galen Weston at his headquarters in London, the gang demanded around £5,250,000 ($8 million) for Tidey's release. Weston conducted a series of negotiations with the kidnappers without the knowledge of the Dublin government, and there was a plan to pay a proportion of the ransom in exchange for Tidey. However, the Dublin police, with the help of British intelligence, heard of the negotiations and made it clear to Weston that they firmly opposed the handing over of any money.

A colour Polaroid photograph of Tidey followed up the ransom demand. He was shown reading an issue of an Irish newspaper dated four days after his capture, and this helped convince the police that he was still alive. They eventually received some intelligence that the gang were hiding in County Leitrim in southern Ireland, and the police hunt concentrated in that area. On 18 December, a man was seen running across a field and disappearing in a nearby wood close to the village of Ballinamore. An intensive search of the area followed, and an army patrol came across the kidnap gang's hideout – a cleverly concealed and well-fortified dug-out about the size of an average living-room, which contained sleeping bags, cooking and heating equipment, supplies of food and bales of straw. The kidnappers had already vanished with their victim but were spotted crossing a nearby field.

A shootout followed, during which Tidey was rescued, two police-men were killed, two members of the gang were captured and four others escaped. In this instance, no money was handed over and the IRA came off with no financial benefit at a time when their need was acute. However, £2 million ($3 million) was subsequently paid into a Swiss bank account held by the IRA by Associated British Foods, Tidey's company, after the IRA threatened more kidnaps and bombings.

Police are now convinced that the same IRA team was involved in the Shergar, Tidey and Weston attacks. Although seriously depleted through arrests, this active service unit is still led by the same man, who comes from County Tyrone but now lives in Dublin. The police originally received some intelligence during the hunt for Shergar that the Weston kidnapping was being set up, and that led to the ambush of the IRA gang involved and to the connection between the two kidnaps. The Tidey affair was linked through the colour Polaroid photographs supplied both in this instance and in the Shergar kidnapping to verify that the victims were still alive. In addition, since the kidnappings, the police have received a considerable amount of intelligence so that they now know the mastermind behind the acts. However, there is not enough evidence to arrest him.

An inquiry was held by the IRA at the beginning of 1984 into the failures of the three attacks. At that meeting, the Army Council of the Provisionals demoted the County Tyrone man responsible for all three incidents. The meeting was also told that Shergar had first been handed over in County Meath to farmers from the north who were sympathetic to the cause. In a change of plan after the negotiations began to go sour, the horse was transferred to a hideout in South Armagh and held there until the negotiations finally broke down. Shergar was then taken back across the border to the Ballinamore area in the south (where Tidey was rescued), where he was shot and buried.

While the three incidents were particularly unsuccessful for the IRA, both the police and the security forces believe that the IRA is committed to further kidnaps. 'You have to remember that they need hard cash fast to finance the elections, and kidnaps are the best way to get the money,' explained one senior police officer. The British intelligence assessment is that there will shortly be another major kidnapping, only on this occasion the victim will be shot soon after being captured, with the IRA blaming the shooting on the police or the victim. This will be followed almost immediately by further kidnapping, and this time, the IRA believe, the negotiations will be swift and the money will be paid.

If the security assessment is correct, then the outlook for Ireland is bleak. Experience elsewhere in the world has been that, when terrorists embark on a major kidnapping campaign, they are swiftly imitated by more run-of-the-mill gangsters, and a minor problem soon becomes an epidemic. With the growth in the number of kidnaps will come the increasing involvement of companies such as Control Risks, and the whole situation will take on an air of legitimacy which is wholly inappropriate to the circumstances.

Kidnapping for ransom has proved to be the single most profitable source of income for terrorists. Unlike banks, which can be protected, or governments, which tend to change leaders and allegiances, kidnapping is a relatively sure bet. There are always enough potential victims to go round and there is never enough security to protect them all.

Ever since kidnapping became a serious weapon of terrorism, there has been a reluctance by governments around the world to take firm action against the gangs. Unlike situations where simple property is involved, counter-terrorist squads understandably tend to adopt a softer approach when trying to free kidnap victims. These are often important figures in society with powerful friends, and their deaths would attract considerable unwelcome publicity.

With priority being given to the freedom of the victim, the initiative is always left with the terrorist. This is particularly the case if gaining the victim's release is left to freelance operators such as family or friends whose only aim is ending the kidnap without bloodshed.

The arrival of kidnap insurance and private kidnap negotiators has led to a huge rise in the popularity of kidnapping as a way of raising money. Over the years, banks and large stores have been better protected from the terrorist fund-raiser, but it has proved far more difficult to protect individuals. From the terrorist's point of view, kidnapping becomes especially attractive when all negotiations are done out of sight of local law enforcement agencies, which in turn must reduce the chances of capture.

The cosy relationship that has built up in many countries between negotiator and terrorist, where the independent negotiator simply moves in to seal the bargain, has done immense damage to counter-terrorism. It is interesting to note that those parts of the world which prove a particularly profitable outlet for Lloyd's of London – Italy, Spain, Latin America – all have serious problems with kidnaps for ransom. Of course, it is difficult to assess cause and effect, but it does seem logical that if the insurance factor were to be removed, victims would not be able to pay such large ransoms and the terrorists would have to negotiate directly with law enforcement agencies.

Individual governments who have consistently taken the soft option of securing a victim's release and leaving the question of capturing the terrorists to some future date must largely be blamed for the current state of affairs. Certainly, freeing a kidnap victim must be high on the list of priorities, but it should be remembered that every ransom that is paid can do a great deal to ensure the survival of a terrorist organisation.

Spain, which has a terrorist problem with ETA, a group wanting a Basque homeland, is the only country so far to have announced sufficiently tough measures against kidnap for ransom to act as a deterrent. In 1984, the government announced that it intended to prosecute people who act as intermediaries in kidnapping cases, and it is also taking legal steps – such as legislation enabling it to freeze the bank accounts of victims and their families – to prevent the movement of money to finance terrorist groups. Although these moves are welcome, they do not go nearly far enough. Italy has already banned kidnap negotiators from operating on its territory, and that seems to have made no difference whatsoever. Most kidnap victims are insured, and negotiators still carry on business as usual, although with slightly more discretion.

To break the popularity of kidnap and ransom for the financing of terrorism, concerted international action is necessary. While President Reagan and Prime Minister Margaret Thatcher talk of leading an international crusade against terrorism, they could start in their own backyards, Reagan in Washington and Thatcher in London, by banning companies from offering insurance to potential kidnap victims. At the same time, there should be international agreement that no private individual will be allowed to negotiate for a victim's release.

While this would undoubtedly mean that some large insurance and security companies would lose a percentage of their income, it would be a small sacrifice if the worldwide growth in kidnaps for ransom were to stop.

Part Five

DRUGS

9

The Narc-Farc connection

AT DAWN on the morning of Saturday, 10 March 1984, a flight of Colombian police helicopters swept out of the dull, wet mist hanging over a remote clearing on the banks of the river Yari, 700 miles south of Bogotá. As the helicopters began to settle, the doors in their bellies opened and heavily armed men of an élite anti-terrorist unit poured out, quickly took up an attacking diamond-shaped formation and began a scuttling, jerky run towards the complex of buildings 200 yards away.

Immediately, they came under heavy machine-gun and rifle fire from around the clearing and particularly from the group of buildings on the riverbank that was their main objective. The gunfight lasted some two hours before the compound was secure.

Minutes after the forty police had secured the perimeter, they came under attack from the surrounding jungle. They later estimated that around 100 men had launched the counter-attack, having moved from a base just north of the clearing where they had been stationed as security guards for the camp. Although the counter-attack was beaten off, it alerted the police to the staggering nature of the complex they had captured.

That afternoon, accompanied by a senior member of the US Drug Enforcement Administration (DEA), the police found 13.8 tons of cocaine with a street value of $1.2 billion – a world-record bust. Apart from that, what particularly stunned the Colombian police was the sophisticated nature of the jungle camp. The site contained forty-four wooden structures, runways for light aircraft that were equipped for night landings and ten cocaine-processing laboratories. The police also captured seven aircraft, including two twin-engined planes and a helicopter, six sub-machine-guns, seven rifles and four shotguns, and enough food to keep eighty people well fed for six months.

The site had originally been spotted by a US surveillance satellite and the information had been passed by the Americans to the Colombian government with a request for early action. Elated after the raid, the US ambassador in Bogotá, Lewis Tambs, said: 'It is the largest drug raid ever in the world. Never has anyone been found with so much cocaine. It is the largest success we have ever had. It is the largest drug arrest by any standard – money value, product, the amount seized.'

Such on-the-ground enthusiasm is perhaps understandable, particularly when it is recalled that the United States has some 450 DEA agents based in Bogotá, whose sole duty is to cut the traffic of cocaine from Colombia to the United States – a trade estimated at around $80 billion a year.

However, while the DEA's Colombia operation is the largest outside the United States, it has been remarkably unsuccessful in stemming the flow of drugs. As one DEA official put it: 'There is really very little we can do under the present circumstances. We push and we push and the best we can hope for is some small successes. But at the end of the day, we will never stop the manufacture and the smuggling out of Colombia. Our only hope is to hit the dealers in the States where we can at least rely on the courts and the law to back us up.'

Such disillusion is perhaps more understandable when put into the context of the other items that were found at the jungle clearing on the Yari river. Ample documentary evidence was discovered linking the group that provided the armed protection for the camp and launched the unsuccessful counter-attack to Fuerzas Armadas Revolucionarias Colombias (FARC), the armed wing of the Colombian Communist Party, which US officials describe as the 'largest, loudest, best-equipped, best-trained and potentially most dangerous subversive group in Colombia'. Subsequently, the embassy dubbed their link to cocaine production and distribution as the 'Narc-Farc connection'.

FARC was founded in 1966 and was led by Manuel Marulanda Velez, known to his friends as *Tirofijo* or 'Dead Shot', because of his prowess as a marksman. Dead Shot was Latin America's pioneer terrorist, having been on the job since his student days more than forty years before, but until FARC was founded, his was a lonely furrow to plough. When at last he decided that the only way to change the corrupt political structure in Colombia was through armed struggle and FARC was established, he attempted to mobilise both the rural and the urban masses to demonstrate or join the cause.

In fact, the organisation proved remarkably unsuccessful. There was little evidence of popular support, and with poor funding, mainly from kidnappings and the odd robbery, Dead Shot found it difficult to keep his armed followers to a fighting strength of more than 100. Throughout the 1970s, which for many terrorist groups was a time of unparalleled growth and prosperity, FARC struggled to make ends meet, and there was little sign of any political success. Yet, by 1984, the group was boasting 2050 members under arms and the additional support of 5000 political cadres in the towns and countryside. This dramatic change was brought about by one thing – drugs.

In 1981, 2500 metric tons of coca leaf was produced in Colombia for refinement into cocaine and shipment abroad, primarily to the United States. By 1985, it is expected that production will have risen to 17,600 metric tons. Currently, the US National Institute on Drug Abuse estimates that at least twenty million Americans have now tried cocaine at least once, while about four million can be considered regular users. In Western Europe, the trend is also sharply upward, and according to the United Nations, 953 kilograms of cocaine were confiscated by law enforcement agencies throughout Europe in 1983, a 140 per cent increase over the previous year. In the United Kingdom alone, seizures increased five-fold over the same period.

To meet the rising demand, the Colombians, as the market's primary supplier, have substantially increased production. This has brought with it a number of problems, most of which are related to security. For the drug growers, the sums of money involved in the cultivation, refining, smuggling and sale of cocaine are so enormous that they provide a temptation to any individual or group wishing to take advantage of a cash-rich industry with little security.

This problem is mirrored in California, where the popular Humboldt County marijuana (known as 'Humboldt home-grown') is cultivated. The growers have pumped such an enormous amount of cash into an area that had suffered terribly from a depressed lumber industry, that they face little danger of being arrested by local law enforcement agencies. On the contrary, the greatest threat to their position comes from those who wish either to steal the crop or to grab the proceeds. The result has been an enormous expansion of self-protection devices, from booby-trapped tripwires to armed guards.

The situation in Colombia is rather different. With a number of terrorist groups already operating on the ground, there appears to have been a natural marriage of requirements, whereby the terrorists supply well-armed protection and the growers and smugglers give the terrorists a much-needed source of regular income.

For a group like FARC, an accommodation with drug producers seemed the perfect solution. Most of the refining plants are in rural areas far from prying government eyes, and the actual growing is well disguised. The growers and the refiners could hardly operate in areas under the control or influence of terrorist groups without coming to some mutually beneficial arrangement. It was logical, therefore, that at a meeting of the FARC national directorate, formal arrangements should be entered into with a number of drug dealers. Under the agreement, FARC levied a ten per cent protection payment on all coca growers in areas under their influence (which produces for them an estimated $3.38 million a month). It was also agreed by FARC's governing body that such arrangements were perfectly legitimate and politically acceptable in the pursuit of the armed struggle.

As in any other business, a steady income from a reliable source enables budgets to be prepared and longer-term plans to be made, and so it was with FARC. Bolstered by new-found wealth, the armed struggle continued but now rather more successfully. In two short years, the organisation managed to increase its hard-core members from around 150 to over 2000 and began to pose a real threat to the government.

It is a seemingly inevitable fact that, when terrorist groups pass a certain stage in their development and become successful in financial terms, their high political principles are compromised. FARC is a very good illustration of this. The more wealth the group has obtained from the drugs business, the more dependent it has become on the latter's continued survival. This, in turn, partly depends on the continuation of the current corrupt administration, so it makes little sense to overthrow the very government that is providing the circumstances for your profitable existence.

At the beginning of April 1984, about a month after the raid at the river Yari, a government commission headed by John Agudela took off at dawn by helicopter from Bogotá. Their destination was a well-kept secret even to most of the government team, the pilot having been given his instructions only minutes before take-off. The helicopter eventually landed in a clearing in the Alto de la Mesa rain forest, where Agudela was met by Dead Shot Marulanda, head of FARC.

The government team had flown to this unlikely destination to discuss a peace initiative proposed by Colombian President Betancur. Apparently the discussions went well, and a provisional truce was agreed that was to last a year, beginning on 28 May 1984. During that time, the government agreed to consider amnesties for various FARC members and some political and land reforms, as well as offers of loans and other inducements to help the terrorists to return to life in normal society.

In Bogotá and other cities throughout the land, the 28 May ceasefire was initially marked by a two-minute silence. After that church bells rang, people waved handkerchiefs and flags, and doves were released to soar over Bogotá's Plaza de Bolívar, which is named in honour of the country's most famous revolutionary. On the face of it, the agreement was a considerable coup for the Colombian government. Others take a less sanguine view, arguing that all the government did was to give legitimacy to an organisation which has played a prominent part in promoting drugs as Colombia's major export earner.

The 'truce' seems to have been an uneasy bargain for both sides. The terrorists were unwilling to give up the substantial income they earned from protecting the drug growers, and the government, under pressure from the United States, was unwilling to curtail its vigorous anti-cocaine campaign. In a climate in which the cocaine dealers had offered $5 billion to the government in exchange for total amnesty, and in which they have placed a $500,000 price on the head of the US ambassador to Colombia and $300,000 for any US narcotics agent, dead or alive, a truce between government and terrorist seemed unlikely to survive. Since the truce came into force (it was extended at the end of the first year), FARC appears to have held to the agreement, while M19, the other major terrorist organisation in Columbia, has continued its bloody battle against the government.

Certainly, there appears to be little doubt that the drugs business has heavily corrupted Colombian society. For example, when the police searched through documents found in the river Yari drugs bust in March 1984, they found evidence linking the operation to two men who the DEA consider to be the godfathers of the South American drugs industry: Fabio Restropo Ochoa and Pablo Escobar Gavria. According to the DEA, among that evidence was a receipt, signed by Restropo, for $1 million given to a Bolivian drug dealer. These two leading drug magnates have become enormously powerful as a result of their business operations, and they operate in a style reminiscent of medieval robber barons. The Restropo clan breed the finest trotting horses on the continent, while Pablo Escobar has imported planeloads of lions, tigers, elephants, giraffes and kangaroos to fill the finest zoo in South America. He won local support by donating lighting systems to the stadiums of his favourite soccer teams, and his largesse has earned him the nickname of the 'native Robin Hood'. He was even elected to Congress in 1982, although he is now a fugitive.

The drugs dealers hotly deny any links with the guerrillas. 'You can accuse me of being a narcotics dealer,' says Pablo Escobar, 'but to say I'm in league with the guerrillas, well, that really hurts my dignity.' However, such denials are largely dismissed by police and DEA officials.

Their worry is that, as the terrorist groups become richer, they will come increasingly to dominate the society they originally set out to overthrow. The methods of achieving that success may have altered to take advantage of new developments, but the end result may well be the same – the total corruption of the existing government. However, it seems increasingly unlikely that any terrorist group will wish to establish a Communist government, their original motivation. Such a development would undercut a business that has become a way of life.

While FARC is the most noticeable example of how a terrorist group can evolve to the point where it becomes so cash rich that present society once again becomes attractive, the group's movement into the drugs business was actually inspired by the example of Colombia's most successful terrorist organisation, the M19 movement, which grew out of a political organisation, the National Popular Alliance. The NPA had actually been successful enough to be represented in the Colombian parliament but, in the elections of 19 April 1970, had suffered serious reversals. To the more extreme of the party, the only solution appeared to be armed struggle to achieve political ends, and so, in 1973, M19 ('*Movimiento 19 Abril*') was founded.

As with FARC, M19 had uncertain beginnings and, for three years after its establishment, had no real impact on the Colombian scene. Then the group initiated a series of kidnappings aimed at the largely American-based multinational companies that were represented in Colombia. Although the ransoms of these kidnappings produced several million dollars spread over five years, the group appears to have been unable to use the money either to buy support or to expand its cell structures in the cities.

Of the two founders of M19, Jaime Bateman Cayon is the most important influence on the organisation's development. Born to a peasant family, unlike most revolutionaries he had no university education. However, he is highly intelligent and, according to those who have met him, has considerable charisma. His early socialist leanings led to sponsored travel in the Eastern Bloc and Cuba, where he received a detailed grounding in Marxist-Leninist philosophy.

In his early years as a budding revolutionary, Bateman used to run with Dead Shot and FARC, but he went his own way after ideological differences began to come between them. The two have remained friends, however, and there have been a number of attempts to bring FARC and M19 together, but all have floundered on their differing interpretations of the course for the armed struggle.

It is, in fact, Bateman's relations with Fidel Castro that have caused considerable interest in the West and particularly the United States, leading to a variety of allegations – from Cuban attempts to subvert South American governments as part of a Communist masterplan to overthrow the world, to a Castro-inspired and Bateman-supported scheme to undermine with drugs the flower of America's youth.

US Senator Jeremiah Denton is head of the Congressional sub-committee on security and terrorism, a body that is widely thought of as anti-terrorist and anti-left-wing. Unfortunately, given its political perspective, it tends to call evidence which simply reinforces a particular bias, rather than assessing a problem in an analytical fashion. For example, at the hearings on 23 April 1984, Senator Denton said in his opening address:

> It has long been alleged that subversive and terrorist groups, and governments such as Cuba that encourage and support such groups, have utilized drug trafficking to fund their activities. The testimony received during our Cuban hearings is consistent with those allegations and with the stated aim of the Cubans to contribute to the destabilization of the United States by encouraging and enhancing the drug trade.

The truth of the relationship between Cuba and terrorist groups is – perhaps inevitably – neither as complex nor as Machiavellian as some would believe. At the same sub-committee hearing, Francis McMullen Jr, then acting administrator of the DEA, put the Cuban role into context:

> It appears basically to be to finance activities, not to use drugs to destabilize. I would agree that it does not make unfriendly governments or terrorist organisations unhappy to see the United States with the difficult drug problem it has, but we have not detected any activity to facilitate the drug trafficking to destabilize the populace or the government. . . I do not personally know of any government that is involved in drug trafficking for destabilizing or for income to finance terrorist activities.

However, while Cuba's role in the supply of drugs to the United States may not be as comprehensive as some fear, Castro undoubtedly gives considerable support to the operations of some drug smugglers. The reasons for this have more to do with economic necessity than with any political ambitions. Given the shambolic state of Cuba's economy, Castro is grateful for any injection of foreign cash, and drugs make a substantial contribution to his country's ailing finances.

Jaime Bateman, the co-founder of M19, used as his main arms-runner a close friend, Jaime Guillot Lara, who acted as the link between the terrorist organisation and the Cubans. In the mid-1970s, Guillot's role was relatively simple: he would travel from Colombia to Miami, Florida, buy some guns and transport them back to Colombia either by plane or, more usually, by boat. However, as the drugs business grew, the United States attempted to shut the easy smuggling routes, thus forcing the traffickers to look elsewhere.

The growth in the market for Colombian cocaine and the ease with which the drugs were distributed in the United States came to the attention of the Cubans at the end of the 1970s. In 1979, a preliminary meeting took place at the Bogotá Hilton between Guillot and Fernando Ravelo Renedo, Cuban ambassador plenipotentiary to Colombia, and Gonsalo Bassols Suarez, the Cuban minister counsellor to Colombia. In August that same year, another drug dealer, Juan Lazaro 'Johnny' Crump, organised a further meeting for Guillot at the Cuban embassy, which was attended by representatives from the Cuban Central Intelligence Directorate (DGI), the country's intelligence service.

At this second meeting, the Cubans provisionally agreed to the use of their country as a temporary stop-over and transfer point for drugs on their way to the United States from Colombia. In return, the smugglers would pay the Cubans for each shipment that passed through their territorial waters, and would purchase guns for their fighters from the Cuban government. Thus, the terrorists got a safe haven within striking distance of the American shore and the Cubans got a steady source of much needed foreign exchange.

The original agreement between Guillot and the Cubans called for the smugglers to pay $500,000 for each vessel that passed through Cuban waters. However, there is conflicting evidence as to the exact nature of the agreement, and it seems likely that it was adapted to take into account changing loads and differing circumstances as the business expanded. Certainly, there is evidence that the Cubans charged $10 per pound of marijuana passing through Cuban waters. Also, it was reported that the Cubans were paid one-third of the profit on a $7-million contract for a cargo of the addictive sedative *methaqualone* (trade name: Mandrax): $1 million was paid to cover the initial cost of the cargo; $1 million for various intermediaries including boat captains; and the remaining profit was divided into three – one-third to Cuba, one-third to Guillot and one-third to his partners, including a share to M19.

The process was actually quite simple, with the Cuban government doing very little for its money. The mother ship would leave Colombia laden with drugs. Once in international waters, it would hoist the Cuban flag and radio ahead with an estimated time of arrival in Cuban waters. Once safely in Cuban territory, the mother ship would rendezvous with smaller boats based in Florida or in the Bahamas, who would take the cargo to the mainland.

One such case occurred when Guillot worked closely with an American drug dealer, the Miami-based David Perez. Perez agreed to transport drugs from Cuba to Miami, and he sent boats to Guincho Key, fifteen miles off the north-central coast of Cuba, to rendezvous with the Guillot mother ship, the *Viviana*, named after Guillot's daughter, which had around twenty tons of marijuana and ten million methaqualone tablets on board.

Perez was eventually arrested for his part in the smuggling operation. At his trial in Miami, he testified that he was forced to go to Guincho Key himself when one of his boats went aground and another never arrived. Perez arrived in Cuban waters in November 1980 on board the *Lazy Lady*, a vessel owned by two Cuban government agents, Hector Gonzalez Quinones and Mario Estevez Gonzalez. The *Lazy Lady* was escorted into Cuban waters by two Cuban gunboats, and during the three days Perez spent transferring the cargo, he met and talked with a number of senior Cuban officials. He later testified that he was told that the Cubans expected to net around $800,000 from the sale of the cargo.

Apart from deriving a profit from the traffic in drugs, the Cubans also took advantage of the need for a regular supply of arms to flow to the various terrorist groups involved in the smuggling. In January 1981, acting on instructions from the M19 national directorate, Guillot travelled from Colombia to Panama where he met with Cuban First Secretary, Gonzalez Bassols Suarez (the former minister counsellor in Colombia), and Jaime Bateman. At that meeting, Bateman emphasised the importance of getting arms through to M19, and arranged for Guillot himself to receive a shipment delivered to Colombia's Guajira Peninsula. On 15 October 1981, after a further meeting with the

Cubans in July, Guillot travelled to the Colombian port of Dibulla where his boat, the *Zar de Honduras*, arrived loaded with arms. The arms were transported to a nearby farm which had an airstrip. In exchange for the arms, Guillot loaded 5000 lbs of marijuana on to the vessel to be transported to Cuba and then to the United States. On 21 October, M19 terrorists moved the cached arms – which consisted of fifty-five crates containing 550 FAL rifles and ninety crates containing 90,000 rounds of 7.62 mm ammunition – on to an Aerospace cargo plane that had been hijacked by M19. The cargo was eventually delivered to an M19 camp on the Orteguaza river in the Caqueta department of Columbia.

This two-way traffic has benefits for all sides: it gives the terrorists a steady income, a source for arms and a secure outlet for their drug exports; for the Cubans, the drugs business provides much needed foreign exchange and a means of having some influence on the way the terrorists do business. However, there is no evidence to suggest that, just because they have a business relationship with the Cubans, Castro automatically had a strong voice in the terrorists' affairs, and no intelligence agency and certainly no member of the DEA would make a conspiratorial connection between Cuba and the terrorist movements of South America. As one senior official in the DEA put it: 'If Cuba left the drugs business tomorrow, it would have absolutely no impact on the current traffic. All that would happen is that other avenues would be used. The current relationship is simply a marriage of needs and based entirely on a need for cash on both sides.'

While most of the Colombian terrorist groups are involved in drugs trafficking and have taken advantage of the Cuban offers of help, their financial success is undermining the more political aspects of the relationship. FARC is now back in the establishment fold, but M19, although initially agreeing to the truce, announced in June 1985 that the armed struggle would continue as insufficient progress had been made by the government in social reform. This will suit Cuba's political masters, since the Castro treasury is benefiting to the tune of over $200 million a year in foreign exchange.

What is far more disturbing about the current trends is that terrorist groups appear to be prepared to become involved in establishment politics for economic ends. As odd as this may seem, this can, in fact, be far more damaging to a country than a long-drawn-out war of terrorism. In Colombia, for example, there are currently some ten underground movements committed to various forms of armed struggle. Most have been around since the early 1970s and, until recently, all have been largely ineffective, with numbers remaining small and their activities limited to isolated bouts of violence and occasional kidnapping. However, the picture has changed dramatically in the last five years. During that time, the terrorist groups have moved with the times, and with the explosion of trafficking in drugs has come wealth. With wealth have come new followers, better arms, new international status and, more particularly, political influence inside the country.

The drugs business is now so huge in Colombia that the country has the healthiest balance of payments in South America, and the hard currency earned from the export of cocaine far exceeds the revenue generated by the country's two official export earners, coffee and cut flowers. Inevitably, such a gigantic business has corrupted the political system. The DEA, who provided the original intelligence for the river Yari drugs bust in March 1984, cynically point out that this was the first major step ever taken by the Colombian government since the beginning of the decade, when the DEA began to try in earnest to stem the flow of cocaine. It is also surely no coincidence that, although the bust took place on 10 March, it was not announced until ten days later, the very day the US Senate Foreign Relations Committee was considering its aid programme to Colombia.

Such an opportunistic approach to enforcing the drug laws has led to corruption of political will, which has enabled the terrorist to flourish. Such has been the change in Colombia in the last few years that few politicians there would dare suggest any serious effort to counteract the drugs business. On the contrary, the best the president can offer is a rehabilitation programme for the terrorists so that they can shed the pretence of being freedom fighters and don their suits and take their rightful places in society as successful businessmen.

'And why not?' commented one US government counter-terrorist specialist. 'The days of Che Guevara living out of a knapsack and playing at the romantic guerrilla have long gone. They are either pragmatists who become absorbed by the system and often turn into very successful capitalists, or they fail. It is only our view of the terrorist that hasn't changed.'

There have been periodic attempts in Colombia to counter the influence of the drug barons, but they have been desultory at best and have always failed, sometimes for very violent reasons. In May 1985, Rodrigo Lara Bonilla, Colombia's thirty-eight-year-old minister of justice was riding home in his Mercedes. The road was abruptly blocked by a car and a motorcycle immediately drew up alongside Lara's car. The man riding pillion riddled the vehicle with machine-gun bullets, and Lara died instantly.

In the chase that followed, the man on the motorbike was killed but the gunman was arrested. After questioning, nineteen-year-old Velasquez Osorno revealed that he had been paid $20,000 to shoot the minister because he had been calling for action against the drug barons.

Two days after the assassination, President Betancur himself received a death threat. A crude paste-up made from local newspaper cuttings read: 'CAREFUL – IT ISN'T OVER.' The president reacted with uncharacteristic fury and declared: 'We are unleashing a war without quarter against the crooks who sow terror in cities, towns and the countryside.' He declared a state of siege, which meant that drug traffickers could be held in jail without bail and tried in military courts.

These brave words were greeted with some disbelief by those familiar with the Colombian political scene. Lara was thought to be an exceptional man in that he had been uncorrupted by the drug barons; few others can make the same claim. There is no doubt that Betancur is sincere in his wish to stamp out the drug barons, but there is little prospect of his campaign having any significant impact. Too many people now have a vested interest in the survival of a business that contributes over $5 billion a year in untraceable cash to the Colombian economy.

Immediately after Betancur announced his campaign, the drug barons let it be known that, should any move be made against them, they would close down 1800 businesses and arm a terrorist force of 18,000 to oppose the government. There is no doubt they could deliver on such a threat, and for the first time, some public criticism was provoked. Writing in the respected Bogotá daily, *El Tiempo*, columnist Enrique Santos Calderon observed: '[The gangsters are] bent on subverting and destabilizing the state. Unlike countries like Italy and the US where the Mafia strives to work within the institutions and avoid excessive provocations, the Colombian mafia . . . has launched the greatest challenge imaginable to the state apparatus.'

It is difficult to see what future Colombia has as a democracy if present trends continue. What is more alarming is that Colombia is only one example on the South American continent: its experience is being mirrored by terrorist groups in Bolivia, Peru and Chile. The key to the problem lies with the United States, which provides both an outlet for drugs and a ready source of arms and ammunition for the terrorist groups involved in the traffic.

The DEA estimate that the current value of the cocaine business in the United States is around $80 billion. In 1984, cocaine was selling on the street for between $225,000 and $300,000 a kilogram – approximately a third of the 1983 price. At the same time, DEA officials claim that the drugs seized were two or three times purer than they used to be. While these figures might indicate a glut on the market, others show that the number of users is rising by at least ten per cent a year. The number of cocaine-related deaths, too, has doubled in the last four years.

It is a gloomy picture and one which the DEA feel will not get much better. Nonetheless, if more is not done to counter the traffic, the sheer size of the business will have far more effect on the stability of South American countries than Cuban or Soviet subversion ever would.

Currently, the figures for illegal transactions within the United States are quite staggering. The US Customs Service has made much of the successes of their 'Operation El Dorado', established in May 1982 and designed to cut into some of the illegal cash transactions that resulted from the drugs business. In a statement before the US Senate committee on the judiciary on 20 May 1983, the Commissioner for Customs, William von Raab, pointed out that, in 1982, in Dade County, Florida, drug-related arrests were up by thirty per cent, cocaine seizures by fifty-six per cent and marijuana seizures by thirty per cent. The street value of all drugs seized in the area in that year exceeded $4 billion.

In fact, so successful have the DEA and Customs officials been in capturing cocaine and heroin that they now hold over 12,655 kilograms of cocaine and 546 kilograms of heroin worth $10 billion, nearly twice the total value of the gold stored in Fort Knox. This embarrassing stockpile grows larger each week since the drugs have to be retained as evidence for prosecution and cannot be disposed of until a trial is completed.

While the bald figures may indicate some measure of success against the drug inflow, the reality is rather different. There is still a surplus on the market, and DEA and Customs officials are the first to admit that, while their arrest and seizure figures increase each year, so does the flow of drugs into the country. Indeed, the amounts of money now involved in the transactions are so huge that it is difficult to see how effective policing can ever be organised to stem the growth.

In 1983, a Miami court was told of a local accountant, Ramon Millian Rodriguez, who was stopped just before he took off in his Lear jet bound for Panama. Customs officials found $5 million in cash on board the aircraft, and subsequently discovered that it left for Panama every Friday evening with that amount in $20 bills stacked in cardboard boxes inside. In an eight-month period, the jet carried $151 million to Panama, all of it proceeds from drug deals.

A Colombian, Beno Ghitis Miller, who is now serving a six-year sentence in a Florida prison, stored $3.6 million (in ninety-nine stacks of $100 bills and smaller denominations, weighing 700 lbs) in his office for use in emergencies. He had a further $5.8 million in his local bank account. Ghitis Miller acted as a fence for Colombian drug dealers who would deliver US currency in Miami: for a fee of two cents in the dollar, he would write cheques in pesos that could be cashed in Colombia. In the eight months before he was raided, $242.2 million had passed through his account at the Capital Bank in Miami.

Such enormous sums of money have effectively corrupted the Florida financial establishment, which appears to have adjusted to largely cash-orientated business. Cynically known to law enforcement agencies as 'Coin-o-Washers', the banks play a key role in underpinning the efforts of the drug dealers. Although, in theory, they have to report all deposits and withdrawals of over $10,000, most ignore this rule and allow the drugs money to circulate freely in the system. This is hardly surprising as drugs now contribute more than $15 billion to the Florida economy and may well be the state's largest industry.

There is an awareness that drugs represent a serious threat to the established order, but it is doubtful whether either the will or the ability exist to do anything about the problem. Although President Reagan, in October 1982, declared drugs trafficking to be the most serious crime problem in the United States and formed the South Florida Task Force under the supervision of Vice President George Bush, it appears that any resultant activity has been an irritant at best.

Currently, Customs officials believe they stop only one per cent of the estimated 18,000 illegal flights bringing drugs into the United States, and manage to prevent only five per cent of the drugs from being illegally imported. This is an insignificant effort, given the enormous profits that are being made by the smugglers and the dealers.

Unfortunately, it is not simply a matter of the United States suffering from a boom in a particular aspect of organised crime. American inability to stem the flow has a knock-on effect throughout Central and South America that is of considerable economic and political import-ance. Indeed, there is a strong argument for more investment to be made in counter-drug operations in the continental United States than there is for simple counter-terrorist operations in Latin America.

The American government still believes that terrorism can best be fought by firm counter-terrorism in the countries concerned. This is both naïve and old-fashioned. Terrorism has become big business, and until the sources of income are removed, all that counter-terrorism can do is temporarily cut the numbers of terrorists in the field. Terrorists come cheap, but a regular source of hard cash is much more difficult to achieve. Terrorists operating in Bolivia, Colombia, Peru and other Central and South American countries had a very lean time of it during the 1970s, and it was only when they began to benefit from the growth in the drugs business that they became a serious threat.

While enormous resources are being devoted to counter the perceived Communist threat in Latin America, this effort is directed almost entirely at highly visible terrorist and guerrilla forces. As has been seen with the IRA, such a concentration of effort on conventional counter-terrorism will allow other areas of illegal and subversive activity to blossom, which is exactly what has happened in Colombia.

In Bogotá, there are 450 DEA agents, all of whom are directed to try and stop the narcotics traffic. At the same time, there are only three people at the DEA headquarters in Washington whose job is to monitor terrorism. This is a ridiculous imbalance, and as no one appears to have understood the influence terrorism has on the drugs business, the different groups have managed to achieve unprecedented power.

An early lesson in the political impact of the drug economy on terrorist movements occurred in the Middle East with the Palestine Liberation Organisation. The PLO has been one of the most successful terrorist movements of modern times, both in its ability to survive and in its accumulation of wealth. Inevitably, drugs have played a part in the investment portfolio.

The Lebanon's Beka'a valley covers some 4280 square kilometres on the country's eastern border with Syria and southern border with Israel. It is one of the most beautiful and tranquil spots in the Middle East, and has traditionally provided much of the Lebanon's fruit and vegetables. The gently sloping valley on the east of the Chouf mountains benefits from regular rain as the clouds coming from the Mediterranean break on the high ground. For centuries, the Hermel area in the north of the Beka'a has been used to grow hashish. This was originally for local consumption and was merely part of the harvest, with no particular value attached to it. The development of a fashionable drug culture in the late 1960s and early 1970s began to alter that pattern. In particular, the influx of American and European students anxious to buy and smuggle home significant quantities of hashish encouraged increased production.

At the same time, the government and senior officials in the country began to see an opportunity for personal gain. In a country where it is believed that every chance of making money legally or illegally should be grabbed at the first available moment, such activity should not be seen as exceptional, merely as part of the local way of life. Such was the involvement of officials that, by 1972, the President of the Lebanon, Suleiman Franjiya, was able personally to command a bribe of $3000 to release an American imprisoned for hashish smuggling.

Even with such covert official support, the drugs business remained at a fairly low and largely containable level until the civil war of 1975–76, which destroyed much of the Lebanon and gave control of the country to a combination of warlords, Palestinians and Syrian troops. By the end of the civil war, there were some 40,000 Syrian troops based in the Lebanon, many of them in and around the Beka'a valley. In addition, operating under the umbrella of the PLO, different Palestinian terrorist groups had carved out large sections of the country as their own particular fiefdoms.

As government writ began to fade away – totally in some parts of the country – groups anxious to establish a steady income and unconcerned with legal niceties turned to hashish as a natural source of ready cash and large profits. The hashish-growing areas, which had been limited to the more obscure northern parts of the country, gradually expanded south until, by the beginning of 1980s, they had reached the Beirut–Damascus highway, and today, around eighty per cent of the land in the Beka'a is producing hashish. Opinions vary as to the size of the crop, with some sources suggesting production in excess of 2000 metric tons, while the DEA estimate for 1984 was between 600 and 700 metric tons. The current value of hashish production is well over $100 million a year at local prices. There have also been recent reports of heroin-refining laboratories opening up in the Beka'a to process opium brought in from Afghanistan and Iran.

From the statistics available, it is interesting to note the decline in effective policing of the drugs business in the Lebanon: in 1981, between ninety and 200 metric tons of hashish were produced and 9.5 metric tons were seized; in 1983 (the latest date for which complete figures are available), at least 600–700 metric tons were grown and only 3.2 metric tons of hashish were seized.

Israeli propaganda has made much of PLO involvement in the drugs business, realising that considerable damage could be done to the PLO image by portraying it as a major influence in the expansion of drugs traffic worldwide. For example, an Israeli Defence Force publication, dated September 1983 and entitled *The PLO's Sources of Income*, pointed out:

> The PLO's control over part of the marijuana export trail over Lebanon, together with its existing international substructure, have enabled it to successfully engage in the Lebanese drug trade. Details of its income from these operations are lacking, but it was clearly an important source of funds prior to the Peace for Galilee War.

Such broad accusations are a serious misrepresentation of the real situation. There is no doubt that some groups falling under the umbrella of the PLO have been and are engaged in both the production and the distribution of drugs, but there is absolutely no evidence to support the contention that this is an officially PLO-backed enterprise. On the contrary, Yasser Arafat is known to be personally opposed to any traffic in drugs for the very reason that the Israelis would make so much use of the information in their propaganda – it would be bad both for the PLO's image and for their other business interests. As in all such matters, the truth is both more complex and ultimately more disturbing than is conventionally portrayed.

After the Israeli invasion of the Lebanon in 1982, much was made of the strategic importance of the Beka'a valley to the Syrians. It was 'vital' to Syria's military security to maintain a strong presence in the valley, and there was so much posturing by both Syria and Israel that some feared another war between the two countries would begin in the Beka'a. In fact, the importance of the Beka'a to the Syrians is more economic than political.

After the Lebanese civil war in 1975–76, the Syrians, along with the Palestinians, realised that the hashish business offered considerable opportunities for expansion. The result of their ambitions was an unholy alliance between groups who, just the other side of the Chouf mountains, are at each other's throats.

The land in the Beka'a has traditionally been owned by Christians and worked by Muslims, although many of these divisions have now disappeared. The Christians still own the land, but it is now worked both by indigenous Muslims and by Palestinians who are primarily members of the Syrian-backed Saiqa and the Popular Front for the Liberation of Palestine General Command (PFLP-GC). In addition, Rifaat Assad, the younger brother of President Assad of Syria, provides the security that guards the hashish crops from attack by any of the many paramilitary groups that frequent the region. Rifaat Assad is commander of the Syrian defence companies whose main job is to guard the president and his family; he also heads the country's secret service and is considered one of the most ruthless and brutal men on the Middle East scene. It is easier to understand Syria's reluctance to give up control of any area in the Beka'a valley when it is appreciated that Rifaat and the group that surrounds him have personally benefited to the tune of several million dollars from the hashish business in the Beka'a.

Over ninety per cent of the hashish crop is currently earmarked for export, and is moved abroad through a series of routes inside the Lebanon. One of the most popular runs over the Lebanese mountains, through the Christian Phalange town of Deir al Ahmar and then on to the port of Tripoli or to any one of five other ports which have been involved in the traffic. As the country is controlled by so many different paramilitary bands, there tend to be roadblocks every few kilometres, and each group demands tribute from the smugglers. This results in a product that is quite expensive, but Beka'a hashish has such a fine reputation – particularly in Egypt, a major market – that there is no difficulty in disposing of the dope at a premium price.

Naturally, the impact of the hashish business on the local economy has been enormous. For instance, Baalbeck, the principal town in the Beka'a valley, has all the trappings of a modern marketplace, with stores crammed full of every conceivable consumer good, and where the shoppers prefer the Mercedes to the more traditional donkey to carry their wares home. However, while local benefit in a poor economy is an advantage, it is in the political and foreign dimension that the current involvement of governments and terrorist groups in the hashish traffic is of concern.

The Israeli invasion of the Lebanon, which resulted in the expulsion of thousands of Palestinian terrorists, does not seem to have affected the drug traffic. Indeed, since 1982, there is some evidence that elements in the PLO have actually expanded their influence in the international drugs trade, giving rise to what US State Department officials describe as 'narco-terrorism'.

Early in 1984, certain members of the PLO sold 4.3 metric tons of 'Lebanese Gold' hashish with a street value of more than $12 million to a group of British dealers, who stowed the dope on board their yacht, the *Robert Gordon*, and sailed for Britain. The Customs Service laid an ambush for the five men involved and captured both them and the drugs. At their trial in July 1985, they were sentenced to a total of thirty-six years in jail.

While that case was a simple example of a crooked business deal, police in Australia uncovered another drugs ring in August 1985 that was trading drugs for guns with the PLO. Police in Sydney arrested thirty-five people, including a prominent doctor and lawyer, for their part in smuggling high-grade hashish worth $40 million, which had been purchased from the PLO in the Lebanon, having been transported from the Beka'a valley.

The influence of the Beka'a on the political scene in the Middle East should not be underestimated. It has been of crucial importance in private discussions between the Israelis and the Syrians, and represents their largest single source of income to some Palestinian terrorist groups. However, it is difficult to see what can be done to reduce the level of hashish production there. The DEA used to be heavily involved in a programme designed to persuade local farmers to move to other crops, but the agency has now closed down its office in Beirut and has no plans to return. Equally, there seems to be no prospect in the foreseeable future for the Lebanese government based in Beirut to widen their writ to take in the Beka'a, which while officially in Lebanese territory is totally under the control of either the Syrians or the Palestinians.

While control of the drugs business rests in the hands of corrupt government officials or politically motivated groups, the impact of drugs will be far greater than would otherwise be the case.

The direct involvement of terrorist groups with drugs is a relatively recent and growing phenomenon. Experience seems to show that, in every instance where terrorists have become involved with drugs, they have earned very large sums of money in a short time. With the cash has come the ability to buy both new followers and political influence.

Even in those areas where terrorists do not get directly involved in drugs trafficking, such as in Northern Ireland, drugs can still be used to gain political influence. The Provisional IRA, largely on moral grounds, have always refused to deal in drugs of any kind, and they have been at the forefront of an underground war in both the north and south of Ireland aimed at undermining the distribution network of drug dealers. Kneecapping and kidnapping drug dealers has become commonplace, and the IRA calculate that, by attacking the drugs business, they will win support among the more conservative working-class groups, who will then tend to view them more as guardians of the community than as terrorists.

There is still a tendency to view the growth in the production and distribution of drugs as a purely criminal matter, but this is not an adequate response to a problem that has far wider ramifications. If society is to cope with the involvement of terrorist movements in drugs, and their resultant expansion, a new approach to the problem is called for. There is currently very little liaison between intelligence services and police forces in assessing the financial resources of terrorist groups. This must change so that a total picture is built up – one which bears more resemblance to a company report than to a psychological profile and *modus operandi* of a terrorist group. Only by cutting off the terrorist organisations' sources of income will their power and influence ever be seriously reduced.

Part Six

CONCLUSION

10

Profit and loss

As a SERIOUS, direct threat to modern society, terrorism in general has been remarkably unsuccessful. The rollcall of famous terrorist organisations which arose in the 1960s and 1970s, briefly starred and then disappeared, is long and includes such famous names as Baader –Meinhof, the Japanese Red Army, the Weathermen and the Symbionese Liberation Army. These groups faded away, not because they had achieved any of their political ends and therefore the justification for their existence was over, but rather because they all failed signally to achieve any of their political aims or to attract the level of popular support they had expected.

Other groups that began back in those days, when it appeared to many that revolution was sweeping the world and democracies were all under threat, have done rather better. The reason is that they were better capitalists. To thrive, terrorism has had to compromise and adapt to changing circumstances. In every case, it has been an extraordinary metamorphosis.

Terrorism is generally perceived as being the pursuit of political ends through violent means and certainly, in the popular perception, involves such things as bank robberies and the kidnapping or killing of innocent civilians. In part, this remains true, but a high degree of sophistication has been added to this so that the terrorist is now more likely to conform to the image of a middle-ranking clerk than to a gun-toting hoodlum.

It seems that, to survive, terrorist groups need to cross an economic divide that separates those who live a hand-to-mouth existence from those who can actually plan ahead. All those groups which have come and gone in the last twenty years have failed to cross that divide. They have either been plagued by leaders who could not plan beyond the next bank robbery and therefore never had enough funds to expand their power base, or they had leaders who were seduced by the easy money and forgot their political principles among the fast cars and fancy apartments. The few who remain have cooler heads and have been able to see that good financial planning means having enough cash to buy and keep support, to pay for arms and to build a propaganda base among the people the organisation claims to represent.

However, while the terrorist has learned to survive and, in some cases, prosper in a hostile world, counter-terrorism has remained largely static. This is partly because politicians, who dictate the response to the terrorist threat, always look for quick and easy solutions that will placate a fearful electorate. Therefore, the emphasis in counter-terrorism is always on the arrest or killing of terrorists – in other words, a 'head count' of terrorists killed or captured is the yardstick by which success is measured.

This attitude is obviously inadequate given the hundreds of IRA prisoners currently in British jails, the hundreds of PLO supporters held by the Israelis and the thousands of Red Brigade members imprisoned by the Italians. In every case, the incarceration of large numbers of their members seems to have made little impact on the ability of a terrorist organisation to survive.

In response to the wishes of their political masters, counter-terrorist specialists tend to target the areas which they know will meet with approval; thus, all counter-terrorism is aimed at dealing with the armed threat as and when it arrives. It is, of course, right that considerable effort should be put into active counter-terrorism, with a high level of training and the best equipment being allocated to respond to the threat, but this is obviously not enough to counter those organisations which have managed to cross the economic divide and appear to prosper no matter what is done to reduce their numbers by conventional methods.

While the way terrorism is popularly perceived has remained largely static, a number of myths have been created around the whole phenomenon. These have tended to confuse the issue and the judgements made concerning what should be done to counter the threat.

One major myth is that the Soviet Union and its allies have been largely responsible for the growth of international terrorism. This theory suggests that the Soviets and their friends are the architects of a grand conspiracy which is designed to undermine and eventually to overthrow the Western democracies, which will then automatically fall into the Soviet orbit.

Western journalists and authors have found it convenient to repeat the grand conspiracy theory without making any effort to check their facts. For those who come from the political right, it is obviously self-serving to paint the image of the Russian Bear as an all-embracing evil that is behind every wrinkle in what would otherwise be a smooth blanket covering the democratic world. Israel, too, finds it convenient to blame the USSR for the activities of the PLO. In the same way as some Americans can see a Cuban hand in much that goes on in Central America, so the Israelis, by pointing to Soviet support of the PLO, can rally the West to their position. They argue that, if the Palestinians are allowed to establish a state, it will, given the USSR's continued support for the organisation, merely be a Soviet client state. The spectre of this in an area of such strategic importance inevitably causes concern in the White House and in other Western seats of government.

However, the Soviets have never provided funding for the PLO, and all the Palestinians interviewed during the research for this book talked in the most insulting terms about their alleged ally. Not only have the Soviets never contributed financially to the PLO cause, but they make the Palestinians pay in hard-earned foreign exchange for all arms delivered, and, for all their propaganda, the Israelis will privately admit that the USSR gives no *financial* support to the PLO. As one senior intelligence officer in Jerusalem put it: 'The Russians have never given the PLO anything except for a few scholarships.'

It is certainly the case that the Soviet Union and her allies have consistently supplied arms (almost invariably for hard cash) to a number of terrorist organisations, but this seems to be done on the basis that anything which undermines the West is to be encouraged. It is very difficult to discern an effective or coherent strategy behind all of this. Indeed, in every country – with the single exception of Cuba – where the Soviet Union has sponsored and supported a revolution, it has either failed to secure an ally (Egypt, Ethiopia, Mozambique, Zimbabwe) or brought to power a regime that is too independent for Moscow's liking (e.g. Angola's recent treaty with South Africa). Even Nicaragua is not proving as co-operative as the Soviets had hoped.

The conspiracists also make much of the point that terrorism is a uniquely Western phenomenon and that it therefore must be inspired by the Communists. Of course, from the Soviet point of view, the CIA is as guilty of supporting terrorism as we believe the KGB is of masterminding much anti-Western activity, and the Soviets point to CIA support for the Contras in Nicaragua, the anti-Khomeini guerrillas in Iran, the mujahedeen in Afghanistan and UNITA in Angola to illustrate their point. While this may be true, the United States is a more reliable friend and ally than the Soviets have ever been, tending to be more generous and to supply more sophisticated weaponry with fewer political strings attached.

Terrorism has been able to flourish in the West because a free society is full of the blood on which a terrorist leech can feed: easy access to money supplies, good communications, a free press and a liberal judiciary. By contrast, the Eastern Bloc is invariably totally repressive and has scant regard for human rights, while any pretence at a judicial system is little more than a joke. Add to that the overwhelming might of the different police agencies that form such a pervasive part of Communist life and there is very little opportunity indeed for terrorism to survive. Despite this, the West has made the occasional attempt to get terrorism started in the Communist Bloc by, at various times, financing and arming groups in Yugoslavia, Cuba and the Soviet Union itself. All have failed miserably.

Apart from any political benefit, all the Communist countries that have been involved in terrorism have made large sums of money from aiding different groups. Cuba, Bulgaria and the USSR itself, the three main arms suppliers, all insist on cash on the nail for arms deliveries, and all are invariably paid in much-needed foreign exchange. Bulgaria in particular has made an industry out of supplying arms to anyone who has the money – from gangsters to terrorists – and has a thriving trade in all manner of illegal goods, from drugs to cars, passing through the country's capital. The involvement of the Eastern Bloc in supporting international terrorism seems to have more to do with opportunism and economic expediency than with some grand political strategy which would overthrow the West. If there is a grand strategy, it has been a notable failure, as no group relying entirely on terrorism has yet achieved its aims.

Of all those who have supported terrorism, the person who best illustrates the changing nature of that support, as well as the static perception of terrorism by the public, is Colonel Muammar al-Gadaffi, the leader of Libya. For many years, Gadaffi has been portrayed as the godfather of international terrorism, the man to whom all terrorists can go caps-in-hand to have their pockets filled with gold and as many Kalashnikovs as they might require to further a revolution. Astonishing as this may seem, particularly in the light of recent US government statements about Libya's support of terrorism, this image is hopelessly out of date and is nothing like an accurate reflection of Gadaffi or the nature of international terrorism today.

When Gadaffi came to power by revolution, he was thirty-two years old and it was 1969. Throughout the Western world, there appeared to be chaos: terrorism was beginning to emerge and there were mass demonstrations all over the free world which had one thing in common – the need to change the established order.

Gadaffi was in charge of a country that had a current-account surplus, through the sale of oil, that was so huge it was an embarrassment and way beyond the requirements of the tiny population. With the first flush of revolutionary fervour, Gadaffi thought he should pass some of his wealth around in the hope of spreading revolution across the world. He was not particularly fussy about whom he gave money to; they simply had to be opposed to the existing order in their own countries, whatever form that order took.

Apart from generous donations to help a number of terrorist groups get off the ground, Gadaffi even introduced what was, in effect, a bonus system for terrorists, believing that good work should be suitably rewarded. Thus, those terrorists who carried out what he considered to be prestige projects, such as the Munich Olympics massacre or the kidnapping of the OPEC ministers in Vienna, received cash rewards varying from $1 million to $5 million. He also introduced a sort of welfare system for terrorists.

Quite understandably, this form of political idealism was very worrying to the West, which was only just beginning to wake up to the fact that modern society is terribly vulnerable to terrorist action. Gadaffi swiftly became the personification of evil and the father of modern terrorism. However, all that is history, and Gadaffi and the world have moved on.

The Libyan leader's largesse inevitably attracted the worst criminal elements from the terrorist fraternity, and Gadaffi found himself the victim of some cruel confidence tricks, which included paying over $1 million for a nuclear device that proved to be an elaborate fake, and donating large sums to alleged terrorists who, hardly believing their luck, spent the lot on fast cars and high living. Also, as counter-terrorist forces began to get into gear and much of the initial impetus fell away from the revolutionary movements, Gadaffi began to realise that his dream of a Libyan-orchestrated world revolution would never become reality. This period of growing maturity has fortunately coincided with a serious cash shortage in the Libyan economy. Oil revenue is down from $22 billion in 1980 to $8.5 billion today, leaving Gadaffi with hardly enough to pay for his ambitious plans for his own citizens, let alone worrying about the ambitions of foreigners.

For the last five years, Gadaffi has supplied almost no money to terrorist groups. Even the PLO, which still receives the full brunt of supportive propaganda from the Libyan publicity machine, has received no money since 1982, much to the disgust of the PLO leadership, who have come to realise they cannot trust even the most extreme of the Arab leaders.

Gadaffi, of course, still has ambitions outside his own borders, but they have had to be contained within budgetary constraints. His agents still operate extensively in the countries of North Africa, and Gadaffi has proclaimed that he would like to see Libyan-style revolutions occur all over that region. However, this is a far cry from the early 1970s, when Gadaffi was supporting everybody from the Baader–Meinhof gang to the Japanese Red Army.

Gadaffi has also remained in the public eye because of his current habit of sending hit squads abroad to liquidate members of the Libyan opposition. However, the activities of these assassins have been confined to shooting their own people, and there is no evidence of a Gadaffi masterplan to send his hit squads around the world to attack world leaders and thus force revolution upon reluctant democracies.

While Gadaffi seems to have matured, the West continues to view him as if it were still 1969 and he still the young radical threatening to change the world. In particular, the United States maintains the myth that Gadaffi is the main architect behind the continued existence and growth of international terrorism as a threat to modern society, and has called for a total boycott of Libya and a trade embargo to try and force Gadaffi to mend his ways. There is, however, little enough evidence to support American allegations that Gadaffi is the prime mover behind world terrorism, and her allies have tended to dismiss such calls as mere rhetoric that shows a rather naïve view of Gadaffi and a lack of understanding of the evolutionary process that has affected terrorism.

It is also interesting to note that, while Gadaffi has become the bogeyman of international terrorism, others who could be viewed as *more* supportive of terrorist groups have emerged comparatively un-scathed. By any standards, Saudi Arabia has, in the past, supplied more money to the PLO than any other country, and almost alone among Arab nations, it continues to fund the organisation – and yet, with the possible exception of Israel, no nation claims that Saudi Arabia supports and finances terrorism. On the contrary, its leaders are portrayed as models of moderation and are praised for their pro-Western policies.

The PLO is the group that has most benefited from cash donations from governments, but even with this most famous and closely examined of terrorist organisations, there are serious misconceptions, including the widely held view that the PLO depends on Arab governments for its survival. This is another myth – it is no longer the case. Even if all Arab aid to the PLO were cut off tomorrow, the PLO would merely have to cut back its annual budget by one-sixth. It would still have $500 million to play with, and the organisation would undoubtedly survive.

Indeed, the PLO has been used more as a tool by its state sponsors than as the recipient of generous aid. Every Arab country contributes to its own favoured group within the PLO, and the money that is given is invariably expected to bring with it political loyalty to the donor nation.

Despite all their rhetoric and public support for the PLO, the Arab nations have never managed to divorce their own personal ambitions sufficiently to donate money to the PLO as a single unit rather than to their own pet groups within it. This has led to the PLO and its leaders having to spend more time trying to hold the different groups together under the control of the executive committee than to political initiatives aimed at establishing a new Palestinian state.

In fact, some would argue that the Arabs have no interest in ever seeing the PLO establish a state. Like the Jews in Europe in the 1930s, the Palestinians as an ethnic group are despised for their business qualities, education and clannishness, all of which keep them remote from other Arabs. However, every Arab nation needs the Palestinians to run its industries and its hospitals, and if a Palestinian state were established, there would be a mass exodus of Palestinians from all Middle East countries resulting in chaos.

Over the last twenty years, the PLO's income profile has completely reversed. In the early days, the organisation was entirely dependent on hand-outs from rich Arabs. Today, out of its $600 million annual income, more than $500 million comes from investments, with donations from Arab leaders making up the balance. If finances of all the different groups that fall under the PLO umbrella are taken into account, a total annual income of $1.25 billion and assets of around $5 billion are involved.

Following the example of the PLO, those terrorist groups that have survived the first flush of revolutionary fervour have quickly realised that they cannot count on outside aid for their survival. All too often, such aid depends on personal whim or has unacceptable conditions attached. It is hardly surprising, therefore, that successful terrorist groups have in recent times become largely self-financing. Certainly, outside aid is always a help, but today, for groups such as the IRA and the PLO, it is not crucial to survival.

While there certainly is not one single chain linking all international terrorism to one central command, a great deal of information is pooled. In just the same way as scientists around the world share a certain amount of information, so terrorists exchange intelligence and occasionally help each other out. It is hardly a coincidence that all the significant terrorist groups have evolved in exactly the same way: from a small group of gunmen to a much larger group of relatively sophisticated business executives who use guns and bombs as only one of many tools in their revolutionary kitbag.

However, while there has never been a significant amount of co-operation among different terrorist groups at an international level, this may be changing. For the first time in recent history, a new alliance has developed between a number of different groups, which could mark a new and worrying escalation of international terrorist activity.

At a meeting outside Lisbon in June 1984, attended by representatives of many of Europe's leading terrorist groups, including Action Directe and the Red Army Faction of West Germany (the re-organised Baader –Meinhof gang), it was agreed that there would be a co-ordinated series of attacks against NATO targets. This campaign has so far resulted in some thirty attacks occurring within twelve months and a number of Western industrialists and servicemen being assassinated. It appears that the term 'NATO targets' has been interpreted to mean anything from a US soldier on patrol in West Germany to a director of a multi-national corporation that does business with any of the armed services of NATO members.

What is especially disturbing about this new wave of attacks is that the terrorist alliance appears to have united groups with widely differing political aims, among them Maoists, Marxists, anarchists and all shades in between.

The bombings and assassinations that began in 1984 caught all the Western intelligence agencies by surprise. All had begun to relax following their successes at the end of the 1970s, which saw the Baader–Meinhof gang smashed and the Red Brigade apparently seriously weakened. However, Europe is now paying for its complacency with inadequate intelligence and poor operational capability.

This new European terrorist alliance underlines the need for constant vigilance against the threat of terrorists as well as an appreciation of their ability to change tactics to keep ahead of counter-terrorist forces. It also underscores the need for greater international co-operation between police and intelligence forces to counter terrorism. At present, this co-operation is at a very low level, and a united terrorist front can only benefit from disunity among its enemies.

The terrorists' transition from simple revolutionaries to business executives can have startling results. In Colombia, for example, the two main terrorist groups – FARC and M19 – were for more than ten years no more than an annoyance to the government in Bogotá. At best they could each muster only 200 followers to rob the odd bank, kidnap some local businessmen or ambush an army patrol. It was strictly small-time stuff, and they had little or no prospect of forcing political change on the government, which was perfectly satisfied that the organisations could be contained. Like many other South American revolutionary groups that have appeared in the last twenty years, FARC and M19 seemed destined eventually to fade away, the revolutionary fire having turned to ashes.

However, the leaders of both groups began to see the potential in providing protection for the drug barons who each year grow and smuggle to the United States cocaine and marijuana worth billions of dollars. In the space of the last four years, each group has successfully generated income of around $150 million a year, and individually have attracted troops numbering more than 10,000 to their flags.

This rise to power has been accompanied by an increase in political influence undreamed of by either Marxist organisation at the beginning of this decade. With their huge incomes, they have been able to bribe senior politicians and worm their way into positions of influence. Their conversion to economic terrorism has given FARC and M19 political successes that would have been impossible to achieve through simple terrorist warfare.

While FARC and M19 have been adapting to achieve their revolutionary ambitions, the United States government, through the Drug Enforcement Administration (DEA), has been spending millions of dollars in an attempt to cut the flow of drugs to America. At the same time, hundreds of millions of dollars are being spent in El Salvador, Honduras and Nicaragua on conventional counter-terrorist measures to stop the spread of Communist regimes in the region. In Colombia, for example, 450 DEA agents are charged with stemming the flow of drugs; there are only three dealing with the terrorists who benefit from it.

The United States has made much of its opposition to the Nicaraguan government – which many feel is far less of a threat than President Reagan believes – and yet has apparently failed to make the link between terrorism and drugs in Colombia. This blinkered approach may well lead to the establishment in Bogotá of exactly the kind of government that the US sees as a threat to stability in the region.

Precisely the same process has occurred in Northern Ireland. Year after year, despite the warnings from the police and the army, the government has insisted on using 'head counts' as a criterion for judging the success of counter-terrorism in Northern Ireland, while the IRA has been quietly strengthening its position in Northern Ireland so that it is now so much a part of the province's economy that it is going to be impossible to eliminate. With that economic base has come far greater power than the IRA ever achieved before. While small in numbers, the organisation actually spreads through every aspect of working-class life.

In some respects, it could be argued that terrorism, once it has evolved sufficiently, actually performs a valuable social service. After all, the primary aim of the terrorists is to win over the broad mass of the people, and in the case of the IRA, this has involved the introduction of an employment programme (albeit illegal) and various social benefits. These might be welcome in other circumstances, but nothing should be allowed to give the impression that terrorism pays. If it is allowed free rein to alter its direction and build a strong financial base, then it is able to advance politically. In crude terms, money buys votes and as the IRA have learned, the combination of the bullet and the ballot box is a very powerful one.

In 1981, 30,000 people voted for Bobby Sands, the imprisoned IRA leader who was on hunger strike in the Maze prison and died four weeks later as MP for Fermanagh and South Tyrone. A year later, 64,000 people voted for Sinn Fein, the political wing of the IRA, in the Northern Ireland Assembly elections. At the 1983 General Election the Sinn Fein vote rose to 103,000 and in the 1984 elections for the European Parliament, the Sinn Fein candidate, although beaten, received 13.3 per cent of the vote. This has been achieved by a terrorist organisation which, ten years ago, was dismissed, with some justification, as a bunch of hoodlums with machine-guns. The IRA has moved on, but counter-terrorism has remained stuck in the same rut.

Using the resources generated by their income and their power base among the working class, the IRA have been building a network of advice centres across the country that will, in effect, act as a counterpoint to the government's own social service outlets. This, combined with their taxi service and other social pressure groups, will win the IRA many supporters.

It is now difficult to find anyone in the British government, the army or the police who actually believes that the IRA can be defeated. The best that everyone hopes for is a holding operation that can contain the IRA as a terrorist organisation and prevent its candidates defeating the voices of moderation at elections. It is now too late to do much to stop the flow of cash into the IRA coffers, and as every politician has discovered, it is easier to get power if you are rich than if you are poor.

Similarly, other successful terrorist groups such as the PLO and ETA in Spain, while not necessarily as near to some form of power as the terrorists in Colombia or Northern Ireland, have now built an economic base so sound as to be almost impossible to defeat.

In part, the rise to wealth of the terrorists can be blamed on the willingness of business organisations – banks, oil companies, investment houses – to do business with terrorists. Certainly, most terrorist groups attempt to disguise the origin of investment money by setting up dummy companies in Lichtenstein or Zurich, but it is hard to believe that many of the recipients of terrorist investments do not know precisely where the money is coming from. There is no doubt, for example, that the Arab Bank, now one of the biggest private banks in the world, is the conduit for a large amount of PLO money, and yet there has never been any question of sanctions being introduced against the bank.

There has also been a regrettable tendency to exploit the threat of terrorism for simple profit without thought of the consequences. An example of this is Lloyd's of London, which has led the field in establishing an insurance market for those who are threatened with kidnapping by terrorists. This has proved extremely profitable for Lloyd's and for other companies that have jumped on the bandwagon. Kidnapping for ransom has also become an extremely profitable and regular source of income for terrorists around the world, and it has become a business where the terrorists do not suffer, only the victims themselves and society at large.

There are professional negotiators on both sides; the kidnap victim claims back the ransom on his/her insurance; and the insurers are happy to pay out on the odd policy since the whole scheme is so immensely profitable. Unfortunately, it is not simply a matter of a little kidnapping. Every ransom paid has a multiplying effect on the terrorist groups that have received the money. Gunmen come cheap, and with no taxes to pay, much of the income can be reinvested in projects that will bring in a steady long-term income.

It is not good enough for big business to wash its hands of responsibility: they have a role to play in the fight against terrorism that, in many respects, is as important as that played by police forces and army counter-terrorist specialists. However, for business to be persuaded to act, they have to be supplied with information and that can only come from government-supplied intelligence.

There has been a tendency to divorce a government's fight against terrorism from the performance of the business community. Industry is generally portrayed as the victim of terrorism, while in some instances, for reasons that it justifies simply by pointing to improved profits, business is actually underwriting the growth in international terrorism. This should not be tolerated. In the same way as industry has the right to protection from the assaults of terrorists, so society has the right to expect that the business world will act responsibly in dealing with terrorists. Those companies that exploit terrorism for their own ends should be penalised in exactly the same way as a person who harbours a gunman on the run.

So firm is the established image of terrorism in the minds of politicians and civil servants around the world that it is going to be exceptionally difficult to bring about a change in perception. Even the Israelis, who have suffered more at the hands of terrorism than any other country, have devoted their counter-terrorist efforts to planned military actions against the PLO. Their primary aim has been to stop the bomber or capture the assassin before he or she presses the button or pulls the trigger, and comparatively little has been done to stop the economic growth of the organisation. As a result, the Israelis have been quite successful at limiting terrorist acts inside their borders, but at the same time, the PLO has grown into a multi-billion multinational business which is now impossible to defeat.

What is required is a two-tier approach which stops the bombers while at the same time undercutting the economic base that feeds them.

Unfortunately, the changing nature of international terrorism has not yet been appreciated by those who dictate policy in the West. The current US administration has done much to raise the consciousness of the Western world regarding the threat that terrorism poses, and the United States has set itself up as the guardian of the free world and as the leading nation among the Western democracies, a role that it rightly assumes. The bombing of the American embassy and the Marine compound in Beirut in 1983 graphically and tragically brought home to the American government and the world just how real the terrorist threat is today. These attacks gave added impetus to the US campaign against terrorism, but unfortunately even that impetus and subsequent policy appear to have been based on assumptions about terrorism that are at least ten years out of date.

In a major speech on 3 April 1984, US Secretary of State George Shultz said:

> In this fast-moving and turbulent world, to sit in a reactive posture is to risk being overwhelmed – or to allow others, who may not wish us well, to decide the world's future.
>
> Terrorism – particularly state-sponsored terrorism – is a contemporary weapon directed at America's interests, America's values and America's allies. We have no choice but to address ourselves boldly to the challenge of terrorism.
>
> State-sponsored terrorism is really a form of warfare. Motivated by ideology and political hostility, it is a weapon of unconventional warfare against democratic societies, taking advantage of the openness of those societies.
>
> How do we combat this challenge?
>
> Certainly we must take security precautions to protect our people and our facilities; certainly we must strengthen our intelligence capabilities to alert ourselves to the threats. But it is increasingly doubtful that a purely passive strategy can even begin to cope with the problem. This raises a host of questions for a free society: In what circumstances – and how – should we respond? When – and how – should we take preventive or pre-emptive action against known terrorist groups? What evidence do we insist upon before taking such steps?
>
> As the threat mounts, and as the involvement of such countries as Iran, Syria, Libya and North Korea has become more and more evident, then it is more and more appropriate that the nations of the West face up to the need for active defense against terrorism.
>
> Once it becomes established that terrorism works – that it achieves its political objectives – its practitioners will be bolder, and the threat to us will be all the greater.
>
> Americans are not a timid people. A foreign policy worthy of America must not be a policy of isolationism or guilt, but a commitment to active

engagement. We can be proud of this country, of what it stands for, and what it has accomplished. Our morality should be a source of courage when we make hard decisions, not a set of excuses for self-paralysis.

On the same day as Shultz made this speech, President Reagan signed National Security Decision Directive 138, which endorses the principles of both pre-emptive strikes and reprisal raids against terrorists.

The following month, President Reagan announced four measures aimed at combating terrorism that he would like to see become law. Under these proposals, it would be unlawful for an American citizen or business to provide training or maintenance (mechanical or other services) to specified terrorist groups, or to serve in, or act in concert with, such groups. The penalties for such acts would be a $100,000 fine or imprisonment for up to ten years or both. In addition to these two measures, the Secretary of State would have the authority to designate certain groups as terrorist. There would be no appeal and any individual or group associated with them would have thirty days to cut off all contact. Finally, a reward of as much as $500,000 would be paid to Americans who provided information leading to the arrest or conviction of terrorist group members, or of those conspiring to commit terrorist acts.

One of the primary objectives of urban terrorism is to provoke the establishment into instituting repressive measures which help convince the mass of the population of the justice of the revolutionary cause. The measures proposed by the Reagan administration not only endanger a broad range of civil liberties, but they are also hopelessly misdirected to meet the current threat. In addition, both Shultz and Reagan seem to view terrorism in the abstract. For those in the military who have to carry out government policy, this new and widely publicised stand against terrorism has led to some debate. Led by Defense Secretary Caspar Weinberger, who is normally considered a 'hawk', the military are arguing that it is impossible to use armed force effectively against terrorism in isolation. Instead, Weinberger has told the President that more effective intelligence-gathering is essential, first to understand the nature of the threat and then to decide what to do about it.

Apart from questions of morality, neither President Reagan nor senior members of his administration appear to understand the nature of modern-day terrorism, and are still seeking the quick and easy solution which will have an instant political pay-off. There is little point in achieving that limited aim if, by concentrating their resources on that specific task, the targeted terrorist organisation is allowed to develop in other areas.

It is time for Western governments to realise that there is no such quick and easy solution to the terrorist problem. Occasional short-term gains, while politically satisfying, will have to be sacrificed to achieve longer-term benefits which will do more to undercut the economic power base of international terrorism. As much effort should be devoted to tracing the sources of money, the bank accounts and the investments of terrorist groups as is spent on countering the bomber and the assassin.

There has been only a single instance in modern times when there was a concerted attack against one of the financial sources of a terrorist organisation, Noraid, which contributed significant sums to the IRA, was decimated after a series of court cases brought against them by the FBI using existing legislation. The virtual destruction of Noraid, while certainly not retarding the IRA's expansion to any great degree, did produce a salutary lesson, and this has yet to be widely appreciated.

Jail or kill some terrorist leaders while leaving their economic base intact and the organisation will simply change direction and grow once again, as has happened with the Red Brigade. Destroy the economic base and a terrorist group will wither and die. After all, terrorists cannot live on idealism alone, and even if their services do come cheap, they need to eat and to buy ammunition for their guns.

Current American policy – which is mirrored in large part by other Western countries – is woefully inadequate to respond to the threat. If the West continues to devote resources simply to attacking the military arm of terrorism, the threat that the phenomenon poses to Western democracies and vulnerable Third World nations will grow until, in some countries, it will be impossible to combat.

Tradition dictates that combating terrorism is largely the role of intelligence agencies and, where necessary, of élite special forces, such as Britain's SAS and the US Delta Force. But if terrorists have moved on and countering the threat has remained stagnant, the terrorists have been left with a substantial advantage.

One of the main aims of Israel's move north into the Lebanon in 1982 was to expel the PLO from the country and thus remove it as a threat to Israel. This showed a profound misunderstanding of the PLO animal of the 1980s. Certainly, the PLO army was defeated, a number of fighters were expelled from the country and a vast quantity of arms was captured, but the Swiss bank accounts, the gold stocks, the Wall Street money market certificates have remained intact, along with the computer centres to keep track of it all. The PLO are now buying more guns, hiring more gunmen and inevitably moving back into the Lebanon.

251

More importantly, perhaps, with the enormous assets at their disposal they will continue to buy influence, and so long as Israel insists on measuring success by the number of PLO terrorists it can kill, the PLO will continue to grow in wealth and strength.

There is a natural reluctance among both the intelligence and military communities to share information or to pass on responsibility for a role that has hitherto been their remit. Yet, it is time for their political masters to insist that the job of combating terrorism is broader than simple kill-counts.

Even if nothing is done, there are still some grounds for optimism. Terrorists set out to overthrow the society in which they are operating. However, the more they succeed, the richer they become and the more dependent they are on the survival of that society for a regular source of income to fund the revolution. Capitalism can evidently corrupt the most idealistic of terrorists.

APPENDICES

A glossary of terrorism

AD *Action Directe* was formed in France in May 1979 under the leadership of Jean-Marc Rouillan and Nathalie Menignon, both of whom were arrested in September 1980 by the French authorities and then pardoned in a later amnesty; they now run AD. The organisation has never been numerically strong – it currently has around ten active members – but it has carried out a widespread campaign of bombing and assassination, against targets that range from government figures to Zionists or businesses with Jewish connections. The AD is part of the Europe-wide anti-NATO terrorist alliance that emerged in late 1984.

ALF The *Arab Liberation Front* was formed in 1969 under Iraqi sponsorship as a direct rival to the Syrian-backed Al-Saiqa. The group is on the fringes of the PLO, although it is a member of the Rejectionist Front (a group of militant Palestinians who oppose a negotiated settlement of the Palestinian issue) and therefore allied with the more militant wing. It has had up to 500 members, but in reality, its influence is so small that active membership is probably one-tenth of that. The ALF is now based in Iraq.

ANC The *African National Congress* was founded in South Africa as a political party in 1912 and is thus the oldest terrorist organisation currently in existence. Until recently, it was also the least successful, largely because it refused to attack civilians even though it had organised agitation against apartheid since 1952 and was banned in 1960, after the Sharpeville massacre. However, this targeting policy changed in 1984, when a number of bombs were planted in city centres causing casualties to both blacks and whites. In addition, the younger, more militant members of ANC embarked on a campaign of intimidation of all those urban blacks whom they considered were friendly to the government. This campaign was remarkably successful and has, in part, been responsible for the deterioration in law and order.

The ANC has bases in Mozambique, Botswana and Zimbabwe, where its several hundred members receive training in guerrilla warfare, often from Eastern Bloc instructors.

255

ASALA   The *Armenian Secret Army for the Liberation of Armenia* was formed in Beirut in 1975 to win independence for the Armenians in Turkey. According to ASALA propaganda, the Turkish government has persecuted the Armenians for many years by repressing its culture and people, including the massacre of 1.5 million Armenians in 1915/16. The number of ASALA's supporters is not known but their activities are characterised by unusually savage attacks, generally against Turkish diplomats serving abroad. ASALA has been most active in the United States, particularly in California, as well as in Europe.

Baader–Meinhof   This West German group is more accurately known as the Red Army Faction (RAF) but is commonly called after the group's two founders, Andreas Baader and Ulrike Meinhof. It had its genesis in the anti-Vietnam war era at the end of the 1960s, and its early attacks were aimed at capitalist targets and those thought to be 'imperialist', including both people and buildings. The group was successful in attracting hundreds of active sympathisers and thousands of passive supporters, and was admired by aspiring left-wing revolutionaries worldwide. A massive counter-terrorist effort launched by the West German government decimated the group in the 1970s, and both founders committed suicide in prison. Without its leaders, the organisation foundered, and while there are a handful (probably fewer than ten) members still active in West Germany, the group is not the threat it once was. In the last two years, it has re-organised, and there is some evidence of a more effective cell structure and better planning, which has resulted in some well-executed terrorist attacks. The Baader–Meinof gang/Red Army Faction is part of the European terrorist alliance against NATO targets.

Black June   This was formed in 1976 in protest at the involvement of Syrian forces in the Lebanese civil war in June of that year. It was founded by Abu Nidal, a former associate of Yasser Arafat who fell out with the Al-Fatah leader over what Nidal saw as a rejection of a simple military solution to the Palestinian question. Nidal and his group, alone among Palestinian terrorists, are dedicated to destroying Israel and the current PLO leadership, and they have been responsible for a number of attacks on Yasser Arafat.

Originally based in Baghdad, Nidal now seems to shuttle between Iraq and Syria as a 'gun for hire', operating all over the Middle East. He is genuinely feared by all Middle East leaders and is widely thought to be psychotic. There were reports that he had died from cancer, but intelligence sources claim that he is still operating and has been responsible for attacks on Western diplomats in India and Greece, as well as a series of attacks in Jordan aimed at undermining the growing *rapprochement* between Arafat and King Hussein. Recently he has been reported in Libya, but there is some doubt about the exact nature of his support.

A glossary of terrorism

Black September *See* Al-Fatah.

BR *Brigate Rosse*, or the Red Brigade, are perhaps the most enduring of all modern terrorist groups. They first emerged in the late 1960s in the wake of worldwide student demonstrations that had opposition to America's involvement in Vietnam as their common theme. The BR began in about 1969 with an 'historic nucleus' drawn from the sociology department at the University of Trento. The 'nucleus' expanded some three years later to take in other, more violent and less intellectual members, and the BR began a nationwide campaign of exceptional violence, which involved the terrorising of the judiciary, the police and big business. At one time, there were fears of the total collapse of Italian society, largely due to the incompetence of the police.

However, following the assassination of the former premier and Christian Democrat party leader, Aldo Moro, on 16 March 1978, a major police effort to capture the terrorists was launched, and more than 2500 suspects were arrested. Despite this, it was not until the successful release of one of the BR's kidnap victims, US General James Dozier, in December 1981 that the organisation appeared to be finally destroyed.

Recently, however, Italian police have noticed a sharp increase in terrorist violence, and they now believe that the remnants of the organisation have regrouped and retrained. The Red Brigade claimed responsibility for the murder in February 1984 of Leamon Hunt, the director of the multinational peace-keeping force in Sinai. The communiqué in which the BR claimed responsibility included anti-American slogans, a demand that Italy withdraw from NATO and opposition to American missiles being based in Italy. The Red Brigade is now part of the anti-NATO alliance of terrorist groups.

CCC The *Cellules Communistes Combattantes* (Fighting Communist Cells) first emerged in October 1984 with an attack on Litton Data Systems in Belgium. Over the next eighteen months, the CCC was responsible for more than twenty bombings and killings in Belgium, all of them aimed at NATO targets or at companies that allegedly have dealings with members of NATO's armed forces. The CCC is believed to have around ten members, some of whom have had military training, and they are thought to be led by Pierre Carrette, a former member of Action Directe (AD) who fled to Belgium in 1981. The CCC is part of the European alliance of terrorists that began in June 1984 as a result of a meeting of international terrorists in Lisbon.

Christian Militia *See* Christian Phalange.

Christian Phalange This was formed before World War II as a response to the rise of Muslim influence in the Lebanon, a country traditionally ruled by Christian families. The Phalange (also known as the Christian Militia),

257

numbering several thousand, are extremely well-armed and funded, often by the Israelis who have long viewed them as a useful cat's-paw in a country where the PLO have been based. Indeed, the Christians have fought the PLO in two civil wars and more recently welcomed the Israeli invasion of the Lebanon. The current President of Lebanon, Amin Gemayel, is also the leader of the Phalange.

Contras The Marxist-Leninist revolution that brought the Sandinistas to power in 1979 deposed the right-wing government of Anastasio Somoza Debayle, and several thousand members of the former dictator's national guard were forced into exile in neighbouring Honduras and Costa Rica. These first united under the umbrella of the Fuerzas Armadas Revolucionarias de Nicaragua (Nicaraguan Armed Revolutionary Forces, or FARN), but later split into a number of different groups, including the Nicaraguan Democratic Force (FDN). All are now generally known as the Contras.

The Sandinistas have acted as an inspiration to all Latin American revolutionaries, and since their victory, revolutionary warfare has spread with alarming speed throughout the continent. As the Sandinistas are left-wing and, while on the road to victory, received considerable support from Cuba and the Soviet Union, the Reagan administration believes that they, rather than political and economic circumstances, are the cause of the unrest in the region. As a result, the US government has been funding the Contras, both covertly via the CIA and more overtly in the guise of 'humanitarian aid', the latter currently to the tune of $27 million. Thwarted by Congress in its wish to give more direct military support, the Reagan administration has also been encouraging right-wing groups to donate $25 million to the Contras.

Militarily, the Contras have shown little sign of winning a victory. Their forces currently number between 12,000 and 15,000 (against the Nicaraguan government's 62,000), and most are forced to remain in the countryside. The government has been extensively supplied by the Soviet Union, most recently with Mi-24 Hind D helicopter gunships, which can bring devastating firepower to bear in a rural environment. It seems unlikely that the current stalemate will change, as the Reagan government sees the role of the Contras as vital in controlling the spread of Communism in Latin America.

DFLP The *Democratic Front for the Liberation of Palestine* was formed in 1969 when Naif Hawatmeh and three colleagues broke away from the PFLP, arguing that political dialogue rather than purely military action could bring about a solution to the Palestinian problem. The DFLP has confined its terrorist activities to Israel. It is supported by the Soviet Union, has good relations with China and bases in Iraq, Syria, Tunisia and the Sudan for its estimated 1500 members.

A glossary of terrorism

ETA The *Euskadi ta Askatasuna* (Freedom for the Basque Homeland) was established in 1959 with the aim of gaining independence, through violence, for the Basque homeland in northern Spain. Like the IRA (with whom they have very good relations), ETA see themselves as a persecuted minority in a country with which they do not identify. Again like the IRA, ETA has split into a number of different wings – including ETA-M, which is the most violent, and the 'autonomous commandos', who also favour a more violent path to independence.

ETA have been quite successful in forcing the Madrid government to grant some autonomy to the region, and have made some gains at local and general elections.

FARC The *Fuerzas Armadas Revolucionarias Colombias* (Armed Revolutionary Forces of Colombia) was formed in 1966, but for the next ten years, it had very little impact on the Colombian political scene, limiting its activities to the occasional shooting or symbolic occupation of a rural village. In the mid-1970s, however, FARC went into the kidnap-for-ransom business, and as its income grew, so did its ambitions. As a result, in the early 1980s the group began organising protection for the cocaine producers in the country. In two years, from a group that numbered less than 200 followers, FARC grew to have several thousand well-armed and trained guerrillas under its control. Large sections of the country are now dominated by FARC, and it has a major influence in the cities. In 1984, it agreed to a truce proposed by the government, which would attempt to integrate the terrorists back into society in return for social reform and a prospect of government posts for some of the terrorist leaders. At the time of writing, FARC is holding to the truce, but M19 (*see below*) has not.

Al-Fatah The Harakat al-Tahrir al-Watani al-Filistini (Palestine National Liberation Movement) was the first military group to appear and fight on behalf of Palestinians. Although Al-Fatah was not formally established until 1962, it has its origins in the mid-1950s. It came to prominence after the 1967 Six-Day War and, in 1968, joined the PLO, gaining control in 1969 when Al-Fatah's leader Yasser Arafat was elected chairman of the PLO Executive Committee. Since then, despite attempts to curb Al-Fatah's power by jealous rivals, the group has held sway within the PLO.

The members of Al-Fatah, like their leader, are both nationalistic and pragmatic. They have committed numerous acts of terrorism both inside and outside Israel, and set up and run Black September, the organisation responsible for some of the worst terrorist attacks, including the massacre of Israeli athletes at the Munich Olympics in September 1972. However, in more recent years, Al-Fatah has stressed a political rather than a military solution to the Palestinian question. Although publicly Al-Fatah demands total Israeli withdrawal from the occupied territories, recognition of the Palestinian people's rights and the establishment of an independent Palestinian state, privately Arafat and others in Al-Fatah adopt a more moderate line. Some form of joint Palestinian–Jordanian federation might be acceptable, provided Arafat could be confident of getting the agreement of other, more militant groups.

Al-Fatah may have as many as 7000 guerrillas in Tunisia, Syria and Iraq, and it receives support from most of the moderate Gulf states, including Saudi Arabia and Kuwait. PLO diplomats abroad are often members of Al-Fatah, as Arafat tends to promote his own followers into positions of influence in the PLO.

FP25   The *Forcas Populares do 25 Abril* (Popular Forces of 25 April) was formed in Portugal in 1980, and has since carried out a series of bomb attacks and assassinations aimed at both military and civilian targets. Numbering fewer than twenty, they have been unusually co-operative with other terrorist groups. For example, in 1981 they launched a series of attacks against British targets in Portugal in support of the Provisional IRA, and in 1984, they joined the anti-NATO alliance of European terrorists.

INLA   The *Irish National Liberation Army* was formed in the late 1970s as an offshoot of the Provisional IRA. It is the most brutal of all terrorist groups in Northern Ireland and is totally committed to expelling the British from Northern Ireland by violent means – a tactic that other groups now believe to be unrealistic. It is a Marxist-Leninist group and is committed to establishing a united and socialist Ireland. The security forces have recently arrested a number of INLA members, and its combat strength is now no more than twenty.

IRA   The *Irish Republican Army* emerged in its modern form in 1956, when it initiated a new wave of terrorism in protest at Protestant discrimination against Catholics in Northern Ireland, and with the longer-term aim of forcing the British government to leave North Ireland and thus allow the north to unite with the Republic of Ireland. In 1969, the IRA split, with the Provisionals arguing that force was the only way to get the British to leave, and the Officials suggesting a political solution. The Officials no longer have any real influence on the political and terrorist scene in Northern Ireland, and ironically, the Provisionals have now adopted much of the Officials' strategy which caused the original rift.

The Provisionals now have some 300 active supporters operating in Northern Ireland and in the Republic. In recent years, there has been a marked falling-off in support for the military activities of the organisation, which has been matched by a rise in the fortunes of Sinn Fein, the political wing of the

Provisional IRA. There are only thirty active Provo members operating in Belfast, and all of these are under constant surveillance by the security forces.

Islamic Jihad   This Shi'ite fundamentalist group first emerged in April 1985 when it claimed responsibility for the bombing of a restaurant near Madrid where American servicemen and their families from a nearby US air base regularly eat. The bomb killed eighteen people – fourteen of them women – and wounded another eighty-two. It was thought at the time that the bombing was the work of ETA-M, but it is now accepted that Islamic Jihad was responsible.

Shi'ite fundamentalists based in the Lebanon and funded by Iran have been responsible for a wave of terrorist attacks in Europe and the Middle East under a wide variety of names. All the attacks have a common theme: hatred of anything and anybody that represents a potential threat to the régime of Ayatollah Khomeini in Iran.

JRA   In their time, the *Japanese Red Army* were among the most feared of all terrorist groups. They were responsible for the Lod airport massacre in 1972 when twenty-five people were killed and seventy injured, and carried out a number of spectacular hijackings, some on behalf of the PFLP with whom they worked closely. They first emerged in 1966, but at the end of the 1970s, the group formally renounced violence as a way of achieving political change and little has been heard of them since. There have been reports that as many as twenty former members of the JRA are still travelling with the PFLP, but there have been no reports of their being involved in terrorist acts.

M19   The *Movimiento 19 Abril* was formed in 1973 by Carlos Toledo Plata and Jaime Bateman Cayon, both of whom had been supporters of the Colombian political party, the National Popular Alliance (ANAPO). The party did poorly in the elections of 19 April 1970, and the two men decided on armed struggle as the way to political power. Toledo was captured in 1981, but Bateman continues as the group's leader. In the 1970s, the group carried out a series of kidnaps and bank robberies, which gave them a certain notoriety but little significant political influence. After Toledo's capture, Bateman followed the example of FARC (with whom he had served prior to setting up M19) and began providing protection for the drug barons growing and distributing cocaine in the country. Along with FARC, M19 is a major political force in Colombia, and Bateman can call on as many as 10,000 well-armed and well-trained troops. President Betancur's 1984 offer of amnesty to the terrorists, which included the prospect of government posts for some of the groups' leaders, was at first accepted by the M19 leadership. However, in June 1985, they abandoned it because of the lack of progress by the government in social reform, and M19 resumed armed conflict.

MNR The *Mozambique National Resistance* emerged out of the collapse of Portuguese rule in Africa in 1975, and was trained, financed and supported by both Rhodesia and South Africa, who were concerned that the new left-wing government in Mozambique might attempt to spread revolution north and south. Since the fall of the Rhodesian government, South Africa has continued to support the MNR, and they are now a well-trained and armed force of around 5000 men. They have been very effective in undermining the government in Mozambique and have also carried out acts of sabotage in Zimbabwe. The MNR control large areas of Mozambique, and despite a 'peace' agreement being signed between the South African and Mozambique governments in 1985, there is little sign of a reduction in MNR activities, and the South African government now appear unable to control the group they originally created.

OIRA *See* IRA.

PFLP The *Popular Front for the Liberation of Palestine* was formed in December 1967 when several small terrorist groups merged with the Arab Nationalist Movement's Palestine Special Group for Armed Struggle in the occupied territories, which itself had been founded before the 1967 Arab–Israeli war by Dr George Habbash. The PFLP, now part of the PLO, is a Marxist-Leninist organisation and heads the Rejectionist Front of Palestinian groups that are opposed to a political settlement with Israel. The PFLP is backed by Libya, South Yemen, Algeria and a number of the minor Gulf States such as the United Arab Emirates.

Although officially limited to terrorist activity in the occupied territories, the PFLP has, in fact, been responsible for a large number of terrorist acts in the Middle East and Europe, including the hijacking of five aircraft in 1970 – three of which were destroyed at Dawson's Field in Jordan. In the mid-1970s, Habbash officially renounced the use of terrorism as a political tool, which resulted in the defection of his deputy Wadi Haddad who continued to carry out terrorist acts, including the Entebbe hijacking in June 1976, until his death from cancer in 1978. Haddad's Baghdad-based PFLP-Special Command, now under the command of Salim Abu Salim, has not renounced terrorism and a question mark remains over the links between that group and the PFLP.

The PFLP is currently based in South Yemen, and it has close links with other international groups, some of whom have received training from the PFLP.

PFLP-GC After the Six Day War of 1967, the Palestine Liberation Front, a small commando group created by Ahmed Jibril in 1959, joined with others to form Section B of the PFLP. The Jibril faction broke away completely in 1968 to form the PFLP-General Command, claiming that there was too much emphasis on politics and not enough on fighting. The group is supported by Libya and Syria, where its estimated 250 members are based.

PIRA *See* IRA.

PLF The *Palestine Liberation Front* split with the PFLP-GC in 1977 in protest at the latter's alleged collusion with Syria and the Lebanon. The PLF is a member of the Rejectionist Front (*see* PFLP), is supported by Iraq and Libya, and its 200 members are believed to be based in Baghdad.

PLO The *Palestine Liberation Organisation* – an 'umbrella' organisation now comprising eight terrorist groups and fifteen social and educational associations – was born at the first Arab summit conference in January 1964, which decided to establish a 'Palestinian entity and personality'. The PLO was formed four months later at a meeting of a Palestinian Congress in Jerusalem, Ahmed Shukairy, the Palestinian representative at the Arab League, was made chairman and a Palestinian National Covenant and constitution were approved.

The PLO was committed to armed struggle to liberate the Palestinian people and form a Palestinian state. In 1969, Yasser Arafat's Al-Fatah became the dominant force in the PLO, after it had gained control of the Palestine National Council – commonly regarded as the Palestinian Parliament-in-exile – and the PLO Executive Committee, and Arafat became chairman of the PLO. Since then, the organisation has been split regularly by differences, which have always revolved around the degree of political negotiation that should be allowed to find an acceptable and peaceful solution with Israel.

The PLO has received official recognition from a large number of nations and has representatives in at least seventy-seven countries. In 1974 Arafat addressed the UN General Assembly, and the PLO subsequently gained observer status at the UN. It is also a full member of the Arab League. Such recognition has enhanced the PLO's claim to be the sole and legitimate voice of the Palestinian people – something the Israelis have always questioned, as they rightly point out that the Palestinian people have never held an election to vote into office any PLO member. However, there is little doubt that any peace settlement will have to involve the PLO, and no settlement will have a chance of success unless it has the PLO's stamp of approval. This, in turn, means directly involving Yasser Arafat who retains personal control over the organisation.

PSF The *Popular Struggle Front* was formed in Jordan in 1968. It briefly joined Al-Fatah in 1971 but went independent once again after the 1973 Arab–Israeli war. It has never been a significant force in Middle East policies, and its acts of terrorism have been uninspired and ineffective. The group is sponsored by Iraq, and its 100 members are based in Baghdad.

RAF *See* Baader–Meinhof.

Red Brigade *See* BR.

RZ The *Revolutionare Zellen*, or Red Cells, were formed in West Germany in 1973, apparently as an offshoot of the Baader–Meinhof gang. They are few in number, possibly only ten active members, and have waged a sporadic campaign of terrorism during the past decade aimed at both buildings and people. Compared with Baader–Meinhof, they are an ineffective group who have had little impact, and this looks unlikely to change, particularly as they are excluded from the anti-NATO terrorist alliance formed in 1984.

As-Saiqa 'Thunderbolt' was formed in October 1968 as the military arm of the Vanguards of the Popular War for the Liberation of Palestine, which itself was formed prior to the 1967 Arab–Israeli war by members of the Palestinian branch of Syria's Ba'ath Party and of the Syrian Army's Palestinian battalion. It officially opposes terrorism but has carried out a few isolated acts of little impact. Being pro-Syrian, the group opposes the Iraqi-backed Rejectionist Front (*see* PFLP), and it generally co-operates with Al-Fatah in taking a moderate anti-terrorism line.

SWAPO The *South-West African Peoples Organisation* was formed in South Africa-governed Namibia in 1960, having developed from the Ovamboland People's Organisation, and is led by Sam Nujoma. SWAPO is supported by the Soviet Union, Cuba and by neighbouring African states. It is based in Angola and its estimated 4000-strong army is trained and equipped by Cuba. SWAPO is not very effective militarily, preferring to run a very low-intensity operation which ties up considerable numbers of South African troops. The South African government has found the war financially very expensive, although it has proved to be a useful training ground for government forces.

There have been a number of peaceful overtures from South Africa recently, and there seems to be a willingness to give some form of autonomy to Namibia. The sticking point appears to be the role that SWAPO, a left-wing group pledged to bring 'democratic socialism' to the country, will have in any new government.

UDA The *Ulster Defence Association* was formed in 1971 as a Protestant response to the rise of IRA activity in Northern Ireland. The group swiftly gained members and is today around 50,000 strong, making it by far the most powerful paramilitary group active in Northern Ireland. It has sympathisers among the police and the Ulster Defence Regiment, and is generally well-armed and well-trained.

The UDA have been responsible for a number of assassinations and revenge killings of Catholics in the province. It opposes any form of power-sharing with the south and wants Ulster to retain close links with the British mainland. They are a constant political pressure, looming large in the background of any talks between the British and the Republic of Ireland, as they have the power to provoke civil war in the province.

UFF The *Ulster Freedom Fighters* are a small band of killers who emerged from the UDA in 1973, and are responsible for most of the Protestant terrorism that occurs in Ulster. While few in number, they (like the INLA on the Catholic side) are exceptionally violent. They officially deny links with the UDA, but some intelligence sources suggest that the UFF carry out killings that would be politically unacceptable to the UDA.

UVF The *Ulster Volunteer Force* was formed in 1966 as an underground movement to oppose the rise in IRA terrorism. It is against any settlement that involves union with the south, and has used terrorism to put over its point of view. The group officially renounced terrorism in 1976, but has remained heavily involved in crime in the province since then.

Vanguards of the Popular War for the Liberation of Palestine   *See* Al-Saiqa.

Notes

Chapter 1: Terrorism: the multi-national corporation

p. 14 'For the Soviet Union and her allies': The most detailed accounts of Soviet involvement in international terrorism appear in Claire Sterling, *The Terror Network* (Weidenfeld & Nicolson, London, 1981); and in Samuel T. Francis, *The Soviet Strategy of Terror* (The Heritage Foundation, Washington, 1981). Both these books subscribe to the conspiracy theory of world terrorism and tend to be from the political right.

p. 15 'The Hotel Vitosha': Information on Bulgaria involvement and Turkish terrorism comes from the *International Herald Tribune*, 1 February 1983; statement by Professor Aydin Yalcin before the US Senate Subcommittee on Security and Terrorism on 25 June 1981 (US Government Printing Office, serial no. J-97-43); *New Republic*, 28 February 1983, pp. 9–10; and interviews with DEA officials in Washington, the Department of State and private arms dealers.

p. 15 'to assassinate Pope John Paul II': The most detailed account (so far) of the plot to kill the Pope is by Claire Sterling in *Time of the Assassins* (Angus & Robertson, London, 1984). However, much of this book has a strong right-wing bias and many of her conclusions are suspect.

p. 17 'Through the years': From *Alleged Assassination Plots Involving Foreign Leaders*, Report of the US Senate Select Committee, 20 November 1975 (US Government Printing Office, Washington, 1975). Quoted in Jeremy Pearce, *Under the Eagle* (Latin America Bureau, London, 1981), p. 34.

p. 19 'in the rolling hills': *Daily Telegraph*, 2 December 1983. This was confirmed by the US State Department in interviews in January 1984.

p. 19 'since 1978, Cuba has': *Cuba's Renewed Support for Violence in Latin America* (US Department of State, Washington, December 1984).

p. 20 'the Reagan administration officially authorised': Jay Peterzell, *Reagan's Secret Wars* (Centre for National Security Studies, Washington, 1984), pp. 75–100.

p. 20 'the US Defense Department': *International Herald Tribune*, 6–7 July 1985; *The Times*, 13 July 1985.

p. 20 'a CIA-written manual': Tayacan, *Operaciones Sicologicas en Guerra de Guerrillas*. Neither publisher nor date of publication is listed.

p. 23 'US Secretary of State': *The Times*, 27 October 1984, p. 6.

p. 23 'the US State Department claimed': Told to the author by the Office for Combating Terrorism, September 1985.

p. 23 'A massive car bomb': *Newsweek*, 27 May 1985, pp. 14–15.

p. 24 'the Italian cruise liner': *The Times*, 12 October 1985; *Sunday Times*, 13 October 1985; *Observer*, 13 October 1985; *Newsweek*, 21 October 1985, pp. 12–30.

p. 26 'after Operation Prairie Fire': The material for this section comes from interviews conducted by the author in Washington and London, April 1986; *Sunday Times*, 13 April and 20 April 1986; unpublished material supplied by Jon Connell, Washington correspondent of *Sunday Times*; US Department of State: *Libya under Qadhafi: A pattern of Aggression*, Special Report No 138, January 1986; Public Report of the Vice President's Task Force on Combatting Terrorism, February 1986.

Chapter 2: An international conspiracy?

p. 37 Skyjack Sunday: Detailed accounts of the events of that day can be found in Edward F. Mickolous, *Transnational Terrorism: A Chronology of Events, 1968–1979* (Aldwych Press, London, 1980), pp. 208–13; Edgar O'Ballance, *The Language of Violence* (Presidio Press, San Rafael, Calif., 1979), pp. 83–92.

p. 38 'the British abandoned Palestine': The British Foreign Office has compiled a detailed background brief on the PLO, which is a thorough and balanced account. The most detailed published sources are: Aryeh Y. Yodfat and Yuval Arnon-Ohanna, *PLO Strategy and Tactics* (Croom Helm, London, 1981); Helena Cobban, *The Palestinian Liberation Organisation: People, Power and Politics* (Cambridge University Press, 1984); Jillian Becker, *The PLO: The Rise and Fall of the Palestine Liberation Organisation* (Weidenfeld & Nicolson, London, 1984). Cobban is pro-PLO and Becker is pro-Israel.

p. 42　'In his autobiography': Abu Iyad with Eric Rouleau, *My Home, My Land: A Narrative of the Palestinian Struggle* (Time Books, New York, 1981), pp. 66–7. Further details of China's links with the PLO came from two senior members of the PLO Central Committee interviewed in November 1983.

p. 43　'More than seventy-five per cent': Quoted in Yodfat and Arnon-Ohanna, *PLO Strategy and Tactics*, op. cit., pp. 78–80.

p. 44　'Israel's attack': An exceptionally detailed account of that war is described by Ze'ev Shiff in his outstanding book, *Operation Peace for Galilee* (Simon & Schuster, New York, 1984).

p. 45　'Among these documents': The most important collation of documents has been provided by Raphael Israeli, *The PLO in Lebanon: Selected Documents* (Weidenfeld & Nicolson, London, 1983). Other information has been supplied by Israeli Defence Force Officials, the Shiloah Institute at Tel Aviv University and intelligence sources.

p. 46　'The Israeli Defence Force claims to have seized': Richard A. Gabriel, *Operation Peace for Galilee* (Hill & Wang, New York, 1984), p. 113.

p. 47　'Robert Moss': From *Terrorism: The Role of Moscow and its Subcontractors*, hearing before the US Senate Subcommittee on Security and Terrorism, 26 June 1981 (US Government Printing Office, serial no. 97-44), p. 13.

p. 52　This list of meetings has been compiled from a number of sources, including Israeli, British and European Community counter-terrorist experts.

Chapter 3: The oil incendiary

p. 55　'Experience has shown': Abu Iyad, *My Home, My Land*, op. cit., pp. 32–3. For detailed background on the relations between the PLO and the Gulf countries, *see* Rashid Khalidi and Kamil Mansour (eds.), *Palestine and the Gulf* (Institute for Palestine Studies, Beirut, 1982); Yodfat and Arnon-Ohanna, *PLO Strategy and Tactics*, op. cit.; and Cobban, *The Palestinian Liberation Organisation*, op. cit.

Notes

p. 56   'At a meeting of the Palestine National Council': O'Ballance, *The Language of Violence*, op. cit., pp. 100–101.

p. 57   'The momentum was': *Jerusalem Post*, 11 November 1977.

p. 57   'Of the $250 million': *Middle East Reporter*, 22 January 1979.

p. 58   'According to a story': *Middle East Reporter*, 11 May 1982.

p. 59   'Consequently, the Saudis banned': Information from a senior PLO official.

p. 59   'Jamal Sawrani': *Al Khaleej*, 13 October 1985.

p. 61   'The organisation is led': The best details on Abu Nidal and Black June are to be found in an unpublished manuscript by the Israeli journalist Yossi Melman; additional information came from the *Washington Post*, 5 February 1984; *Guardian*, 24 November 1983; *Wall Street Journal*, 11 April 1983; *The Times*, 7, 9 and 30 March 1983; and intelligence sources in Washington, Tel Aviv and London.

p. 63   'US State Department and CIA sources': Information supplied to the author in Washington, 3–5 December 1985.

p. 64   'In a rare interview': 'Abul Nidal Parle', *France Pays Arabes*, February 1985.

p. 65   'We welcome Arafat': Libyan Information Agency, 2 September 1981, quoted in *Libyan–PLO Relations*, and Israeli Defence Force publication. Additional details on Gadaffi's role in terrorism come from: *Los Angeles Times*, 28 August and 7 September 1981; *New York Times*, 26 and 30 August 1981; *Daily Telegraph*, 22 October 1983; *Sunday Times*, 21 December 1980; *Newsweek*, 20 July 1981; Christopher Dobson and Ronald Payne, *The Weapons of Terror* (Papermac, London, 1979), pp. 81–5; Marius H. Livingston (ed.), *International Terrorism in the Contemporary World* (Greenwood Press, Westport, Conn., 1978), pp. 172–3. Further material came from the US State Department, Israeli intelligence and two senior members of the PLO.

p. 66   'We have had a long history': *Der Spiegel*, 17 December 1979, pp. 26–9, quoted in Yodfat and Arnon-Ohanna, *PLO Strategy and Tactics*, op. cit., p. 122.

269

p. 66   'other reports suggested': Mickolous, *Transnational Terrorism*, op. cit., pp. 570–72.

p. 66   'The most extraordinary long-term arrangement': The most detailed account of the lives of Wilson and Terpil can be found in Joseph C. Goulden, *The Death Merchant* (Simon & Schuster, New York, 1984).

p. 66   'Terpil was fired': Details on Wilson and Terpil come from the *Sunday Times*, 21 December 1981; *Los Angeles Times*, 28 August 1981; *New York Times*, 26 and 30 August 1981; *New York Times Magazine*, undated; *Newsweek*, 2 May 1983, p. 17, and 20 July 1981, p. 20.

p. 69   'The last confirmed sighting': Information supplied by Israeli intelligence.

p. 70   'In the cycle of international terrorism': Details for this section on Iran come from: Robin Wright, *Sacred Rage* (Linden Press, New York, 1985), the most definitive account of the rise of Shi'ite militancy; Robert Graham, *Iran: the Illusion of Power* (Croom Helm, London, 1979); Aryeh Y. Yodfat, *The Soviet Union and Revolutionary Iran* (Croom Helm, London, 1984); M. S. El Azhary (ed.), *The Iran–Iraq War* (Croom Helm, London, 1984); *Washington Post*, 1 and 3 February 1984; *Guardian*, 13 February 1984; *Observer*, 29 January 1984; *The Times*, 22 March and 23 December 1983; *International Herald Tribune*, 12 December 1983 and 3 January 1984; interview with Dr Ariol Marari, Tel Aviv University, January 1984; interviews with sources in Tel Aviv, Jerusalem, London and Washington.

p. 70   'such religious devotion': An interesting account of Sabbah's life appears in O'Ballance, *The Language of Violence*, op. cit., pp. 2–6.

p. 72   'The first country to suffer': Events witnessed by the author.

p. 73   'The Saudis turn came next': David Holden and Richard Johns, *The House of Saud* (Sidgwick & Jackson, London, 1981), pp. 511–38.

p. 75   'As Iran has achieved': *Observer*, 13 October 1985.

p. 76   'Since the capture': *Sunday Times*, 14 April 1985.

p. 76   'samples of the bomb': Information supplied to the author by counter-terrorist sources.

p. 76   'Further evidence': *Sunday Times*, 16 June 1985.

Chapter 4: Criminal capital

p. 83　'The Lebanese did not welcome': Much information for this section comes from Dr Zvi Lanir of the Centre for Strategic Studies, Tel Aviv University, who made a special study of the Palestinian refugee camps following Operation Peace for Galilee in 1982. His book, *Meetings in Rashidiya: Anatomy of a Palestinian Community in Lebanon* (Dvir, Tel Aviv, 1983) is the definitive work on the subject. He was interviewed by the author in April 1983. Additional details come from sources in military intelligence and in the PLO; *Jerusalem Post*, 6 August and 22 October 1982 and 7 July and 23 September 1983.

p. 86　'the organisation established Samed': Details from *Samed Diary*, 1983; interview with Ahmed Abu Ala, general manager and chairman of Samed; senior PLO sources; *Jerusalem Post*, 6 August 1980.

p. 90　'The BSO was the result': For detailed background on Black September, *see* Michael Bar-Zohar and Eitan Haber, *The Quest for the Red Prince* (Weidenfeld & Nicolson, London, 1983); pp. 205–10 contain details on Abu Hassan Salamah. See also *Wall Street Journal*, 10 February 1983; *Jerusalem Post*, 23 and 25 January 1979; O'Ballance, *The Language of Violence*, op. cit., pp. 105–27. Additional material on the BSO comes from Israeli and PLO sources.

p. 91　'a secret meeting in Rabat': Henry Kissinger, *Years of Upheaval* (Weidenfeld & Nicolson/Michael Joseph, London, 1982), pp. 624–9.

p. 93　'an extraordinary deal': Details of the robbery came from sources within the PLO; *8 Days* magazine, 4 August 1979, pp. 6–10; Norris McWhirter (ed.), *Guinness Book of Records* (Guinness Superlatives Ltd, London, edition 26), p. 192; sources inside the Chubb Safe Co. and the British Bank of the Middle East; Jonathan Randal, *The Tragedy of Lebanon* (Chatto & Windus, London, 1983), pp. 98–104.

p. 97　'This enabled the PFLP': O'Ballance, *The Language of Violence*, op. cit., pp. 103–105.

p. 99　'the Arab Bank emerged': Most of the information on the Arab Bank came from interviews with bankers in the Lebanon and elsewhere in the Middle East. Israeli intelligence supplied some details, and financial records were obtained using a database in the City of London; also, on 10 April 1984, the *Wall Street Journal* published an article on the subject.

271

p. 100 'Arafat paid $2.4 million': Information supplied by the Shiloah Institute and confirmed by the PLO.

p. 103 'The PLO always maintained': *The Times*, 21 October 1983.

p. 103 'However, Abu Musa': *Middle East Reporter*, November 1983, pp. 18–20; *Jerusalem Post*, 3 June and 10 and 25 November 1983; *International Herald Tribune*, 26–27 November 1983; *Guardian*, 13 July 1984.

p. 104 'the British Embassy': Story told to author by a senior British diplomat involved.

p. 105 'When the PLO were expelled': *International Herald Tribune*, 21 November 1984.

p. 105 'that of North Yemen': Information supplied by North Yemeni government sources, June 1985.

p. 105 'In Tunisia': *New York Times Magazine*, 18 August 1985, p. 26 *et seq.*

p. 105 'Arafat clearly has not': Eyewitness account, September 1985.

Chapter 5: Gilt-edged terror

All the details in this chapter came primarily from interviews conducted with leading members of the PLO, the PNF and various factions. Descriptions of the PNF facilities are a result of visits made to the relevant office. Some of the financial details were received from Israeli intelligence and have been confirmed by PLO members. Interviews were conducted in Beirut, Damascus, London, Washington, New York, Geneva and Paris. It was not possible to persuade any individual with the required knowledge to agree to have his or her name mentioned in this book.

In addition to personal interviews, the following sources have been used: *Jerusalem Post*, 16 June and 11 November 1977 and 24 October 1979; *Middle East Reporter*, 22 January 1979 and 11 May 1982; *The Financial Resources of the PLO* (Israeli Ministry of Foreign Affairs briefing, 11 November 1983); Israeli Defence Force's secret assessment of PLO income (document no. 651/0125); *Time*, 18 July 1977, p. 20.

p. 109 'The PNF was given': Details of the history, structure and finances of the PNF come from interviews with senior officials in that organisation.

p. 110 'According to Khimawai': Background biographical details on the senior figures in the PNF come from Israeli officials.

p. 113 'Dr Salah Dabbagh says': Interview in April 1984.

p. 117 'PLO ran a budget deficit': *Middle East Reporter*, 15 February 1984.

p. 117 'The PLO received': Arab diplomatic sources, July 1985.

p. 118 'The Marxist DFLP': Interview with senior official, June 1984.

p. 120 'Nicaragua also appears': The information in the following section comes from intelligence sources familiar with airline security who were interviewed in September 1985.

p. 124 'Rumours have circulated': The figures are widely used in Israel and the US within the counter-terrorist community.

p. 125 'The PLO lost': This figure came from bankers in Beirut and Sidon in the autumn of 1983, and has been confirmed by PLO sources.

Chapter 6: Noraid

p. 131 'the Irish Republican Army': Statistics supplied by the Royal Ulster Constabulary, February 1985.

p. 131 'England . . . has been associated': Good historical information on the relationship between Britain and Ireland as well as the development of terrorism can be found in Charles Townshend, *Political Violence in Ireland* (Clarendon Press, Oxford, 1983); Don Mansfield, 'The Irish Republican Army and Northern Ireland' in Bard E. O'Neill *et al.* (eds.), *Insurgency in the Modern World* (Westview Press, Boulder, Colo., 1980), pp. 45–87; Dennis Clark, 'Terrorism in Ireland: Renewal of a Tradition' in Marius H. Livingston (ed.), *International Terrorism in the Contemporary World*, op. cit., pp. 77–84.

p. 134 'The IRA divided': There are three main source works on the IRA: Tim Pat Coogan, *The IRA* (Fontana, London, 1980); J. Bowyer Bell, *The Secret Army: The IRA 1916–1979* (Academy Press, Dublin, 1979); Kevin Kelley, *The Longest War: Northern Ireland and the IRA* (Zed Books, London, 1982). More general information can be found in Peter Janke, *Guerrilla and Terrorist Organizations: A World Directory and Bibliography* (Macmillan, New York,

1983), pp. 98–101; and *Ulster: Politics and Terrorism* (Institute for the Study of Conflict, London, June 1973).

p. 135　'The key figure today': *Irish Times*, 19 January 1978; *Belfast Telegraph*, 15 May 1979.

p. 135　'Flannery established': Unless otherwise specified, details on Noraid come from the following sources: a secret briefing paper prepared by British intelligence in 1983 for the British army and the RUC; interviews with the RUC and the Northern Ireland Office in Belfast and London; and briefings by the British Embassy in Washington.

p. 137　'At the 1975 dinner': *Daily Express*, 4 February 1975.

p. 137　'Among the guests': *Irish Press*, 14 August 1980.

p. 138　'Encouraged by his fellow IRA': *Daily Telegraph*, 18 March 1984.

p. 140　'Eighteen British soldiers': Mickolous, *Transnational Terrorism*, op. cit., p. 868; Kelley, *The Longest War*, op. cit., pp. 304–5; British army sources serving in Northern Ireland at the time; and numerous press reports.

p. 141　'Originally, Flannery': Quoted in *Irish Times*, 19 January 1978.

p. 143　'They had few modern armaments': Details of weapons in the hands of the IRA and of arms deals come from British army sources.

p. 145　'The key to the first major FBI case': Information from the FBI; unpublished material filed for the *Sunday Times*, 3 November 1982; *New York* magazine, 22 November 1982, pp. 58–68; and the transcript of a *World in Action* (Granada Television) programme entitled 'Operation Hit and Win', broadcast on 21 March 1983.

p. 150　'Megahey was so skilful': Much of this information comes from FBI sources; 'Operation Hit and Win', op. cit.; *Daily Mail*, 16 March 1983; *The Times*, 13 February and 1 April 1983.

p. 152　'The FBI believed that Ryan': *Sunday Times*, 28 April 1985.

p. 152 'On board were rockets': *New York Times*, 1 and 2 October 1984; *Washington Post*, 1 October 1984; *The Times*, 17 October 1984.

p. 153 'A glossy brochure': *Daily Telegraph*, 25 April 1983.

p. 153 'the measure is not expected': Information supplied to the author in Washington, 4 December 1985.

p. 154 'Gerry Adams' response': *Newsweek*, 16 January 1984, p. 52.

Chapter 7: The IRA mafia

p. 157 'belongs to Thomas Murphy': Information on Slab Murphy comes from British military intelligence, who grade their information on him 'Al' – the highest classification – as well as from the RUC and serving army officers. The general question of financing the IRA is extremely difficult to research on the ground. Various British journalists have attempted to write about the subject, and all have been threatened by different terrorist groups. The most knowledgeable journalist is Chris Ryder of the *Sunday Times*, who has been most helpful. See also *Financial Times*, 13 March 1982; *Daily Telegraph*, 6 May 1983; and *Sunday Times*, 10 June 1984.

p. 158 'One of the cases': *Special Report of the Court of Auditors of the European Economic Community* (no. 85/C/215/01, 26 August 1985); *Sunday Times*, 6 October 1985.

p. 163 'in 1977 by Gerry Adams': For the evolution of the IRA's election strategy, see the *Sunday Times*, 8 May 1983. In addition, Gerry Adams has written a colourful and sentimental autobiography entitled *Falls Memories* (Brandon Book Publishers, Dingle, 1982). Primary material on this and other Northern Ireland terrorist matters comes from a series of interviews conducted by the author with army, police, intelligence, British government and terrorist sources in Northern Ireland and London, 1983–5.

p. 165 'The gun existed': *Newsweek*, 16 January 1984, p. 52.

p. 165 'at the ballot box': *The Times*, 17 and 23 May 1985; *Daily Telegraph*, 17 May 1985; *Guardian*, 17 May 1985.

p. 165 'Of the fifty-nine Sinn Fein': *Sunday Times*, 2 June 1985.

p. 165 'the Dublin government': *Daily Telegraph*, 21 February 1985; *The Times*, 20 and 21 February 1985; *Sunday Times*, 24 February 1985.

p. 166 'The loss of the money': *Sunday Times*, 21 April 1985.

p. 166 'Adams continues to dismiss': Quote recorded by Chris Ryder, *Sunday Times* Ulster correspondent, and passed to the author.

p. 167 'frauds on building sites': Information on building sites racketeering comes from the RUC and Northern Ireland Office, as well as paramilitary sources. In addition, *Irish Times*, 27 January 1984; *Belfast Telegraph*, 2 October 1981 and 24 January, 10, 17, 21 February and 23 October 1984.

p. 170 'In the early 1970s': Information comes from the RUC and intelligence sources in Northern Ireland; *Belfast Newsletter*, 22 March 1984; *Belfast Telegraph*, 19 January 1982; *The Situation in Northern Ireland: Report of the Political Affairs Commiteee of the European Parliament* (20 December 1983).

p. 171 'That threat is': *Daily Telegraph*, 22 August 1985; *Daily Mail*, 22 August 1985.

p. 173 'The IRA have chosen taxis': Information comes from the RUC; *Irish Times*, 1 June 1978; *Belfast Telegraph*, 26 January 1970, 1 March 1978, 14 February, 26 April and 6 September 1980, 15 February and 13 August 1981, 15 March and 5, 6, 7 September 1983. Additional information was received from the Northern Ireland Office and unpublished material from various journalists in Belfast.

p. 175 'In the autumn of 1972': Information on the Andersonstown Co-operative comes from the RUC; *Sunday Times* journalist Chris Ryder; records of a court case brought by the Andersonstown Co-op and two of its officials in October 1979; newspaper coverage of that case in the *Irish Times* and *Belfast Telegraph*. The Andersonstown Co-operative was first exposed in the *Sunday Times*, 3 August 1975.

p. 178 'illegal drinking club': Information from the RUC and the Northern Ireland Office; *Irish Press*, 3 November 1977; *Belfast Telegraph*, 20 June 1978, 26 January and 20 December 1983, 20 October 1979, 2 September 1980, 20 December 1983.

Notes

Chapter 8: The snatch business

p. 187 'masterminding the reconstruction': Information for this section comes from primary sources in Italy, including judges, investigating bodies and police officers, as well as current and past members of the Red Brigade. In addition, the following have been used: Vittorfranco S. Pisano, *The Red Brigades: A Challenge to Italian Democracy* (Institute for the Study of Conflict, No. 120, July 1980); *Guardian*, 22 June 1983; *The Times*, 22 March 1978, 25 July 1981, 18 February 1983; *Daily Mail*, 9 August 1982.

p. 190 'Although the Red Brigade': Aside from sources already mentioned, historical information can be found in Peter Janke, *Guerrilla and Terrorist Organizations*, op. cit., pp. 52–5; Alberto Ronchey, 'Guns and Gray Matter: Terrorism in Italy', *Foreign Affairs*, undated, pp. 921–40.

p. 192 'According to the US State Department's': *International Terrorism: Hostage Seizures* (US Department of State, Washington, DC, March 1983).

p. 193 'it was estimated that Lloyd's': Details on this and other matters relating to kidnap insurance come from: a Lloyd's underwriter involved in the work; three separate sources all working for different security companies; internal documents of Control Risks Ltd; and the following publications: unpublished manuscript from Sam Passow, New York, 2 December 1983; *Guardian*, 6 July and 7 September 1979; *8 Days*, 25 May 1979.

p. 195 'Control Risks has also appointed': *Sunday Times*, 1 December 1985.

p. 202 'Ben Dunne, junior boss': *Irish Independent*, 23 October 1981; *The Times*, 23 October 1981; *Belfast Telegraph*, 22 October 1981; *Daily Telegraph*, 21 October 1981; additional information from a member of the Dunne family and security sources.

p. 204 'Their target this time': The most detailed and accurate account of the Shergar affair can be found in the *Report of the Syndicate Committee to Shareholders of the Shergar Syndicate*, issued on 3 February 1984 by the Committee's solicitors, McCann, Fitzgerald, Sutton Dudley of Dublin; also in Chapter 8 of Richard Baerlein's book, *Shergar and the Aga Khan's Thoroughbred Empire* (Michael Joseph, London, 1984). Many of the newspaper accounts of the affair have been wildly inaccurate. Those that were less so can be found in the *Belfast Telegraph*, 9 February 1983 and 7 February 1984; *Irish Times*, 11 November 1983; *Irish Independent*, 2 February 1984.

p. 207   'All five were found': *Irish Times*, 8 August 1983; *Belfast Telegraph*, 8 August and 1, 2 and 4 November 1983; *Irish Press*, 4 November 1983. Additional information came from police and security sources.

p. 208   'A shootout followed': *Belfast Telegraph*, 24 November and 16 and 17 December 1983; *Irish Press*, 30 November 1983 and 12 December 1984; *Irish Times*, 2 December 1983; and police sources.

Chapter 9: The Narc-Farc connection

p. 215   'At dawn on the morning': AP news file, 20 March 1984; *New York Times*, 21 March 1984; *Washington Post*, 21 March 1984. Details are confirmed or added to in meetings with DEA officials in Washington, April 1984.

p. 216   'In fact, the organisation': Janke, *Guerrilla and Terrorist Organizations*, op. cit., pp. 449–59; *Time*, 16 April 1984, p. 35.

p. 217   '2500 metric tons of cocoa leaf': *Financial Times*, 13 June 1985.

p. 219   'In Bogotá and other cities': *International Herald Tribune*, 26–27 May 1984; *South*, July 1984, pp. 34–5; *Time*, 25 February 1985, pp. 6–18; *Newsweek*, 25 February 1985, pp. 8–18.

p. 221   'at the hearings': *Hearing before the Subcommittee on Security and Terrorism*, 23 April 1982 (US Government Printing Office, serial no. J-97-112).

p. 222   'Cuba's role in the supply of drugs': Much of the evidence for this section comes from three sources: testimony supplied to the hearing of the Subcommittee on Security and Terrorism, published as *The Cuban Government's Involvement in Facilitating International Drug Traffic* (US Government Printing Office, serial no. J-98-36), held in Miami, Florida, 30 April 1983; the results of a Grand Jury investigation and court cases relating to drug smuggling brought by the southern district court of Florida; information supplied to the author by DEA agents in Washington.

p. 226   'The president reacted': *Newsweek*, 14 May 1984, pp. 24–25.

p. 226   'the respected Bogotá daily': Quoted in *The Times*, 30 May 1984; see also *International Herald Tribune*, 23 June and 26 July 1984.

Notes

p. 227   'While these figures': *International Herald Tribune*, 19 May 1984.

p. 227   'In fact, so successful': *Newsweek*, 14 May 1984, p. 9.

p. 228   'A Colombian': *Washington Post*, 17 March 1983; *Wall Street Journal*, 3 November 1983; *Christian Science Monitor*, 20 January 1984.

p. 230   'At the same time': Information supplied to the author by the American concerned, who is now a successful business executive.

p. 230   'The hashish-growing areas': Randal, *The Tragedy of Lebanon*, op. cit., p. 136 *et seq.*

p. 230   'Opinions vary as to size': *The Middle East and North Africa* (Europa Publications, London, 1983), p. 568; *International Narcotics Control Strategy Report* (US Department of State, 1 February 1984), pp. 135–8; *Report of the International Narcotics Control Board for 1984* (United Nations, Vienna, 17 January 1985).

p. 232   'It is easier': John F. Devlin, *Syria: Modern State in an Ancient Land* (Croom Helm, London, 1983), p. 33; *Jerusalem Post*, 22 March 1983; *Wall Street Journal*, 3 April 1984. Details of Rifaat Assad's involvement come from intelligence sources in Washington as well as PLO sources who are highly critical of the involvement of certain members of the organisation in the drugs business.

p. 233   'members of the PLO sold': *The Times*, 5 and 6 July 1985.

p. 233   'police in Australia': *Sunday Telegraph*, 18 August 1985; unused reports sent from Perth, Australia to the *Sunday Times*, 25 August 1985.

A glossary of terrorism

Details for this section come from Peter Janke's *Guerrilla and Terrorist Organizations*, op. cit.; the background brief on the PLO prepared by the British Foreign Office and intelligence sources.

Bibliography

Books

ADAMS, Gerry. *Falls Memories*. Brandon Book Publishers, Dingle, Co. Kerry, Ireland, 1982.

Africa South of the Sahara, 1983–84. Europa Publications, London, 1984.

ALEXANDER, Yonah, CARLTON, David and WILKINSON, Paul. *Terrorism: Theory and Practice*. Westview Press, Boulder, Colorado, 1979.

ALEXANDER, Yonah and EBINGER, Charles K. *Political Terrorism and Energy*. Praeger Publishers, New York, 1982.

ALEXANDER, Yonah and MYERS, Kenneth A. *Terrorism in Europe*. St Martin's Press, New York, 1982.

AMBURSLEY, Fitzroy and COHEN, Robin. *Crisis in the Caribbean*. Heinemann, London, 1983.

BAERLEIN, Richard. *Shergar and the Aga Khan's Thoroughbred Empire*. Michael Joseph, London, 1984.

BARRON, John. *The KGB Today: The Hidden Hand*. Readers Digest Press, New York, 1983.

BAR-ZOHAR, Michael and HABER, Eitan. *The Quest for the Red Prince*. Weidenfeld & Nicolson, London, 1983.

BECKER, Jillian. *The PLO: The Rise and Fall of the Palestine Liberation Organisation*. Weidenfeld & Nicolson, London, 1984.

BELL, J. Bowyer. *The Secret Army: The IRA 1916–1979*. Academy Press, Dublin, 1983.

BLOCH, Jonathan and FITZGERALD, Patrick. *British Intelligence and Covert Action*. Junction Books, London, 1983.

CLUTTERBUCK, Richard. *Guerrillas and Terrorists*. Ohio University Press, Athens, Ohio, 1980.

COBBAN, Helena. *The Palestinian Liberation Organisation: People, Power and Politics*. Cambridge University Press, 1984.

Cambridge University Press, 1984.

Bibliography

COOGAN, Tim Pat. *The IRA*. Fontana, London, 1980.

CRENSHAW, Martha. *Terrorism, Legitimacy and Power*. Wesleyan University Press, Middletown, Conn., 1983.

DEVLIN, John F. *Syria: Modern State in an Ancient Land*. Croom Helm, London, 1983.

DOBSON, Christopher and PAYNE, Ronald. *Terror! The West Fights Back*. Papermac, London, 1982.

—. *The Weapons of Terror*. Papermac, London, 1979.

EISENBERG, Dennis, DAN, Uri and LANDAU, Eli. *The Mossad*. New American Library, New York, 1979.

EL AZHARY, M. S. (ed.). *The Iran–Iraq War*. Croom Helm, London, 1984.

EVANS, Alona E. and MURPHY, John F. *Legal Aspects of International Terrorism*. Lexington Books, Lexington, Mass., 1979.

EVANS, Ernest. *Calling a Truce to Terror*. Greenwood Press, Westport, Conn., 1979.

FIELD, Michael. *The Merchants*. John Murray, London, 1984.

FRANCIS, Samuel T. *The Soviet Strategy of Terror*. The Heritage Foundation, Washington, 1981.

FREEMANTLE, Brian. *The KGB*. Michael Joseph, London, 1982.

GABRIEL, Richard A. *Operation Peace for Galilee*. Hill & Wang, New York, 1984.

GOULDEN, Joseph C. *The Death Merchant*. Simon & Schuster, New York, 1984.

GRAHAM, Robert. *Iran: The Illusion of Power*. Croom Helm, London, 1979.

HALPERIN, Ernst. *Terrorism in Latin America* (The Washington Papers, Vol. IV). Sage Publications, Beverly Hills, Calif., 1976.

HAYCOCK, Ronald. *Regular Armies and Insurgency*. Croom Helm, London, 1979.

HAYES, David. *Terrorists and Freedom Fighters*. Wayland, Hove, Sussex, 1980.

HENZE, Paul. *The Plot to Kill the Pope*. Croom Helm, London, 1984.

HODGES, Tony. *Western Sahara: The Roots of a Desert War*. Croom Helm, London, 1984.

HOLDEN, David and JOHNS, Richard. *The House of Saud*. Sidgwick & Jackson, London, 1981.

ISRAELI, Raphael. *The PLO in Lebanon: Selected Documents*. Weidenfeld & Nicolson, London, 1983.

IYAD, Abu (with Eric Rouleau). *My Home, My Land: A Narrative of the Palestinian Struggle*. Times Books, New York, 1981.

JANKE, Peter. *Guerrilla and Terrorist Organizations: A World Directory and Bibliography*. Macmillan, New York, 1983.

KELLEY, Kevin. *The Longest War: Northern Ireland and the IRA*. Zed Books, London, 1982.

KHALIDI, Rashid and MANSOUR, Kamil (eds.). *Palestine and the Gulf.* Institute for Palestine Studies, Beirut, 1982.

KISSINGER, Henry. *Years of Upheaval.* Weidenfeld & Nicolson/Michael Joseph, London, 1982.

KITSON, Frank. *Gangs and Counter-Gangs.* Barrie & Rockliff, London, 1960.

LAFFIN, John. *The PLO Connection.* Corgi Books, London, 1982.

LANIR, Zvi. *Meetings in Rashidiya: Anatomy of a Palestinian Community in Lebanon.* Dvir, Tel Aviv, 1983.

LAQUEUR, Walter. *Terrorism.* Weidenfeld & Nicolson, London, 1977.

LIVINGSTON, Marius H. (ed.). *International Terrorism in the Contemporary World.* Greenwood Press, Westport, Conn., 1978.

LIVINGSTONE, Neil C. *The War Against Terrorism.* Lexington Books, Lexington, Mass., 1982.

LODGE, Juliette. *Terrorism: The Challenge to the State.* Martin Robertson, Oxford, 1981.

LONDON, Kurt. *The Soviet Union in World Politics.* Croom Helm, London, 1980.

MICKOLOUS, Edward F. *The Literature of Terrorism.* Greenwood Press, Westport, Conn., 1980.

—. *Transnational Terrorism: A Chronology of Events, 1968–1979.* Aldwych Press, London, 1980.

—. *The Middle East and North Africa 1982–83.* Europa Publications, London, 1983.

MOOREHEAD, Caroline. *Fortune's Hostages.* Hamish Hamilton, London, 1980.

O'BALLANCE, Edgar. *The Language of Violence.* Presidio Press, San Rafael, Calif., 1979.

O'NEILL, Bard E., HEATON, William R. and ALBERTS, Donald J. (eds.). *Insurgency in the Modern World.* Westview Press, Boulder, Colorado, 1980.

PEARCE, Jeremy. *Under the Eagle.* Latin American Bureau. London, 1981.

PETERZELL, Jay. *Reagan's Secret Wars.* Centre for National Security Studies, Washington, 1984.

PIPES, Daniel. *In the Path of God: Islam and Political Power.* Basic Books, New York, 1983.

PISANO, Vittorfranco S. *The Red Brigades: A Challenge to Italian Democracy.* Institute for the Study of Conflict, No. 120, July 1980.

PURCELL, Hugh. *Revolutionary War.* Hamish Hamilton, London, 1980.

RANDAL, Jonathan. *The Tragedy of Lebanon.* Chatto & Windus, London, 1983.

ROSITZKE, Harry. *The KGB: The Eyes of Russia.* Sidgwick & Jackson, London, 1982.

SCHAMIS, Gerardo Jorge. *War and Terrorism in International Affairs.* Transaction Books, New Brunswick, NJ, 1980.

Bibliography

SCHREIBER, Jan. *The Ultimate Weapon: Terrorists and World Order*. William Morrow & Co., New York, 1978.

SHAW, Jennifer, GUERITZ, Rear Admiral E. F., YOUNGER, Major-General A. E., GREGORY, Frank and PALMER, Commander Joseph. *Ten Years of Terrorism*. Royal United Services Institute for Defence Studies, London, 1979.

SHIFF, Ze'ev. *Operation Peace for Galilee*. Simon & Schuster, London, 1984.

SMITH, Bradley F. *The Shadow Warriors*. Andre Deutsch, London, 1983.

STERLING, Claire. *The Terror Network*. Weidenfeld & Nicolson, London, 1981.

—. *The Time of the Assassins*. Angus & Robertson, London, 1984.

TANZI, Vito. *The Underground Economy in the United States and Abroad*. Lexington Books, Lexington, Mass., 1982.

TOWNSHEND, Charles. *Political Violence in Ireland*. Clarendon Press, Oxford, 1983.

TZU, Sun. *The Art of War*. Delacorte Press, New York, 1983.

WILKINSON, Paul. *Terrorism and the Liberal State*. Macmillan Press, London, 1977.

WRIGHT, John. *Libya: A Modern History*. Croom Helm, London, 1982.

WRIGHT, Robin. *Sacred Rage: The Crusade of Militant Islam*. Linden Press, New York, 1985.

YODFAT, Aryeh Y. *The Soviet Union and Revolutionary Iran*. Croom Helm, London, 1984.

YODFAT, Aryeh Y. and ARNON-OHANNA, Yuval. *PLO Strategy and Tactics*. Croom Helm, London, 1981.

Documents

BUREAU OF INTERNATIONAL NARCOTIC MATTERS. *International Narcotics Control Strategy Report*. US Department of State, Washington, 1984.

NANES, Allan S. *International Terrorism*. The Library of Congress, Congressional Research Service, Washington, Issue Brief no. IB81141, 1983.

OFFICE FOR COMBATING TERRORISM: The following four titles were published by the US Department of State, Washington:
Combating Terrorism. 1982.
International Terrorism: Hostage Seizures. 1983.
Terrorist Attacks Against US Business. 1982.
Terrorist Skyjackings. 1982.

SENATE COMMITTEE ON FOREIGN RELATIONS. *International Narcotics Control*. US Government Printing Office, Washington, 1983.

The Financing of Terror

SENATE COMMITTEE ON SECURITY AND TERRORISM: all the following titles were printed at the US Government Printing Office, Washington:

The Anti-Terrorism and Foreign Mercenary Act. 1983.

Attorney-General's Guidelines for Domestic Security Investigations: The Smith Guidelines. 1983.

The Cuban Government's Involvement in Facilitating International Drug Traffic. 1983.

DEA Oversight and Authorization. 1983.

DEA Oversight and Budget Authorization. 1982.

FBI Oversight Hearing. 1982.

FBI Oversight and Authorization. 1983.

Historical Antecedents of Soviet Terrorism. 1981.

Impact of Attorney General's Guidelines for Domestic Security Investigations: The Levi Guidelines. 1984.

The Role of Cuba in International Terrorism and Subversion. 1982.

The Role of the Soviet Union, Cuba, and East Germany in Fomenting Terrorism in Southern Africa. 1982.

The Role of the Soviet Union, Cuba, and East Germany in Fomenting Terrorism in South Africa: Addendum. 1982.

Terrorism: Origins, Directions and Support. 1981.

Terrorism: The Role of Moscow and its Sub-Contractors. 1982.

Terrorism: The Turkish Experience. 1981.

Index

Index

Index

Index